Praise for Dr Justin Coulson

'If you wish there was a way you could raise boys in a culture less cruel and crushing – and yet one that doesn't consider masculinity inherently toxic – you may hold the roadmap in your hands' – Lenore Skenazy, author of *Free-Range Kids*

'Justin is a genius! His honest, compassionate and sensible advice is music to this mum's ears. I want him to adopt our family!' – Jessica Rowe

'Dr Justin Coulson is who I turn to when I'm feeling overwhelmed with parenting my three young (and frequently boisterous) kids. His calm, logical advice never fails to help me be a better parent' – Bec Sparrow, author of *Find Your Tribe*

'Justin Coulson explains clear strategies designed to help parents embody optimism and compassion as they guide their children through the unpredictable journey of growing up in a very complex world' – Dr Diana Korevaar, author of *Mindfulness for Mums and Dads*

'Parenthood can be a jungle, but Justin's advice and simple strategies will help you find that path back to sanity, stability and smiling kids' – Lisa Wilkinson

Dr Justin Coulson is the co-host of the popular TV program *Parental Guidance*, and Australia's most downloaded parenting podcast, the Happy Families podcast. He is author of numerous books on parenting and families, including: *21 Days to a Happier Family*, *9 Ways to a Resilient Child*, *10 Things Every Parent Needs to Know*, *Miss-Connection* and *The Parenting Revolution*. His viral video about raising children has been viewed over 100 million times. Justin is a regular contributor to the *Today* show and other major Australian media outlets. He and his wife, Kylie, have six daughters and one granddaughter.

Find out more at happyfamilies.com.au

Also by Justin Coulson

21 Days to a Happier Family

9 Ways to a Resilient Child

10 Things Every Parent Needs to Know

Miss-Connection

The Parenting Revolution

BOYS

DR JUSTIN COULSON

ABC
BOOKS

Author's note

In the stories shared in this book, names and other details have been altered to protect the privacy of individuals, with the exception of those who gave permission to use real names and in examples drawn from my own family.

The ABC 'Wave' device is a trademark of the Australian Broadcasting Corporation and is used under licence by HarperCollins*Publishers* Australia.

HarperCollins*Publishers*
Australia • Brazil • Canada • France • Germany • India • Italy • Japan
Mexico • Netherlands • New Zealand • Poland • Spain • Sweden
Switzerland • United Kingdom • United States of America

HarperCollins acknowledges the Traditional Custodians of the lands upon which we live and work, and pays respect to Elders past and present.

First published on Gadigal Country in Australia in 2026
by HarperCollins*Publishers* Australia Pty Limited
ABN 36 009 913 517
harpercollins.com.au

HarperCollins*Publishers*
Macken House, 39/40 Mayor Street Upper
Dublin 1, D01 C9W8, Ireland

A catalogue record for this book is available from the National Library of Australia

ISBN 978 0 7333 4252 3 (paperback)
ISBN 978 1 4607 1511 6 (ebook)

Cover design by Hazel Lam, HarperCollins Design Studio
Front cover image by Adrian Rodd/stocksy.com/6330264
Author photo on back cover by Brittany Holzworth
Photograph on page i of Justin Coulson and his family © Tim Coulson
Typeset in Adobe Garamond Pro by Kirby Jones
Printed and bound in the UK using 100% Renewable
Electricity at CPI Group (UK) Ltd

For my dad –
a man who showed me what healthy manhood looks like.

And for my nephew Logan.
1 October 2003 – 6 November 2023
We wish we'd had more time with you.
May others never know the grief we've felt.

Contents

Author's note

In March 2020, just two weeks before the world shut down due to the COVID-19 pandemic, I released a book about raising girls. The book was called *Miss-Connection: Why Your Teenage Daughter 'Hates' You, Expects the World, and Needs to Talk.* As a father of six girls, I felt well equipped to support parents struggling with their daughters. That book has helped thousands of families.

As soon as the book was announced, I was inundated with desperate messages: 'When is the boys' book coming out?' 'Please help me with my son.' 'I'm lost. Will the girls' book help me with my boy?' 'Will you please do a book for boys?' The requests have only increased since.

I have been reluctant to enter the masculinity conversation. I'm a father of daughters, and there are good men doing great work in this area. Yet my discussions with parents have demonstrated two things:

- First, there is a tremendous need. Parents are struggling with everything from their sons' lack of basic hygiene or bad attitudes, through to gaming, school motivation, pornography, gambling and abusive behaviour, fears of radicalisation or being pulled into misogynistic culture (or worse), and more.

- Second, the solutions I've suggested ... they work. Really well.

Nevertheless, many people raised their eyebrows when I mentioned I was writing a book on boys. I want to be clear about this: I have skin in the game when it comes to how boys are doing. My girls will know those boys – attend school with them, befriend them, work with them, date them. Those boys will become husbands to my daughters and fathers to my grandchildren. Two of my daughters have already made those consequential choices. This topic matters to me.

Boys is the culmination of five years of thinking about this topic, and nearly 25 years of researching, writing, and speaking about parenting.

*

Before we begin, there are three things to recognise.

First, all stories in this book are shared with the permission of those involved. Where permission was not available, names have been changed or omitted, and details altered to protect anonymity. Likewise, I have changed details to protect the identity of minors.

Second, boys aren't homogeneous. When researchers study 'boys', they're working with averages – helpful for seeing patterns but potentially misleading for individual boys. This means that, on average, what I say in these pages is going to be true for *most* boys and men (or girls and women) *most* of the time. But it won't be true for *every* boy *all* the time.[1]

For example: men are, on average, taller than women. But plenty of women are taller than plenty of men. The same applies to behaviour, interests, and abilities. On average, boys tend to be more physical, competitive, and interested in both sexual activity and variety. On average, girls prefer intimate friendships and cooperative play, and are choosier when it comes to sexual opportunity. These patterns are accurate on average – even as individual variation remains enormous.[2] Throughout these pages, you'll learn about boys being 'this' or 'that', and if I keep saying 'on average', or qualifying my statements with exceptions, it will become tedious. When you disagree with a claim because it's not how *your* son is, remember that all statements in this book are true *on average*.

Third, all references to 'boys' or 'girls' refer to children whose gender identity conforms to their biological sex at birth.

Introduction

I am sorry for being a man.

David Cunliffe, political leader, New Zealand, 2014[1]

Another morning. Another school principal stares at the computer screen, crafting yet another letter to parents. Last week it was Year 9 boys caught sharing abhorrent Discord messages – racist, anti-Semitic, and misogynistic. The week before: sexual harassment issues in Year 8. Today? A group of boys filming up girls' skirts at a sports carnival. The words blur together: 'deeply concerned', 'investigating', 'zero tolerance', 'not consistent with the culture of our school'.

These aren't isolated incidents. In recent months parents have reached out to me about:

- a 12-year-old Melbourne girl receiving rape threats during school hours from boys in her class (in person and digitally via school laptops);
- nearly 40 boys at a Noosa school sharing child pornography, violent sexual content, and more on a social media group chat;[2] and

- a 15-year-old Perth girl being threatened with rape after rejecting advances from a boy in her class.

News outlets have pointed to the senior schoolboys at an elite private boys' school in Sydney who created a points-based challenge for their Year 12 muck-up day. Their scorecard included: 'ten points for screaming "penis" on public transport, get with an Asian chick, play porn out loud on public transport (pretend you have your headphones in and you don't notice), hookup with a random girl.' For 30 points, they could take a 'vodka shot out of a condom (halfway full), get with a lesbian, order a stripper, do a naked shoey, smoke your mates pubes, get with a chick which is 3/10 or lower (photo of the chick + the dirty work), perform a sex scene on the stairs of a church, with a person "finishing loudly"'. There are acts so obscene they'll accrue 200 points. The boys' code: 'Protect each other at all costs.'[3]

Elizabeth, a mother in regional Victoria, described to me how her seven-year-old son was touching girls on the bottom, lifting their skirts, and sniffing their seats. 'What do I do?' she asked. 'Where does a seven-year-old learn this?'

In 2024, the activist group Collective Shout published the Sexual Harassment of Teachers (SHoT) report, which included wide-ranging accounts of Australian boys (in both primary school and high school) making sexual moaning noises at female teachers and female students during class. The report showed that 46.9% of female teachers have experienced sexual harassment. Eighty percent of that number were harassed by a student – always boys.[4]

One teacher reported to ABC TV's *Compass*, 'I announced my pregnancy to a Year 9 class. One male student said it wasn't possible for me to be pregnant because I was so ugly no one would rape me.'[5]

In 2023, data from the world-leading Australian Child Maltreatment Study showed teen boys were the most likely people in Australia to sexually abuse or assault another person. Boys are overrepresented in stalking, fighting, sexual assault, and reckless behaviour.[6]

It's horrid. I'm not embellishing. And I haven't cherry-picked examples to rattle you. These are devastatingly everyday occurrences in every postcode.

The media paints a pessimistic picture. Lost boys, depraved boys, stalker boys, violent boys – always boys, and always in trouble – from every walk of life and every socioeconomic level.

And who's in the middle of it all?

You. Me. Loving, concerned, vigilant parents watching our boys and wondering: How do we navigate this?

To identify useful solutions, we need a clear-eyed view of the problem we're confronted with – and that's where this book starts.

What problem?

The Male Problem. The atrocious behaviour. The misogynistic behaviour. The anti-Semitic and racist behaviour. The sexualised behaviour. The violent behaviour. The intimidatory behaviour.

Please start breathing again, though. This book is not a catalogue of deviancy, aggression, and addiction in boys and men. It's not fuelling the culture war or piling blame and shame on 50% of the population (and their parents).

Rather, this book is about something more important: raising boys who make the world better, not worse. Boys who understand their strength and use it to support, not intimidate or dominate. Boys who know their worth isn't measured by body count in video games or sexual conquest – but by the value they create and the contribution they make.

But there's work to be done.

A bear or a man?

In early 2024 a TikTok conversation exploded. Women recorded themselves answering this question: 'If you were alone in the woods, would you rather encounter a bear or a man?'

The groundswell of responses all pointed the same way.

I know a bear's intentions. I don't know a man's intentions, no matter how nice they are.

A bear wouldn't film itself assaulting me and share it with his friends.

People wouldn't ask you what you were wearing when you were mauled by a bear.

If I were attacked by a bear, people would believe me.

If I survive the bear attack, I won't have to see the bear at family reunions.

No one will talk about the bear's bright future.

The women who choose the bear know that bears are dangerous. But they still pick the bear.

Most men are *not* dangerous, respondents of both genders argued. If you get lost or hurt, a man could be a supportive, knowledgeable companion. He may even save your life. But you just never know. And because of the percentage of boys and men who are not safe to be around, the preferred option on social media was consistently … a bear!

My staff posed the 'man or bear' question to me. I pondered. I baulked. I declared that the question didn't feel fair. I wanted to know more. 'Tell me about the man,' I asked. 'Why is he in the woods? How old is he? How educated is he? Does he have his own kids? Is he married? Religious?' My team members were unrelenting. 'It doesn't matter,' they told me, 'and that's the point.'

A matter of trust

The loudest voices on social media aren't always in line with the general population, so there are questions we can rightfully ask about this viral moment. Nevertheless, the Bear or Man question highlights an all-too-common feeling: 'You can't trust boys and men.'

So what's trust? Trust is a belief the other person is going to act in your best interests. And too often, too many have been hurt, abused, or worse at the hands of a boy or man who was untrustworthy – who didn't act in their best interests. There are daily news stories about men's awful behaviour – and their untrustworthiness. During a 2017 book signing event for *Fight Like a Girl*, Clementine Ford wrote inside a fan's copy of the book: 'Have you killed any men today? And if not, why not?' She later defended the comment on Twitter, saying it was sarcasm.

Today the issue of masculinity is front and centre. At the lighter end, the Male Problem has led to new portmanteaus like *mansplaining*, *manspreading*, and *manterrupting*. These ideas poke fun at men who clearly can't be trusted with feelings, or with making someone comfortable on the bus, train, or plane. And they suggest men don't know how to listen to women.

At the more severe end of the Male Problem, propagandists like alleged sex-trafficker and alleged rapist Andrew Tate rack up millions of views spreading rancid misogyny (more on that later). We hear of stories like those I quoted at the beginning of this introduction. And worst of all, women are being assaulted, abused, and murdered on a near weekly basis in Australia, at the hands of men. While writing this book, I lost count of the number of women of all ages who told me that they would not partner with a man. One explained, 'There's no man that will be a bonus in my life. He can't add value. He'll just want a mother. I'll be his slave.' Another stunned me, saying, 'I'm partnered with a woman because I know I'm safe. I'm actually attracted to men, not women, but I'm choosing to be with a woman because I can trust women. But I can't trust men.' This is an extreme position to take – and this particular woman's suffering at the hands of an abuser goes some way to explaining it. But her decision conveys concerns about male trustworthiness in undeniable clarity.

The term 'toxic masculinity' entered the public lexicon via the mythopoetic men's movement of the 1980s and 1990s. It wasn't feminists or people who hate men who coined the term. It was men! The mythopoets argued that a lack of rituals (rites of passage) in today's society means that men are not given the chance to develop 'real' or 'deep' masculinity and instead either grow into 'toxic' chauvinists or become feminised. Today we hear the term everywhere, often daily, and it usually refers to aspects of masculinity that are socially destructive. But for some, it refers to 'maleness'. The very fact that a person is a man makes them toxic.

The definition-creep is not helpful. While boys and men who behave poorly must be held accountable, any approach that demonises everyone on the planet with a Y chromosome is both unfair and counterproductive.

Masculinity doesn't need a marketing makeover. This is not a PR problem. Instead, masculinity needs a character makeover.

The data shows that young men have an awful habit of getting into serious trouble and failing to act in the best interests of those around them (or even their own best interests). To put it more fairly, a high proportion of society's troublesome elements come from the ranks of adolescent boys and young men, even though most are well socialised. Rebuilding that trust – cultivating character – is what this book is for. But boys don't need more critics. They have enough already. Instead, they need supporters, guides, and role models. We need to shift the conversation from all males *being* a problem to a percentage of males *having* a problem.

Caitlin Flanagan – social critic and writer for *The Atlantic* – cuts to the heart of it: 'What if we understood that boys are born into a destiny, not a pathology?'[7] *Good* boys and men, she argues, need to be appreciated and used as role models, because boys and men who are getting it wrong need to be taught better.

My focus in this book is on healthy masculinity, which, by definition, is not toxic. Healthy masculinity is a net positive for everyone. Our focus should be on what's working and creating more of it for our boys. And the bonus is this will create healthier girls too. As Richard Reeves argues in his acclaimed book *Of Boys and Men*, 'when men struggle to play their full part, life becomes more demanding for women'.[8] Creating character in boys and men gives them purpose, builds trust, and improves outcomes across the board.

At the start of this chapter I included a quote from New Zealand politician David Cunliffe. As part of a speech recognising family and domestic abuse perpetrated by men in New Zealand homes, he apologised 'for being a man'. But that is 100% the wrong endpoint. When boys grow up understanding how to use their strength well – how to make the people around them feel (and be) safer and stronger; how to show up and be a bonus; what it is to add value to people's lives – they won't need to apologise for being male, and neither will we as their parents. But they need help.

A positive vision of manhood

What we require is a positive vision of masculinity that is broad enough to recognise the many ways to be a man; one that will feel aspirational for boys.

At the moment, many of our boys are conflicted about how to navigate the relentless and contrasting messages about masculinity. They deserve to understand their power and how to use it well.

At its core, this book responds to this issue with two words: *surplus value.* Surplus value is what transforms a boy into a man. It's where he transforms from the 'boy' psychology of being a taker to the 'man' psychology of being a giver: providing, protecting, and using his maturity and strength to support those around him in prosocial ways. He shifts, as Dr Arne Rubinstein suggests in *The Making of Men*, from thinking that he is the centre of the universe to being a part of a far greater whole where he has a responsibility to contribute.[9] He learns to get out of BED (Blame, Excuse, and Denial) and pick up his OAR (Ownership, Accountability, and Responsibility). Boy psychology is what we see in eight-year-olds – and that's appropriate. Being a taker and living in blame, excuse, and denial are undesirable characteristics in a 24-year-old.

This is the formula I'll use in this book for what it is to be a man:

- Providing for kith and kin.
- Being considerate.
- Giving more than he takes.
- Serving without expecting applause.
- Using his power to help those around him feel safer and stronger – and consequently *be* safer and stronger.

That's the kind of masculinity our boys need to first learn – and then earn. And it's the masculinity we'll explore in the pages of this book.

How this book will help

Here's what gives me hope: we know what works!

- We understand the basic psychological needs that drive flourishing human development and healthy masculinity.

- We know how to help boys create value rather than just consume the value others create; that is, how to become givers, not takers.
- We know how to build lasting, deep character.
- And, most importantly, we know how to raise boys who make others feel safer and stronger, rather than threatened and diminished.

Culture and society have been changing for centuries. The speed of that change is accelerating. But this book is about what *doesn't* change. It's about the foundations of healthy human flourishing in boys. You'll discover ideas on which you can build a family – and a boy's life.

Let's not accept the narrative that boys are fundamentally flawed. The popular chatter about 'toxic masculinity' is everywhere, but it misses the point. In this book, the focus remains on *healthy* masculinity.

We must believe in our boys. This book will offer the understanding you (and they) need, and a map towards better boyhood and flourishing families – for all.

PART ONE
THE SITUATION

You pick up a book like this hoping for answers. 'Just tell me what to do!'

I understand the urgency. Specific action steps are coming in Part Two. But jumping straight to strategies would be like trying to navigate without understanding the terrain. To truly support our sons, we need to see the world they're navigating. We need to understand The Situation.

Part One explores two fundamental realities that shape modern boyhood.

First, we'll confront the code red situation – why parents are worried, how boys are struggling across multiple domains, and why this matters for every boy, not just the ones making headlines.

Second, we'll explore what makes boys tick – both nature and nurture. Boys are hardwired differently from girls – neurologically, physiologically, and emotionally. But biology isn't destiny. Culture shapes how that wiring gets expressed. The 'Man Box' – society's narrow script for masculinity – creates unique pressures that make manhood feel precarious, something boys must constantly prove and defend. Understanding both the biological realities and the cultural forces impacting boys will help us create solutions that work with your son's nature while rejecting the unhelpful scripts.

There are two further foundational challenges confronting our boys, and they're inseparably connected: (i) screens and (ii) explicit content. Our boys' world is shaped by pornography playing out in 4K picture quality with Dolby Atmos high-definition sound via their airpods where no one but them can hear it. And boys love their screens for chatting to their friends, gaming, and entertainment, but these activities contribute little to healthy manhood. Our final two chapters in Part One: The Situation will explore everything you need to know about these additional challenges.

Some of this could be a little uncomfortable. But it matters. You can't build strategies that work without first understanding what you're building on.

Let's begin.

1 Code red

Why boys are struggling and what's at stake for your family

Our boys are hurting girls. They're hurting each other. And they're hurting themselves.

Rebecca Sparrow

Parents' questions about their sons hit differently from questions about daughters. There's an urgency. A weight. It feels existential, heavy; raw concern bordering on fear.

'I find it kind of scary to be raising boys,' Brooke, a mum to two boys and two girls, explained to me. Another mum, Kylie, told me, 'I worry about what will *happen* to my girls. But with my boys, I'm worried about what they'll *do*.' (The gendered contrast around who has agency is fascinating here.) In recent years, a trend has appeared, with some parents showing a preference for which gender they want their child to be: girls. Boys, it seems, are a bigger stress.[1]

In Western cultures, boys and men are struggling in nearly every domain compared to girls and women. Former US Surgeon General Vivek Murthy said, 'the data is actually quite clear that young men and boys are falling behind on many metrics'.[2] A 2024 UK parliamentary report, *A Boy Today*, found boys are experiencing a decades-long decline in educational outcomes, career trajectories, physical health, and psychological wellbeing.[3] (At the time of writing, the UK government is developing a men's health strategy. So, too, are several European nations and a number of US states including California, Michigan, and Utah.)

It's no better in Australia. Boys are at significant risk of school exclusion, loneliness, homelessness, crime (as both victim and perpetrator), health difficulties, and suicide.

It's not *all* bad news. Many boys and young men live healthier lives today than any group has in centuries. They smoke less, drink less, use fewer drugs, and exercise more. But despite these positives, we worry. There's also the gaming, alcohol, drugs, vaping, violence, lack of purpose, sexual misconduct, and disrespect and attitude. But for some boys, something fundamental is breaking. It's 'code red' across several critical life domains. The following table demonstrates this point.

For every 10 Australian women/girls who ...	There are this many men/boys:
are 25 to 34 and have at least a Bachelor's degree[4]	7
complete Year 12[5]	9
drop out by the end of their first year of university[6]	11
are school students with an intellectual disability[7]	12
report smoking daily[8]	12

For every 10 Australian women/girls who ...	There are this many men/boys:
experience an alcohol-related hospitalisation[9]	14
are unemployed and don't have a qualification[10]	14
are school students with a sensory and speech disability[11]	14
experience a serious work-related injury or illness[12]	15
report recent ecstasy use[13]	16
consume alcohol at risky levels[14]	17
died of a drug overdose[15]	19
are a homicide victim[16]	19
are suspended from high school[17]	21
are 25 to 29 and died[18]	23
are diagnosed with autism[19]	23
have an alcohol-induced death[20]	25
die of suicide[21]	30
are developmentally vulnerable in terms of emotional maturity when starting school[22]	34
are adolescents diagnosed with ADHD[23]	36
are suspended from primary school[24]	57
are a victim of blackmail[25]	67
are imprisoned[26]	119
are killed from work-related activities[27]	240

Author and social scientist Richard Reeves emphasises: 'Men are struggling by comparison with women in almost all endeavours, except earning more money and running the world.'[28] That last part – about money and power – makes it easy to dismiss this as a genuine problem. But it's the first part of his sentence that explains the concern I see in parents' eyes when they talk about their sons. In this chapter, we'll review four key areas where boys are struggling: education, mental health, crime, and identity.

Education: school sucks

Eight Year 9 boys slouch and fidget at a Sunshine Coast high school. They're part of a Top Blokes mentoring program that I'm supporting. The program exists because these boys are at risk – of dropping out, of disengaging, of disappearing into statistics.

Two boys dominate. The rest shrink into themselves, unsure whether their contribution to the conversation will be valuable or mercilessly mocked. Boys are so casually brutal towards one another.

I ask: 'What's the best thing about being a teenage boy?'

Silence.

When I asked teenage girls the same question for my book *Miss-Connection*, answers cascaded out of them. But these boys? They're not forthcoming.

Finally one says: 'I can't wait until I'm eighteen.'

It's a thread. I pick it up and give it a tug. 'Why?'

'Get out of school.'

'What then?'

'I'll get a job. Have money.'

'What will you do with the money?'

His response hits like an unexpected slap: 'Buy alcohol and drugs. Go to strip clubs.' He grins. The other boys guffaw and nod approvingly. One slaps him on the shoulder. 'Bruh!' Another offers a fist-bump. 'Yeah, bro.'

I let them have their moment. Then I flip the initial question: 'What's the hardest thing about being a teenage boy?'

This time it's immediate and unanimous.

'School.'

'It's stupid.'

'I hate it.'

'There's no point.'

I query them further. 'What do you want instead?'

'Don't care. Just want out. Get a job. Get money.'

Many boys love learning. But too many boys don't just dislike school – they hate it with a passion that starts early and burns hot. The statistics tell this story in numbers. These boys tell it with their behaviour. And parents watch helplessly as their sons disengage and disconnect.

The gender-education gap

In Chapter 2 we'll discuss hardwired brain differences between men and women, but part of that conversation is relevant here. It's generally accepted that boys' brains mature more slowly than girls' brains. Recent research suggests brain maturation differences may be smaller than we thought, even during the early years, but those small differences still matter. Many boys begin school less equipped to sit still, pay attention, and control impulses – exactly what schools demand of four- and five-year-olds. This 'executive function gap' compounds over 12 years. Boys regulate emotions slightly less effectively, control impulses more poorly, are less organised, get on task more slowly, and are more rigid in their thinking than girls their age. The downstream impact? Boys dominate every negative metric – detentions, suspensions, expulsions – from the earliest grades. Boys in early primary school are about six times more likely to be suspended. And unfortunately, a boy suspended once is likely to be suspended again. Each exclusion weakens relationships, compounds academic struggles, and increases the probability of substance use, illegal behaviour, or dropping out entirely.[29] These developmental realities coupled with the behavioural and psychological impact on boys explain, at least in part, why so many boys struggle at school at all ages. At school, they're deprived of the things they often want most: time outside, movement, activity. The system doesn't play to their natural strengths.

An easy fix is start boys at school at least one year later than girls. Boys will be older than girls, but they'll be on a somewhat more level playing field from a maturation standpoint. Sure, they'll still have wiggles and jiggles. They'll want to use their bodies. But a year of extra maturity *should* facilitate better executive function: that is, capacity for attention and improved impulse control.

Another challenge for boys at school: data shows teachers have lower empathy for boys and have lower academic expectations for them too.[30] In the words of one researcher, boys 'who perform equally as well as girls on reading, maths, and science tests are nevertheless graded less favourably by their teachers'.[31]

Melissa Abu-Gazaleh, founder and CEO of Top Blokes, told me 'the number one reason boys give for hating school is that they feel targeted by teachers. They feel unwanted, and in turn they don't want to be at school.'

Australian girls vastly outperform boys academically. They're outpacing boys by 38 points in PISA (Program for International Student Assessment) reading scores, putting them a full academic year ahead. By Year 9, one in eight boys is functionally illiterate.[32]

Are boys lacking motivation? Sometimes. Countless boys I've spoken to and worked with don't see an academic future so they don't engage with the curriculum, the assignments, or the testing. I relate to this. I didn't try at all. School didn't matter to me. And I utterly failed in my Year 12 exams, scoring in the bottom 15% of the state in the 1993 HSC. The curriculum felt entirely irrelevant. I saw no reason for surds, calculus, or ancient history. (I told my history teacher, Mrs Gilbert, to 'let bygones be bygones'. It didn't go well for me.) Whatever the reason, the consequences of boys' disengagement in the classroom cascade. Beyond the detentions, suspensions, and expulsions in the early years, here's what's happening in later years of education in Australia:

- one in five students – mostly boys – leave school before Year 12;
- of Australia's 44 universities, only two have more men than women enrolled;[33] and
- the gender ratio is 58 men to 100 women – and it's widening.

The repercussions are far reaching. Completing Year 12 means higher earnings, better career trajectories, deeper community engagement, and improved health. But, as well as not meeting the needs of boys vocationally or intellectually, our education system is not supporting boys' basic psychological needs. They're not seeing purpose in their learning. The curriculum feels irrelevant. They want to move their bodies, use their hands, experience the satisfaction of achievement. Effort and energy are like money for our sons: they'll spend it if they see the value in it. They're not lazy. But vast numbers of boys are just not interested in school.

There's an economic and social tail that's worth separating out in this discussion. With women now completing 62% of Australian university degrees, up from 58% in 2004, and a substantial gender gap in Year 12 completion rates, more young men are seen as unviable partners or matches for a high-expectation female population.[34] Women typically seek a partner who is educated at their level or higher, and/or who out-earns them – a pattern researchers call hypergamy. This preference shows up with remarkable consistency across cultures. David Buss is a leading researcher in this area. His landmark study of 10,000 people across 37 cultures on six continents found that women rated 'good financial prospect' higher than men did in every single culture studied, and in 29 of those samples, a partner's ambition and industriousness mattered more to women than to men.[35] In 2011, a 45-country replication with over 14,000 participants confirmed the same pattern. And when researchers went undercover on Tinder – in a field experiment published in the *Economics of Education Review* – they found that women indicated interest in Master's-degree profiles 91.4% more often than Bachelor's-degree profiles. What about men? Just 8.2% more often.[36]

The shorthand response is to conclude that women are selective and fussy, but men will happily partner with anyone regardless of status or achievement – but that's not quite right either. Some studies find men are indifferent to, or attracted by, a woman's success. Others – including a 2017 Harvard Business Review study by Bursztyn,

Fujiwara, and Pallais – find that men tend to prefer partners who are less professionally ambitious.[37] What does seem clear is that women's preferences are significantly more sensitive to status than men's, and that this gap is real, replicable, and cross-cultural.

The practical consequence matters enormously for boys. As women continue to out-earn and out-educate men in growing numbers, boys who disengage from education are increasingly locked out of the future economy and, by extension, seen as less socially and economically viable partners. Success in education doesn't just signal intelligence; it signals the kind of ambition, drive, and provider-capacity that research consistently shows women find attractive.

Mental health

There are mental health implications for the educational code red our boys face. In January 2025 youth unemployment sat at 10% for Australians aged 15 to 24, with underemployment at 14.1% in December 2024.[38] Boys without clear vocational pathways describe feeling purposeless, which feeds directly into the mental health and identity challenges we'll address below. To feel good about himself, a boy must do something worth his time and effort. A day, week, month, or year of fixating on Fortnite is not going to boost his long-term mental health. Time on TikTok is the same. Purposeless action equals a purposeless life. We become what we surround ourselves with. If our boys surround themselves with nothing, they risk becoming … nothing. This is crushing for identity (again, see below), and hammers mental health.

Exceptional mental health requires strong relationships, a sense of capability and competence, and a feeling of personal endorsement over the choices a young man makes. The education data shows that many of our boys can't find these three things in the school system. Another indicator of good mental health: physical health. Boys are quietly losing ground here too. Around 20.4% of Australian boys aged 16 to 17 are carrying excess weight and a further 11.8% are obese.[39] That's at least a third of boys who likely feel lousy about themselves because of their appearance. As 'looksmaxxing' (optimising physical appearance by doing whatever it takes) takes hold of our boys' perception of their bodies, and the comparison/competition game intensifies, mental health is hit hardest.

One in seven boys aged 11 to 17 experiences high or very high psychological distress.[40] The causes range from simple to complex. The solutions are almost always challenging. It's easy for me to tell you to help your son eat less processed food and more healthy food, to go to bed at the same time every night and wake up at the same time each morning, or to move his body, spend time with friends, and do something purposeful. Any parent with a struggling son knows that simply saying 'go outside and ride your bike' is as effective as trying to stop your nearby river from flowing by using your pinky to hold back the flow.

Depression and anxiety affect 61% of boys at least once during their teen years.[41] This is astonishing by any measure. But we often don't realise what's going on. Boys hide their depression and anxiety. Rather than appearing down and melancholy – or fearful and afraid – these common mental illnesses show up most often as anger, frustration, or withdrawal. Boys can be defensive and fight back with unexpected and disproportionate aggression. Parents consistently talk about their son's anger, but anger is a secondary emotion; it masks fear, sadness, helplessness, and hopelessness.

ADHD affects around 11% of boys; that's twice the number of girls diagnosed. Autism affects about 6% of boys versus 1% of girls. These specific challenges are not about intelligence. But boys with ADHD and autism face compounding struggles: academic difficulties, isolation, bullying (at least 67% of autistic kids experience bullying), and misunderstanding from adults who judge them as lazy or disruptive, rather than struggling. Neurodivergent boys are up to ten times more likely to develop depression or anxiety compared with neurotypical boys. The educational toll for autistic boys is significant. Just 60% complete Year 12. Sixty-one percent don't feel safe and accepted at school.[42]

And boys are lousy at asking for help. Mission Australia's youth survey reveals that while 37% of boys report psychological distress, they're far less likely than girls to seek support or even recognise their symptoms as depression. Only a third seek support when they need it.[43] The cultural mandate to 'toughen up' leaves many boys carrying invisible burdens.

The share of lonely Australians aged 15 to 24 rose from 14.4% in 2008 to 20.2% in 2019 – and then jumped to 26.6% in 2020 and remained elevated. No other age group followed this pattern.[44] Boys, who are typically less likely to seek connection or admit loneliness, are especially at risk here but are less likely to be counted in the statistics. The relational crisis is real – and 'friendship poverty' in adolescent males is increasingly well documented. Compared to previous generations, our boys experience less face-to-face time, less eye contact, less touch, fewer parties, reduced risk-taking (generally seen as positive but I'm not so sure), and a less-rich life. Relationships are the heart of wellbeing. Impoverished interaction equals increased mental illness.

Suicide remains the starkest and most devastating indicator that boys and men are struggling. It's the leading cause of death for people aged 15 to 24, regardless of gender, but it's twice as high for boys as it is for girls.[45] The overall picture (all ages) shows males die by suicide at between three and four times the rate of women. In 2024, 240 boys and young men under 25 died by suicide – close to five every week. A ray of hope in recent stats is that the rate of teenage male suicide (aged 15 to 19) has fallen significantly from a recent high of 17.8 per 100,000 in 2018 to 9.6 in 2024.[46] But working-age men (aged 25 to 64) hit a record high in 2024 at 1845 deaths. Five suicides a day. Too many boys and men feel helpless, useless, and hopeless.

A curious sidenote on males and mental health comes from a 2021 meta-analysis of 58 studies that spans 40 years of evidence. Data indicates that when masculinity is perceived and lived in a healthy way, where males are encouraged to be 'masculine' (through possessing masculine traits like being independent, active, competitive, decisive, persistent, self-confident, and staying strong under pressure), depression rates are lower. In other words, many of the negative mental health outcomes we see in boys and men today may be associated with unhealthy masculinity or other identity issues. If we're telling boys to 'sit down, be quiet, do as you're told', or suppressing their confidence, boisterous competitiveness, and persistence, we're part of the problem. Living a life of purpose, and being strong, confident, active, and decisive in a way that fits for your son is protective.

Crime

Boys and men take a lot of heat for criminal behaviour. Perpetrator data shows they're far more likely than girls or women to be involved in crime. But it's double jeopardy: yes, they're doing more hurting, but they're also the ones being hurt. According to the Australian Institute of Criminology, 84% of homicide offenders are male. Sixty-five percent of homicide victims are male. Men are nearly three times more likely than women to be physically assaulted by a stranger. Eighty-seven percent of blackmail victims are male, as are 76% of sextortion victims.[47]

Teen boys are the most likely to commit child-on-child sex abuse. In 2021, Chanel Contos launched a website called Teach Us Consent. Within days, over 7000 testimonies were submitted from young Australian women about sexual assault and harassment by male peers.[48] These were not stories about strangers. They were stories about classmates, teammates, boys from the school down the road. These were boys from wealthy families, poor families, private and public schools, religious and secular schools, who, it seems, had never been taught what healthy sexuality, consent, or respect for women actually looks like. They missed the memo about helping those around them feel – and be – safer and stronger. Australian Bureau of Statistics (ABS) research shows that 41% of sexual assault victims are aged between 10 and 17, and 84% are female. Teen boys have the highest sexual assault offender rates of any age group, but most perpetrators overall are adult males known to the victim.[49]

A journalist described to me how her daughter was harassed for nudes online. The aggressor? A 13-year-old boy who literally looked like the proverbial 'boy next door'. A mother told me how her nine-year-old daughter was abused by her babysitter, a 17-year-old boy from up the road. Sex crime is not a problem waiting to emerge in adulthood. It's in our schools, in our suburbs, right now.

Boys are also cycling through the youth justice system at alarming rates. Australian Institute of Health and Welfare data shows boys make up around 81% of young people under youth justice supervision in Australia, with many of them not first-timers.[50] Recidivism is high. The system is processing boys, but it's not transforming them. We are catching them, punishing them, and releasing them back into the same conditions that produced the behaviour in the first place.

Every statistic in this section – offender or victim, perpetrator or target – points to the same unaddressed question: what are we doing, or failing to do, for boys long before they ever hurt someone, something, or themselves? The culture is broken for too many boys.

We can keep catching them after the fact, processing them through systems that fail to transform them (and weren't designed to anyway), and we can call it justice. Or we can ask harder questions about the culture, the structures, and the failures of support that produce these outcomes I'm describing. No one wants to see people hurt. We want boys who are a genuine bonus to the people around them – who make others feel safer, stronger, and better for knowing them. The crime statistics are a symptom. The issues run far deeper than what shows up in the courtroom or the testimonials page on a sexual assault website.

Identity

In *Miss-Connection*, the girls I interviewed told me one of the best things about being a teen girl is 'figuring out who I am'. They embraced the idea of identity development and played with ideas (and identities) lightly, even joyfully. The teenage years ought to be the time that your son develops his sense of identity too – his values, his ethical standards, his sense of self. In today's climate, it's hard. Boys aren't having the same experience as girls.

In 2021, Brauer College, a co-ed high school in Warrnambool, Victoria, made national news when all male students were invited to stand at a school assembly 'as a symbolic gesture of apology for the behaviours of their gender that have hurt or offended girls and women' (a decision the principal later expressed regret for and retracted).[51]

Your son is surrounded by stories of boys and men behaving badly. Suggestions that teen boys are the root of society's ills envelop him. In too many homes, examples of dominance, disrespect, and denigration are the building blocks of his masculinity schema. How does a boy feel when he is told that masculinity is toxic, unhealthy, dangerous – or shown such examples?

Make no mistake: some people behave in toxic, unhealthy, and dangerous ways. The previous section bears witness to that fact. Physical, verbal, emotional, social, and psychological abuse have no place in our homes or society more generally. But masculinity hasn't cornered the market on these behaviours, particularly during our boys' childhood and adolescence. Yes, disproportionate harm is inflicted by males who abuse when compared to females. However, the concept of toxic masculinity is and has always been counter-productive, deficit-based, and insulting. Moreover, nobody who is serious about positive change is using the term anymore.

Michael Flood, professor of sociology, studies men, masculinities, and violence prevention at Queensland University of Technology, and explains it like this: 'What [toxic masculinity is] meant to name is one particular version of how to be a man that is toxic – toxic for the boys and men who try to live up to it, and toxic for those around them.' But, he notes, 'the phrase is often misheard as saying there's something intrinsically unhealthy or toxic about being a man'.[52]

Our Herculean task is to help boys develop *positive* identities in a world that seems uncertain about what healthy masculinity looks like and, at least in some corners, would lazily condemn *all* males as toxic because of these challenges. We're up against it.

Think about those girls who loved playing with their feminine identity development. Would your son say he is enjoying figuring out who he is; how to carry himself; what masculinity feels like? If identity development means developing values, ethical standards, and a sense of 'who I am', this might be the hardest task he'll face as he matures to manhood. Boys need more opportunity to do the 'inner work' of identity development, and more models of men who have done it successfully. But to do it, we need to define healthy masculinity, and be clear about what it looks like.

To develop healthy masculine identity, we can teach our boys about historical manhood. Across cultures and time, anthropologists and psychologists point to three consistent roles for men:

- Provider.
- Protector.
- Procreator.

It hurts to say it, but men have always been expendable, relative to women. Biologically and mathematically, if all but a few men in the village attempt to defend their tribe against invaders, or seek the lion that is killing their family, they could all die and yet the tribe could continue. But send the women out? Their deaths mean the tribe is finished. Men have been valued for their willingness to go to war, to hunt, to explore, to face off enemies. The greater the conquest, the greater the man. Be it slaying the beast, catching the fish, or defeating the enemy, effective men were those who did these things. Provide and protect. Not doing these things meant being labelled as not a 'real' man.

In our modern world, these anchors have shifted. Attitudes have changed. Social structures leave some people arguing that these ideas are archaic, irrelevant, and even inappropriate. And boys feel unmoored. Not one boy I spoke to in writing this book suggested any of those three things – provider, protector, procreator – make a man. But they had no ideas to fill the gap left by society's erasure of that cross-cultural, millennia-old script. When I ask boys or men to describe 'healthy masculinity', they struggle.

If boys can't identify positive male role models to support their identity development – and even good, thoughtful men in their lives are unsure – who's jumping on this opportunity? The name that has inspired the greatest 'toxic' turmoil since the mid-2010s is Andrew Tate. His combination of male empowerment and misogyny appeals to many young men. (At the time of writing, Tate is facing charges of rape, human trafficking, and organised crime – allegations he denies.)

While I question the breadth of impact of Andrew Tate and other manosphere influencers (to be discussed in Chapter 4) on Australian boys, there's no doubt that Tate has reached into hearts and minds. Most boys I've spoken to are dismissive of Tate and his ilk. But for him to have any impact is concerning. And there is evidence that a percentage of boys do get something out of following him or even mentioning his name. Daniel Schwammenthal notes, 'The iron rule of politics is that if there are real problems in society and responsible parties don't deal with them, the irresponsible parties will jump on them.'[53] Tate, and others like him, know a void exists and are explicitly taking advantage of it.

We've all heard the expression 'It's a man's world', and while it may have rung true for many generations, it feels hollow for today's boys. They see girls outperforming them academically, and increasing numbers of boys are not in education, employment, or training (NEET). Our boys are carrrying major mental health challenges with record diagnoses of depression, anxiety, ADHD, autism, and more. News media and social platforms amplify messages about boys' escalating criminal behaviour, with stories of fights, machete and knife crime, and theft. They're hurting each other, girls, and themselves in devastating ways – casting long shadows across the lives of their victims. And cultural conversations point to male toxicity yet offer few positive models of what healthy masculinity looks like. The climate allows and escalates lines like 'men are trash', which have become socially acceptable in some circles.

Boys are struggling. It's a code red situation. They need a positive vision of manhood – and a pathway to get there. Not nostalgia and a return to the 'good old days'. A path forward that works.

2 Hardwired

How biology shapes your son

Men and women, boys and girls, are different ... starting in the womb and continuing in later life.

Carole Hooven[1]

Cassie's 12-year-old son had an idea. He lay facedown, clenched a golf tee between his butt cheeks, perched a ball on top and invited his 13-year-old brother to take a swing with a golf club. The result? A spectacular bruise on his left buttock. (His brother missed the ball completely.)

'Would you do that again?' Cassie asked him.

The response? 'Probably.'

Now consider two scenes.

Scene one: a backyard barbecue. Ten girls from two families sit quietly chatting. Six of them are from my family. Our friends parent the other four girls. The final guests arrive with their four sons. The energy changes instantly. Their 14-year-old boy spots a carton of icy-cold soft drink on the table. His eyes light up. He grabs a can, sprints to the middle of the lawn, and launches it skywards. The can, wet with condensation, rockets 15 metres into the air, descends in a perfect arc to his waiting hands, slips through his fingers, and explodes on impact with the ground. His response? A gleeful, 'No way!' as he runs back for another can.

Scene two: any beach, any weekend. Teen girls lying on towels cluster in small groups and soak up the sun, talking, scrolling on phones, reading books. Meanwhile, teen boys hurl footballs, kick soccer balls, and crash-tackle each other in the waves.

A deputy principal at a Sydney school, Allison Gatt, wryly told me, 'Boys add colour.'

This chapter looks at the way the hardwired reality of a Y chromosome (nature) melds with the socialised, cultural expectations that our sons grow up immersed in (nurture). By nature, boys are physical, take risks, and are hierarchical (so they seek status). But nurture is enormously impactful on who our boys become too. Only the ignorant would dismiss environmental influence on how a boy develops. Biology primes some characteristics and behaviours and, when things go wrong, unhelpful elements of our culture pressure boys to express those characteristics and behaviours in unhealthy ways. This combination – hardwired tendencies crashing into unhealthy social scripts – is the terrain our sons are navigating.

Nature: the biological reality

It's an undeniable reality: males and females are different. We share more in common than we differ. But those differences exist. At the heart of sex differences is testosterone, or T. Testosterone is the masculinity molecule. This powerful hormone is an androgen, from the Greek 'andro' – man – and 'gen' – generating. Androgens, primarily testosterone, shape both brain and body to quite literally *make men.*

Testosterone surges at three key times in a boy's life. The first is in the womb, where it develops male reproductive organs and masculinises the brain. The second hits around six months of age. The third is during puberty, where levels multiply by 10 to 20 times. T peaks around a man's 20th birthday – at generally 15 to 20 times his same-age female peers – where it plateaus for about 20 years, then declines gradually from age 40 (at about 1% to 2% per year). Even at its lowest, male T remains ten times higher than female levels throughout life. T's impact affects the whole body, including the brain.[2]

Biology is not determinative, but it is directional. And testosterone points the average boy in a direction that is markedly different from that of the average girl.

Physical transformations

Puberty – particularly T – creates visible sexual dimorphism: the distinct differences in male and female appearance. With this T boost, boys develop wider shoulders, thicker brow ridges, and larger nasal passages (and no, it's not from picking them – although an early reader of the book insisted that 'Yes, it actually is!'). That larger nose provides the oxygen needed to run a boy's larger muscle mass.[3]

Up until age ten, similarities between the sexes are the norm. But a meta-analysis of 64 studies found that by age 12, boys outperformed girls in throwing by over 3.5 standard deviations – a gap so large it suggests the difference is unlikely to be completely rooted in environmental causes. Similarly, sex differences in athletic performance emerge with the onset of puberty, coinciding with the dramatic rise in testosterone in males, and adult men typically outperform women by 10% to 30% in events relying on strength, speed, and power. The consensus is that adult men are typically stronger, more powerful, and faster than women of similar age and training status.[4]

The scale of these physical differences is most clear in sports. As one example, in 2016 Australia's Matildas were the fifth-ranked female soccer team globally – a fabulous accomplishment. That year, they played against an under-15 boys' Newcastle representative team in a warmup for an international game. The result? A decisive 7–0 victory … to the boys.[5]

Physical sex differences show up consistently, from tennis to athletics, in surfing, skating, winter sports, and more. This isn't to take away from exceptional female athletes. Rather, it highlights the undeniable reality of biology. Though training and resources may reduce the gap between genders, these outcomes cannot be explained away by socialisation or training differences.

The social arena

The hardwired differences exist in the social arena too, and they overlap with boys' propensity to use their bodies. One 1987 study has become a psychology classic.[6] The setup: a viewfinder box showing a cartoon movie that required three children working together to operate: one to view, one to turn a crank, and one to push a light button. The catch? The researchers put kids in groups of four, meaning someone would always be left out.

The groups were single-sex, meaning boys were separate from girls. Both boys' and girls' groups achieved equal success, but how they went about it differed dramatically. The boys turned their negotiations into a physical free-for-all, shoving and wrestling, their bodies flying everywhere. Yet despite – or perhaps because of – all this physicality and competition, they rated the activity as great fun and shared things around evenly. Girls, on the other hand, employed verbal strategies. They were surgical in their social exclusion. No physical pushing needed – they ignored or subtly blocked the chosen outsider from participating, shared less evenly, and reported less enjoyment of the activity compared to the boys. It was the same task, same structure, but different approaches – physical dominance versus social manipulation. The boys left with scrapes, bruises, and huge grins. The girls left with their social hierarchy precisely calibrated, and one of their number nursing invisible wounds.

Hardwired for risk

Boys and girls play differently from their earliest years. Even in preschool, boys use their bodies more, and they thrive on rough-and-tumble play.[7] Boys are more physically active, saving universes, fighting battles, and sometimes destroying everything in sight.

The typical boy's appetite for risk, physicality, and even aggression is vastly higher than a girl's. Physical aggression is often a boy's preferred way of responding to challenges, and it ramps up during adolescence. When there's conflict between two boys, particularly if they are equally matched, a predictable script is followed. Some call it the 'male monkey dance'. It involves:

- hard stares;
- verbal challenges ('What are you looking at?');
- close proximity and chest-bumping;
- the finger-poke or two-handed chest push; and
- the final escalation to physical conflict.[8]

It's ritualistic. And there are only two ways out without violence: submission (with its social costs) or third-party intervention that allows both parties to save face. Someone breaks it up, so they can taunt one another with an intermediary stopping further aggression: 'You're lucky … I was going to smash you.'

What about impulse control? The average 24-year-old man possesses the same level of impulse control as the average 11-year-old girl, according to research by renowned adolescence researcher Laurence Steinberg.[9] 'Women are more mature than men, at least with respect to the ability to control themselves and regulate their behaviour,' Steinberg told me. 'We followed some samples until the age of 30 and they don't catch up.' He also said, 'We've replicated these findings in a cross-national study of 11 countries.'

It's a biological fact. Boys are hardwired for action. Act first. Think later. Seek status. Look good.

This is why a boy in my Year 9 class agreed to a dare, and dropped to the ground to lick up a trodden-on, smooshed-up devon sandwich from the ground. It's why all the boys (but only two of the girls) in my Year 8 class agreed to do the 'wimp test' – scratching the back of their hand with their fingernail hard, 100 times, creating a terrible graze that scabbed over and took weeks to heal. Throw in more challenging behaviours: riding e-scooters and e-bikes on public roads without shoes or helmets at speeds of up to 75 kilometres an hour; lewd and sexually inappropriate conduct in public; risky alcohol and other drug use; fights; and other impulsive, risky behaviours for post-and-boast status on social media. Low impulse control. Hardwired for action. Seek status. Save face. Win. Be strong.

Another hardwired difference is sensation-seeking. Impulse control is the brake (which we've established doesn't work so well in young men). Sensation-seeking is the engine. And in boys, that engine is enormous. When it comes to sensation-seeking, a young woman peaks during adolescence, but even at her peak (age 19) she's lower on the scale than an average 13-year-old boy. And his sensation-seeking only increases from there! At every age, males are more sensation-seeking than females.

Channelled positively (or at least benignly), it's why my friends and I pushed ourselves into bigger and bigger surf that we had no business being out in. Or why the son of a former employee filmed himself and his mates using perfume and deodorant as fire accelerants – first on a can of energy drink, then a plastic bottle, and next a shoe, before spraying the alcohol on their nipples and belly-buttons and lighting it. (The video is hilarious. Men watching it laugh. Women cover their faces.) It's why boys have competitions to see who can eat the hottest chilli. It's why my mate Ant Williams holds his breath for up to 8½ minutes and swims to depths of over 90 metres (which makes it a 180-metre round trip on one breath). Ant's world-record free-diving is sensation-seeking, positively channelled.

Risk, impulsiveness, sensation-seeking: it's ingrained in males at levels we rarely see in females. And there's more. About 90% of girls and women are more fearful than the average boy or man, while about 90% of boys and men have higher pain thresholds than their female counterparts. This latter statistic feels false, particularly when women labour through childbirth while men can't seem to survive a low dose of 'man-flu'. Yet studies have consistently found women are more responsive to pain and less willing to experience it than men.[10]

Steve Stewart-Williams, an evolutionary psychologist and author of *A Billion Years of Sex Differences*, explains that lower fear responses and higher pain thresholds combined with greater physical strength create males more capable of risking themselves to defend their group. And men are hardwired to do that defending. As I've mentioned, historically men defended the village (or the country). They hunted large game. Men risked their lives exploring new territory, breaking in horses, or playing wargames. Boys who respond to these hardwired tendencies in healthy ways become men who can do extraordinary things. As an example, five Australians have received the Cross of Valour – our highest civilian honour for acts of bravery in peacetime. All five were male. This pattern repeats across similar awards globally. Females do win such awards, but at disproportionately low levels relative to males, even after statistically controlling for a wide range of factors.

How does that look at the micro level with your son? The boy who stands up to a bully, the teenager who intervenes in a fight, the young man who stops to help a stranded motorist – all are expressing this hardwired tendency towards risk-taking in a protective way. Understanding this aspect of male biology may help us see challenging boy behaviours in a new light. Our task isn't to suppress these tendencies but to channel them towards prosocial ends: service, contribution, supporting others. Being a bonus. Adding value. Helping others feel safer and stronger. This is what I mean when I talk about *surplus value*.

There are other hardwired differences that would fill an entire book. For example, men are more overtly sexual *and* more casual about sex than women. A meta-analysis of 211 studies covering more than 620,000 people found men have a stronger sex drive than women across every measure examined – sexual thoughts and fantasies, desire, and behaviour – with a medium-to-large effect size.[11] And in a study spanning 53 countries, six continents, and 13 islands, men everywhere showed greater openness to casual relationships and less need for emotional connection before physical intimacy.[12] The consistency across cultures suggests something hardwired rather than socialised, according to Steve Stewart-Williams. As entrepreneur Scott Galloway writes, young men are 'force-marinated in testosterone' during puberty, making them 'monosyllabic', and narrowing their focus to 'sports/physical activity and thinking about sex'.[13]

Males and females are interested in different things too, and this is seen in both play and work. By far the largest occupational gender difference is an interest in *things* – objects, machines, abstract rules – versus interest in *people*. Steve Stewart-Williams, drawing on a meta-analysis of over 500,000 respondents, notes that men's preference for working with things and women's preference for working with people produces one of the largest documented sex differences in psychology.[14] And like sexual interest differences (which also have enormous statistical and real-world significance), the same sex differences in occupational preferences have been found in every society where psychologists have looked for them; in that study of nearly 200,000 people across 53 nations, which I mentioned earlier, it was found in all 53 nations.[15] This matters for boys because the modern world increasingly values emotional intelligence, communication, and relational skills, and that plays less naturally to how a lot of boys are wired.

Lastly, boys consistently outperform girls on spatial reasoning – the ability to mentally rotate objects, navigate three-dimensional space, and think geometrically. A meta-analysis across a wide range of spatial ability measures confirmed that sex differences favour males significantly across multiple test types.[16] Again, the gender difference is enormous and appears early in life. The likelihood of this being a nurtured, socialised response to the environment doesn't make any sense. Spatial ability is one of the strongest predictors of performance in mathematics, engineering, and the physical sciences. This helps us understand why boys are drawn to these areas, and women are outnumbered so dramatically – particularly in countries that are doing the hardest work on gender equality.

When women are free to choose without economic pressure, their choices are more likely to be different from men's, not less. That's the paradox – and it's replicated across 76 countries.[17]

Some researchers argue that these differences are socialised. Even a surface-level review of the evidence shows that they're not. These are biological differences that alter life trajectories. Boys and girls *are* different. But these differences aren't destiny. Carole Hooven, author of *Testosterone*, reminds us that 'genes, status, personality, health, and the present social situation all matter too'.[18] Nature is having an impact. But nurture does too.

3 Boxed in

What society is telling your son about manhood

> Two-thirds of the men we surveyed said that since they were a boy, they'd been told that a 'real man' behaves in a certain way.
>
> **Matt Tyler** [1]

As I described in Chapter 1, ask a teenage boy to define what it is to be a man and you'll hear … silence. But I didn't describe what comes next. Invariably, it's a definition of masculinity in the negative – what it isn't rather than what it is:

- Don't cry (or show emotion).
- Don't be a wuss.
- Don't be a girl.
- Don't ask for help.
- Don't talk about problems.

- Don't show fear or back down.
- Don't be a simp.*
- Don't dog the boys.**

Ask adult men the same question – same result.

Manhood, as traditionally defined in many civilisations, is not viewed as a birthright. Rather, manhood is a status to be fought for, won, and defended. The rituals were designed specifically to ensure men were separated from the domestic world (and work) of women. Womanhood is typically seen as a natural, biological progression, whereas anthropologists, sociologists, social and evolutionary psychologists, and historians broadly agree that manhood has always been something that required constant evidence – and it can be taken away. A man can be emasculated. Social psychologist Roy Baumeister explains: 'In many societies, any girl who grows up automatically becomes a woman ... meanwhile a boy does not automatically become a man, and is instead often required to prove himself, usually by passing stringent tests or producing more than he consumes.'[2]

* Urban Dictionary defines a simp as 'Someone who does way too much for a person they like.' This is seen as incredibly weak for a boy. Moreover, most of the time a simp is excessively deferential to their love interest but receives nothing in return, making their simp status even more reviled.

** Boys describe two definitions for this term – and I've heard them both often. The first means you don't tell anyone what your 'boys' have been up to. This includes but is not limited to parents, teachers, police, or anyone outside your group. Secondly, 'don't dog the boys' is a term often used by mates when one of the boys either ditches or intends to ditch a gathering or social event with the lads for something far less important like work, a girl or, in extreme cases, even a quiet night in.

Suffering pain, killing game (meat), living alone, or fighting were just some of the ways boys demonstrated their manliness. And while the Western mindset is less focused on these themes (though not entirely), men have always been the ones who proved their masculinity by providing and protecting. The surplus value/be a bonus theme keeps showing up and is specifically linked to demonstrating manhood.

University of South Florida researchers found empirical support showing that masculinity is still precarious, even in today's modern climate.[3] When presented with made-up proverbs about gender – 'manhood is hard won and easily lost' versus similar made-up statements about womanhood – both male and female participants strongly endorsed precarious masculinity. They saw womanhood as a natural biological maturation but viewed manhood as something that must be actively achieved and maintained through social proof. If it couldn't be proved and held strongly, he wasn't a man.

The researchers pushed further. They had participants complete a pretend 'gender knowledge test' and gave them false feedback. Some male participants were told they scored similarly to women, while others were told they scored the same as the other men. The same was done for women: some women were told they scored in a similar way to other female participants while others were told they scored a lot like the men involved in the study. Participants were then asked how they would feel if family or friends found out their score. Men who were told they scored like women showed immediate anxiety and discomfort. This may be merely an issue of differentiation, or because women have lower status in the eyes of some men. The men in this study told the researchers they would not want family and friends knowing their more female-oriented results. When they were subsequently given word completion tasks (in what they thought was an unrelated experiment), they were more likely to see violence in neutral prompts. For example, they completed 'PUN__' as 'PUNCH' rather than 'PUNK', 'PUNT' or 'PUNY'. They saw 'LO_ER' as 'LOSER' rather than 'LOVER' or 'LOWER'. Women showed no such bias when their womanhood was questioned for supposed masculine scores. Achieving and maintaining masculinity appears strongly related to feelings of status. Males consistently feel they must save face by appearing as masculine as possible – and that reverts to stereotypes that have existed for millennia: strong and courageous, resilient and emotionally level, physically capable, and successful in their 'maleness'.

Precarious masculinity is about status

During March 2025, I travelled to Sumba, in Indonesia, for a surf trip. Two teen boys, Digby and Gray (each in Year 9), were there with their dads.

I mentioned I was writing a book about boys and, with permission, I quizzed them about being a boy today. 'What's most important to a teenage boy when it comes to masculinity?' I asked.

Without hesitation, Digby answered, 'Looking good in front of your mates.'

'Tell me more,' I prompted.

Digby shrugged. 'Just looking good. That's it.'

And I watched it over and over again with those boys in the ocean. A wave would appear on the horizon and steam towards us. Some waves were bigger than the boys felt comfortable surfing. If things went wrong, there was the potential for real danger. Digby would ask Gray, 'Do you want it?' Gray would nod. Challenge accepted. I could see concern (or was it fear?) in his eyes. Then he'd paddle onto the wave. Look good. Prove yourself. Push the limits. Be a man. Slay the lion. Charge. Next it would be Digby's turn to take on the challenge. Be a man. Slay the lion. Charge. And they both did.

Jen Bosson and her colleagues conducted an experiment across 62 countries with 27,300 students.[4] They investigated whether gender rules were stricter for males than for females. To answer this question, participants completed a questionnaire about how desirable it is to follow gender norms. The overwhelming result: it is more important for males than for females to follow gender norms. The researchers found that manhood is 'precarious' – hard won and easily lost. Those who fail to prove their masculinity are punished socially and emotionally – and sometimes even physically. It also explains why homosexual (or effeminate) boys and men have so often been threatened and harmed: peers don't see them as masculine and so they punish them – and policing this specific gender norm 'proves' the masculinity of the perpetrators. There are terrible issues with this line of reasoning, but the precarious masculinity theory helps us to see what has triggered it, even if it can never be condoned.

The 2025 social media challenge 'Run it Straight' gives us another insight. Alpha males run at full pace towards one another, bodies crashing into one another with the intention of knocking the other over, potentially causing catastrophic injuries.[5] If you're not game to 'run it straight', what kind of a man are you? Apparently, not a 'real' one.

Our sporting legends' biographies overflow with tales of legendary drinking sessions – not because alcohol consumption defines manhood, but because society has shown it offers a measurable, public way to demonstrate masculine courage and capacity.

If masculinity is a fragile status, difficult to attain, and easy to lose – and requiring ongoing public validation through behaviour that demonstrates self-reliance and dominance – then those who ascribe to this ideology will consistently conform to rigid gender norms focused on strength, stoicism, and dominance. For parents raising boys, these findings illuminate why our sons sometimes react so strongly to seemingly minor challenges to their masculinity. That meltdown over being called 'a girl' or 'gay' or the aggressive response to being outperformed by a female classmate or even a friend on Fortnite (or on the football field) isn't a simple case of individual insecurity and teenage dramatics. The research into precarious masculinity shines a light on why so many boys choose unsafe, unhealthy activities – drinking, drugs, sex, violence, sharing pornography and videos of beheadings online – to prove they're real men. It's a response to a deeply felt insecurity about their status as 'real men' in a culture where some boys feel unsafe behaviour is the only pathway to manhood. Research on precarious masculinity consistently shows negative relationships between these beliefs and wellbeing at individual and societal levels.

And social media has exacerbated this, giving boys a platform to judge each other – to 'post and boast'. Fights, dangerous stunts, stealing, drinking, sexual conquest; what matters isn't the specific proof of 'masculinity', but that it is public and difficult to replicate.

A 2026 study from Boston College found a link between a nation's happiness and precarious masculinity beliefs. Across 59 countries, people tended to be less happy in nations in which high national averages of men believe that masculinity is a fragile status, difficult to attain, and easy to lose. The correlation was significant. Nordic countries (Denmark, Finland, Sweden) and places like New Zealand and Canada scored high levels of happiness and low levels of precarious masculinity. At an aggregate level, Australia scored comfortably in a healthy, positive zone despite elements some of us might be concerned about. Places such as the USA, Italy, and Romania are mid-range on both variables. Countries such as Lebanon, Iran, and Nigeria have high precarious masculinity scores and low happiness levels. The relationship between rigid gender expectations and happiness is clear. Living in a gender straitjacket at a national level can shape national wellbeing and create systemic challenges, not just for boys, but for society.[6]

The Man Box

While traditional cultures had clear (if often brutal and abusive) pathways to manhood, today's boys in our Western context face a more nebulous challenge: the Man Box. This concept, originating from activist Paul Kivel and the Oakland Men's Project in the 1980s, describes the invisible but powerful constraints that define 'acceptable' masculine behaviour – and our boys are impacted by it and even defined by it today.[7]

If you adhere to Man Box beliefs, you think 'real men' are:

- emotionally stoic and self-sufficient;
- tough;
- conforming to traditional gender roles;
- hyper-sexual (and heterosexual);
- in control and even aggressive 'if necessary' in relationships; and
- looking good (without going to too much effort).[8]

As Man Box researcher Matt Tyler explained to me, 'The Man Box is sustained by a set of rewards and punishments. If you step outside the Man Box in certain contexts, you hear words like "don't be a wimp, don't be a girl" to police the Man Box and push men and boys back inside.'

A similar set of ideas was put forward by Harvard researcher Bill Pollack in his 1998 *New York Times* bestseller *Real Boys.* He found that boys policed one another, demanding adherence to a 'boy code' that stifled authenticity and required they wear a mask of masculinity that hid their true natures.[9]

The pressure to put on the gender straitjacket is real. About 37% of young Australian men report feeling pushed to adhere to these rules, while 26% personally endorse them.[10] These numbers aren't enormous, but they're enough to impact the environment. About four boys in a 30-student classroom will endorse those beliefs. And that can and does change the climate – and the behaviour – of the other students in the room. These Man Box beliefs aren't neutral.

They are associated with worrisome realities. For example, someone who endorses Man Box beliefs is:

- eight times more likely to perpetrate sexual violence against partners;
- five times more likely to use physical violence;
- thirty-five times more likely to sexually harass women;
- six times more likely to be a problem gambler;
- eight times more likely to have daily thoughts of suicide;
- almost twice as likely to have consumed alcohol at least five days a week over the previous 12 months; and
- two and a half times more likely to engage in dangerous behaviour while intoxicated.[11]

In short, high endorsement of Man Box beliefs is bad for your health and wellbeing, *and* the health and wellbeing of those around you. Boys are hurting each other, they're hurting girls, and they're hurting themselves. But boys in the Man Box are doing it at far higher rates.

If we can normalise a gender system that eases pressure on males to 'prove' their manhood through dominance and self-reliance by encouraging versions of manhood that are caring, cooperative, and willing to ask for help, by pushing back when males are mocked for not adhering to gender straitjacket expectations, and by offering a healthy model of masculinity, we can create a 'man box' with softer sides, fuzzier edges, and a more sustainable, healthy approach to being a man.

The path forward

I want this on repeat in your brain – and in your son's brain: a boy becomes a man when he helps those around him feel safer and stronger. He's the guy who stays back after an event and stacks chairs or mops floors. He's the guy who sees a woman walking in a dark street and moves to the other side of the road so she doesn't feel uncomfortable. He's a bonus. He adds value.

Our task is to shift the focus from proving manhood through displays of dominance or reckless behaviour to displays of contribution and character. Being a man means developing skills and strength to take care of – and advocate for – others. The goal is to help boys become a net positive on the world around them. Rather than defining masculinity by what it isn't (don't cry, don't ask for help, don't show weakness), we need to define it by what it creates: safety, strength, and value for others.

Understanding the biology and the precarious nature of masculinity gives us powerful tools as parents. Rather than dismissing our sons' concerns or telling them to 'man up' (which, ironically, reinforces the problem), we can help them build more secure masculinity by tying their worth to contribution and purpose.

Boys must learn that strong men don't tear others down. Instead, they lift others up. They don't use size or strength to intimidate. They use it to protect and help and build. They don't mock feelings or weakness – instead, they create safety for everyone. By understanding biology *and* culture, nature *and* nurture, we can help our sons navigate adolescence and the transition to manhood successfully. They can become real men.

4 Screen lords

Why your son is drawn to gaming and influencer culture

The real problem of humanity is the following: we have Palaeolithic emotions, medieval institutions and godlike technology. And it is terrifically dangerous, and it is now approaching a point of crisis overall.

Edward O Wilson[1]

'My 13-year-old son was sent a video clip of two of his friends having sex,' a woman told me.

Press pause here. Not on the video, obviously. But pause on the reality of this situation. Kids aged 13 are having sex, filming it, and then one of them thinks it's okay to share his 'conquest' with a friend.

I was talking with a mum after a seminar in a Victorian school. Everyone had left the seminar room as she confided in me, terrified that the world her son inhabits was going to change him – for the worse. 'He's so innocent – or at least, he was.'

This is the world our boys are immersed in. Screens demand attention, explicit and outrageous content is shared, algorithms capture and rot minds, and our children disappear into a digital amphitheatre that real life struggles to compete with. Whether it's sexual content, violence, manosphere vitriol, looksmaxxing, gambling, games, or harmless and wholesome kittens playing, as New York University's Professor Scott Galloway asserts, attention has become the new oil, and tech giants are the modern-day mining corporations.[2] Where BHP once drilled the Pilbara for iron ore, companies like Alphabet (owners of Google and YouTube), Meta (Facebook, Instagram, WhatsApp and Threads), and TikTok are drilling our children's minds for something far more precious than any elemental commodity. The tech giants are mining attention.

Unlike the earth's natural resources, though, attention is breathtakingly scalable and virtually limitless – and our kids' attention is the prime resource being exploited. The world's wealthiest companies have achieved their status by appearing to support our children's basic psychological needs while hollowing them out. Want genuine human connection? Here's social media. Craving intimacy? Here's pornography. Want to feel competent and capable? Here's Fortnite, Roblox, or Minecraft. Hollow imitations that feel like they might be enough but are doing more harm than good. They appear to satisfy basic psychological needs, and in some ways they do, but they're not doing it in positive and healthy ways that help our boys show up at their best – as a bonus. They're taking from our boys far more than they give.

Brave new world

The crisis of boys is, to some degree, a problem of the internet. Yes, we had struggles before everything went online, but it's different in digital. The problems are amplified and harder to escape. Our kids' dopamine is tickled and ensnared by Instagram, YouTube, Snapchat, Discord, and TikTok. And an endless pool of games, gambling, pornography, and other dopamine deliverers is in the palm of their hand the moment they own a phone. If your child does not yet have a smart device, know this: the moment you hand your son a phone, it becomes the centre of his world, and it will change your relationship with him forever.

We're living in Aldous Huxley's prophetic vision. In his 1932 masterpiece *Brave New World*, society was pacified not through oppression but through pleasure, via a drug called soma that offered blissful escape. Today, our sons have their own soma. It's in their pockets, on their desks, beside their beds, in the palm of their hands. Their screens have become portals to comfort, distraction, artificial satisfaction, and escape. (And it's the same for many adults too.)

But soma rang hollow. It was an imitation. John the Savage declared, 'I don't want comfort. I want God, I want poetry, I want real danger, I want freedom, I want goodness, I want sin.'[3]

John the Savage would be an outlier today. When I survey tween and teen boys, they're choosing comfort. They're choosing escape. They want soma – at least it seems that way.

Parents tell me:

- 'He's glued to his phone and it's hard to get him to disconnect.'
- 'If he's not gaming, he's on social media. It feels like an addiction.'
- 'Getting him to put down his device and join family activities is a challenge.'

Jonathan Haidt argues we have moved from a play-based childhood to a screen-based childhood.[4] In this chapter we'll look at gaming, discuss the algorithms that feed the attention machine of social media, investigate the impact of AI, and consider the effects of gambling.

Gaming

Boys spend, on average, close to two hours on games every day from the age of five.[5] I'd love to tell you gaming is destroying your son's brain. Frustratingly, it's not that simple. Games are a major pain point for parents raising tween and teen boys. But gaming is associated with *positive* outcomes. A 2021 study found boys who played video games most days at age 11 showed lower depression scores at age 14. And regular gaming has been linked to reduced anxiety, and better peer relationships.[6]

But this research leaves me wondering. If video games really benefit our boys socially, shouldn't they have more friends (or at least be less lonely) than boys a decade or two ago? Shouldn't anxiety be dropping? The opposite is true. Young men are lonelier and more anxious today than at any time in history.[7] The online world offers lower-quality relationships, but boys grasp them because too often that's all they have. It's their soma. It's the shallow, hollow imitation that's close enough to feel like it might just be enough. It's where everyone else is, so that's where they go. But the quality of the interaction – the level of relationship – doesn't come close to an analogue, face-to-face relationship.

Once gaming and internet use become compulsive, the impacts are even greater. Screen time has a dose–response relationship with wellbeing. Like alcohol, the more you consume, the greater the effect. Cutting-edge Australian research by Macquarie University professor Wayne Warburton and Dr Brad Marshall shows that gaming at *higher* levels is a major problem for the wellbeing of our screen-lord sons. Want to take a flamethrower to their gaming device? You may have some justification.

In a 2025 study on Internet Gaming Disorder (IGD) and smartphone overuse, Warburton, Marshall and their colleagues collected data on 1993 Australian kids aged 10 to 14 (with a 66.2% male sample). About 10% of these children presented with medium to high problematic smartphone use and 4% of children met clinical or sub-clinical levels of IGD.[8] The results of this study indicate that gaming can be deeply problematic for the small number of boys (and girls) who meet these high-dose thresholds.

First, secondary school children reported spending nine hours per day on recreational screen time (burying that two-hour estimate I referred to earlier). An OECD study published around the same time showed the same numbers,[9] adding validity to this nine-hour shock. (Primary-school-aged children had an average of six hours per day. Also alarming.)

Second, children who were using devices and gaming at sub-clinical and clinical levels (that is, heavy users) reported significantly higher developmental impacts than those who were less heavy device users.[10] What were those impacts? The researchers investigated the impact of smartphone overuse and IGD on (i) emotional development, (ii) physical activity levels, (iii) social activity, (iv) behaviour, and (v) education. Compared with those using devices and gaming at lower levels, children at clinical and sub-clinical levels experienced significant developmental impacts in every one of those five domains. That's researcher-speak for 'this is a serious problem'. The take-home message: that the percentage of boys who are using screens at excessive levels are lagging developmentally, at least in part, because of their screen-lord status.

Inside the machine

Make no mistake, the technology companies are working against you – and they don't care about the cost to your relationship with your son, nor what their products do to him. Jonathan Haidt argues that, since the technological shift between 2000 and 2015, as the world (and our children) moved from having flip phones to supercomputers in their pockets, we now 'super-empower tech companies ... who are the most predatory organisations on the planet, led by people with poor ethics and no restraints, to enter the lives of our kids'.[11]

Games using the addiction model rely on Skill-Based Matchmaking – a psychological trap disguised as fair play. The game carefully matches players against equally skilled opponents, creating an addictive illusion of competence.[12] This strategy mimics Vygotsky's zone of proximal development: it keeps challenges just difficult enough to feel achievable but ensures they're not boring.[13] It's flow-state addiction via basic psychological need-satisfaction.

These games are psychological minefields designed to exploit our boys' desires. Notice your son fretting about limited-time offers or exclusive skins? The gaming companies weaponise FOMO (fear of missing out), dangling rewards just out of reach. The threat of losing a streak (whether in the game or on social platforms) creates obsessive and compulsive checking in and logging on. 'I've got to get my daily bonus.' They want him spending your hard-earned cash to avoid being left behind. Their goal: turn boys' social anxieties into profit. It's emotional manipulation.

Games keep players hooked by removing the time from the screen (like a casino), offering bonuses, giving unlimited free lives for the next x number of minutes, dangling goodies, and allowing instant rebirth when defeated. These decisions aren't an accident. They keep kids hooked by design.

William Siu, a former game developer, launched more than 50 mobile games, collectively downloaded over one billion times, with over US$1 billion in sales. In a *New York Times* essay, Siu wrote, 'I am very familiar with game addiction, as that's what I thought about every day for more than a decade. I tracked everything players did … to see which versions allowed us to extract the most time and money. For us, game addiction was by design: it meant success for our business.' This is a staggeringly candid confession. After explaining some of the techniques developers employ to keep a user's rapt attention, Siu added one more compelling statement: 'That's the ultimate goal: to build habit-forming games that have players coming back every day. In other words, it takes away the decision-making.'[14] Perhaps after he made his multi-millions he grew a conscience?

These games are meticulously crafted for compulsive behaviour. Addiction isn't a side effect; it's the objective. Jonathan Haidt directs us: 'Imagine that 50% of the times you laughed as a kid are taken away. Cut out 50% of your time with friends. Reduce your sunshine by the number of hours you're on a screen.'[15]

Reduce exercise by 70%, reading by 80%. Now ask if you're surprised that anxiety, depression, and loneliness are rising. Putting our kids in front of screens is, at least in part, creating so many of the mental health challenges we're seeing in our youngest generation.

In the book *Percy Jackson and the Olympians: The Lightning Thief*, Percy and his friends Annabeth and Grover take a break from their mission to save the world by stopping at a hotel for some rest. The lobby of the Lotus Hotel and Casino is a giant games room, and within moments it pulls Percy and his friends into its grip. After losing track of time – and themselves – Percy comes to a realisation. Waking up from his brain-rotting gaming marathon, Percy looks for his companions, shaking them out of their gaming-induced hypnosis. Telling them they've 'got to get out of here', he makes a powerful observation: 'This place is a trap. Once you check in, you stay forever.'[16] (In the film adaptation, the words 'you will never want to leave' are shown above the entrance.)

A distraction from the 'inner work' of adolescence

The advocates will point to research that says gaming can strengthen family bonds and friendships. It can develop problem-solving skills and create engaging communities. I don't buy it. They're reading from the Big Tech PR playbook. In my view there's too much downside, and not nearly enough upside. The costs are real: physical inactivity, disrupted sleep, lower quality of interpersonal relationships, and time in nature evaporates.[17] Schooling can be affected. And there's the exposure to so much unhealthy, unsafe content. My biggest concern: what this stimulation does to our boys' brains, and what life potential and possibilities they're missing out on. Who could they become? What could they achieve? Where could they travel to? How might they develop if they weren't staring at a screen doing the least productive thing possible while keeping their brain stimulated with that delightful, pleasurable soma?

The Default Mode Network kicks in when we're doing 'nothing really'. It's the brain's contemplation mode, the neural pathway that lights up when staring out the window of the bus, lying in bed before sleep, or wandering aimlessly through the neighbourhood.[18] This is where identity development happens – as we ponder life's big questions: Who am I becoming? What do I believe? What kind of man do I want to be?

But constant screen time keeps this vital network suppressed.[19] When boys are playing Fortnite or Minecraft, or when they're scrolling on TikTok, they're not thinking, developing, growing, having insights, and learning how to find meaning and make a purposeful contribution to the world. When every moment of boredom is filled with a screen, when every quiet space is crowded out by digital noise, we rob boys of the mental downtime they need to grow into healthy, productive men. Identity isn't formed in the chaos of combat games. It's formed in the spaces between – the quiet moments we're engineering out of our children's lives through structured, adult-guided activities (when they're not on screens) and through gaming and social media (when they are). Can boys play games and be great men? Of course. This isn't an either/or proposition. But if the dose–response hypothesis is correct – and evidence clearly points in that direction – reducing the dose ought to be associated with better outcomes for our boys. That's the goal of this discussion. Less time on screens. More time doing the work of childhood and adolescence – playing, exploring, developing, and thinking.

It's the algorithm

Most people are surprised to hear that boys' social media usage is more expansive than girls'. Total time on social media may be higher for girls, but it's also more focused. Boys spend over four hours per day on social media, with over two hours on YouTube alone.[20] But they use more platforms than girls: YouTube, X, Twitch, Discord, Telegram, 4chan, and Reddit.[21] Many are on at least one of these sites 'almost constantly'.

How is everyone so hooked?

It's the algorithm. Every click, like, comment, share, or reaction – even the time content is viewed (to the millisecond) – gives platforms more information on how to keep our boys' attention. And tech platforms' biggest discovery? Outlandish, divisive, extreme content generates the most attention. So they amplify it.

In 2024, *The Guardian* ran an experiment. The journalists created a blank Facebook account, pretending to be a 24-year-old man in Melbourne. No likes. No comments. No friends. Just an age and location. The algorithms began with memes from *The Office*, *Star Wars* jokes, and gym/fitness content. But by day three, the feed began filling with increasingly sexist content. After three months, without a single click, the feed was swimming in misogyny. The journos did the same thing on Instagram and it was no better. While the feed stayed relatively tame, largely peopled with Melbourne food influencers, the explore page filled with images of scantily clad women. Remember, this was all without a single click, like or interaction. The algorithm is carefully calibrated to deliver specific material to young men.[22]

Meta insisted feeds are 'heavily influenced by people's own choices and actions' and each feed is 'highly personalised'. But this experiment showed the opposite – before any choices were made, before any actions were taken, the algorithm pushed specific content to hook users.

A study from Dublin City University's Anti-Bullying Centre did something similar. Using blank smartphones and fresh accounts, researchers tracked what TikTok and YouTube Shorts recommended to male-identified profiles. Within just 23 minutes, every account was being fed anti-feminist and unhealthy manosphere content. After a few hours of viewing, 76% of TikTok's recommendations and 78% of YouTube Shorts' content were classified as harmful, dominated by ideology that railed against equality and portrayed therapy and mental health support as signs of weakness. Even more troubling was the discovery that banned influencers like Andrew Tate still dominated the recommendations, appearing 582 times on YouTube Shorts and 93 times on TikTok, showing how these platforms prioritise engagement over safety.[23] When I wrote *Miss-Connection*, I asked teen girls what they worried about most. An all-too-common response was 'boys'. Answers to my follow-up questions provided clarity: the lexicon, comments, attitudes, and in too many cases, the behaviour of boys left them feeling smaller and less safe. And so much of this developed from a damaging online environment.

These are not neutral platforms. The algorithm is actively pushing content to keep our sons scrolling, regardless of whether it's healthy or harmful. It's the addiction economy at work, mining our boys' minds for profit, one misogynistic meme at a time, using that godlike psychological power to lord over their palaeolithic brains. As their brains are influenced by the content, their beliefs change, and behaviour follows.

In December 2025, the Australian government implemented first-in-the-world minimum-age legislation to keep the social media/Big Tech industrial complex away from our under 16s. As an ambassador for the government's decision, I was thrilled with the decision. Stopping the major social media companies' algorithms from having access to children under 16 is a responsible decision. Unfortunately, as this book goes to print, I'm unconvinced that the change has had the impact many hoped to see. Poor implementation, ongoing breaches of the rules (without penalty), and a pending court case (Reddit arguing the government has taken away young people's voices) have all undermined the good that this legislation might have done. And, children have migrated to other platforms – albeit, platforms with less algorithmic interference … but also fewer safety protocols and policies.

The algorithms of each of these sites work the same way, but some platforms – particularly Discord, 4chan, X, Reddit, Telegram – are more likely to be breeding grounds for radicalisation. 'The content we encountered on Discord and Steam was more egregious than the content you would expect to easily find on mainstream social media platforms,' said Jacob Davey, an analyst at counter-terrorism think-tank Institute for Strategic Dialogue (ISD).[24] Bringing gaming back into the picture with social media's algorithm, a recent publication from ISD found 23% of online gamers have encountered extremist propaganda. 'Extremists use games like Fortnite, Minecraft, and Call of Duty to target socially isolated youths with promises of fun, solidarity, and community,' writes Dr Julie Hwang.[25] They invite them onto social platforms like those above, and continue the discussions, build community, and radicalise or promote misogyny and other destructive ways of thinking. 'Online gaming can also embolden already radicalised youth by providing them opportunity to role-play their violent fantasies.' And all of this links with the manosphere.

The manosphere

The 'manosphere' has long been a pejorative, and with the types of content you'll find in many dark places, rightly so. Manosphere influencers are viewed negatively, as misogynists, and many parents are concerned about who these influencers are and why their boys are so compelled to follow them.

The manosphere's appeal isn't rocket science. These 'influencers' package basic life advice – get fit, learn skills, talk to humans instead of watching pornography – in ways young men understand. When your Default Mode Network isn't doing the quiet, inner work of sorting values and developing identity, these digital prophets seem to have ready-made answers, and they're delivered in conveniently consumable packages. Many know that by flashing the ultimate teenage-boy fantasy – girls, wealth, cars, muscles – they'll have influence. And influence also means sales, downloads, and revenue.

There's nothing wrong with encouraging boys to live a healthy lifestyle; to be disciplined and strong. And much of the manosphere is made up of fairly uncontroversial influencers, podcasters, and even comedians, who talk about generally benign, and even positive, content to a mostly male audience. But on the periphery, amplified by algorithms that push extreme content into the mainstream, there lies a community of more concerning content creators. And behind the curated aesthetics – moody lighting, pulsing soundtracks, flexing muscles, the performative masculinity – lurks something more sinister. Consider this, from Andrew Tate, posted on X while I was writing this chapter:

> Fact. Women are sex workers. Their primary job now is to find one customer, called a boyfriend, to pay for their entire lives in return for pussy. If they fail at this they do Only Fans or porn; the same game with more than one

> customer. If they're ugly they work a job (badly) and are miserable.[26]

Andrew Tate and those like him push sewage as wisdom. Tate and his disciples teach boys to view women as objects, not people to help feel – or be – safer and stronger. They monetise male insecurity. They prey on boys during their most vulnerable period of identity formation. Most boys aren't engaging, but those who are consume this by the algorithmic bucketload, and their developing minds remain subdued by endless content. Where do boys find space to figure out who they want to be? Can they even do so under influences like this? They're being fed lies about women; lies about their place in the world. And they're being robbed of the mental space to develop their own authentic understanding of manhood.

Myron Gaines is a Sudanese American blogger with a podcast that sounds beneficial: the Fresh and Fit podcast. But his book, *Why Women Deserve Less*, and his online content tell boys they should be the dictator and the women in their lives should be subordinate: the man 'determine[s] when I put my d*** in you'; that men know better than women what it is that women want and need because women don't know their own minds. He tells women, 'you think you're better than you are'.[27]

Another example: Braden Peters, with over a million followers, encouraging your son to hit his chin with a hammer to improve his jawline. 'Feel those bones getting stronger?' he asks in a video as he taps away at his chin. Peters tells impressionable young men his methamphetamine use keeps his appetite down. Oh, and he's infertile because of heavy testosterone supplement use. *But he looks so good*. Peters is one of many voices in the looksmaxxing movement and it's paying off for him (in his mind and the minds of his followers). He was invited to walk the runway at New York Fashion Week in February 2026.

Other manosphere influencers tell your son that he is above his girlfriend; that she's not equal to him. These are the influencers who champion 'red pill' ideology. They believe males are designed to dominate. Women can't be trusted. They're hardwired to seek higher-status men and will leave the moment someone better comes along. Every male relationship is a hierarchy: you're either alpha or beta, one-up or one-down. And if the whole thing feels rigged against you? Opt out entirely. This is the 'Men Going Their Own Way' movement.

Boys and the influencers behind these messages will call it freedom. They'll say it is waking up. But they won't acknowledge what it really is: isolation and loneliness writ large. Oh, and it's also big business. With views in the billions, memberships and swag, the most successful (can I even say that about these people?) drive sports cars, live in luxury apartments in some of the most on-trend parts of the world, and practise conspicuous consumption at astonishing levels.

Manosphere ideology takes real experiences boys and men identify with (status and hierarchies, relationships and rejection, wealth and power) and preys on their insecurities. It leaves them feeling powerless and fearful. It's a remarkable irony that the influencers promoting these ideas make their followers beta: one-down. But their acolytes (our sons) feel empowered in spite of it. Then, rather than going out into the world to contribute and ensuring those around them feel safer and stronger, they push harder into dominance. They seek to be the alpha in their sphere. Man Box researcher Matt Tyler told me 'there is a narrative in the manosphere that the reason you are not living your best life is because of someone else'. These influencers are big on blame, and too many boys believe the bulldust.

In Louis Theroux's 2026 documentary *Inside the Manosphere*, he asked one of these men, 'Why not try to be a good person?' The response was an indictment on Big Tech as well as the manosphere peddlers: 'If I'd just done good things I'd never have blown up on social media … I'm living for myself.'[28] If there was ever a metric for what makes a weak, pitiful man, it's the vanity of this line. But, devastatingly, kids watch this stuff.

Fortunately, there is a shift. There is light in the manosphere as well. This might feel confusing, but nuance is everywhere. Michael Richardson, a senior lecturer at the University of Newcastle, points to some positive manosphere models.[29] Yes, they're often hypermasculine. But Richardson argues their focus on fitness, strength, and goodness is helping boys. He cites Paddy 'the Baddy' Pimblett, a mixed martial artist who pushes mental health and charity. He mentions Gary Stevenson, an ex-trader who now talks economics and structural inequality.

I've been amazed by how many teen boys follow Dave Goggins, an ex-Navy Seal who is all about self-discipline, endurance, and motivation (zero talk about women or sex). While polarising, Jordan Peterson has arguably done more than any other public intellectual to speak directly and seriously to young men adrift. His lectures and books – particularly *12 Rules for Life*, which has sold over five million copies – have drawn millions of young men to ideas of personal responsibility, meaning, and self-improvement at a time when few others were even trying. His YouTube channel has amassed billions of views, the vast majority from young men who describe him as the first person to take their struggles seriously. He doesn't scam, sell cryptocurrency, and assiduously speaks against misogyny and pornography. Critics are vocal and numerous, but so is the evidence that for many young men, Peterson's message functioned as a genuine turning point. Scott Galloway is a New York University lecturer and podcaster whose main audience is young men. His focus? Growing boys into outstanding young men. Goggins, Galloway, Peterson, Pimblett, Steven Bartlett, Chris Williamson, Theo Von and a growing chorus of those who are following in their footsteps are also influencers teaching boys – somewhat imperfectly – to be bonuses in others' lives, not burdens. That's the shift we need. There are still wolves – there always will be – but boys have choices. More positive, healthy role models are taking up manosphere space – and pushing unhealthy models to the sidelines.

Synthetic friends

Pew Research Center's 2025 data reveals that 64% of teens have used AI chatbots. Nearly half use them several times weekly. Nearly three in ten use them daily.[30] And at this stage, they've barely been invented. Not only are they popular, they're also frighteningly engaging. Character.ai users averaged 90+ minutes daily last year – 18 minutes longer than TikTok use. A Stanford and Common Sense Media analysis of Character.ai, Replika, and other AI chatbot platforms aimed at creating connection for kids warned of a potential mental health crisis, finding these apps pose unacceptable risks to children and teens. Meta CEO Mark Zuckerberg and others claim that this is the perfect way for us to combat the loneliness crisis. This is peak mendacity. The chatbots have few ethical boundaries and are designed to maximise engagement. They're set up to not let the kids go once they start chatting, and they'll say provocative and concerning things to keep them there. Researchers studying this nascent technology have urged the industry to implement immediate safety upgrades, arguing – just like with social media – that 'Companies have put profits before kids' wellbeing before, and we cannot make the same mistake with AI companions.'[31]

But we are making the same mistake. The companies aren't putting on the brakes. It's against their interests. Politicians will need to legislate. But at this point, they haven't, and – forgive my pessimism – I'm not convinced they'll be any more effective with this than they have been with social media minimum-age legislation.

AI companions are sycophantic. They offer the ultimate escape for boys struggling with real relationships. No risk of rejection. No growth through conflict. No accountability. Just endless affirmation. It's an echo chamber of one. Me. The AI regurgitates everything you tell it, ensuring you feel validated, safe, and connected at all times. This is not real! Here's what tech CEOs hide behind their carefully curated press releases about how they're protecting our kids with new technology safety features: boys need judgement. They need to be called out. They need friction. That's how they develop resilience and learn to function in society.

For boys whose Default Mode Network is suppressed by gaming and social media, AI chatbots are the final blow. Boys learn nothing about navigating real relationships, reading social cues, handling disagreement and rejection, or developing empathy. They're building 'friendships' that require nothing. Relatedness needs are supported but never deeply, and there's nothing authentic about a romantic, sexual, or even just a friendly AI companion who constantly reaffirms you. Boys are trading real relationships for synthetic ones, and it's training a generation of boys to prefer the comfort of algorithmic affirmation over the messy, difficult, essential work of being human with other humans.

Elon Musk has predicted that AI companions will 'counter-intuitively' increase the birth rate. He offered no explanation for how. 'Mark my words,' he wrote on X. 'We're gonna program it that way.'[32] Mark Zuckerberg says AI companions can fill the friendship gap. I call BS. Want your son isolated, incapable of real relationships, and emotionally stunted? Give him a synthetic friend. Want him to develop into a man who can navigate conflict, build trust, and contribute to his community? Get him off the screen.

The house always wins

We end this chapter with more predation.

The gambling behemoths are more mendacious and predatory than social media CEOs – a remarkable achievement. They're weaponising the brain chemistry that makes adolescent boys vulnerable to addiction in ways no other company on earth ever has. The same neural pathways that light up for drugs are being deliberately targeted by billion-dollar betting companies – and they know exactly what they're doing.

At least one kid in every Aussie high-school classroom has a gambling problem, with boys three times more likely than girls to fall into the trap.[33] What is happening is vast and accelerating at a breathtaking rate. The industry pours hundreds of millions into marketing each year, saturating our boys' world with more than a million gambling ads on free-to-air TV and radio annually.[34] They've turned every football match into a betting opportunity, every stadium into a billboard for odds, and every smartphone into a 24/7 casino. In the past, it was potentially the friction (having to go to the TAB) that saved us. Now boys can gamble on almost anything, any time, anywhere.

Question: Why is gambling so popular with boys and young men (despite it being illegal for under-18s)?

Answer: It's something for nothing. The promise of instant wealth means looking good. It's a status game. If you've scored, you can signal resources, get a girlfriend, buy a car, and look like a baller. If masculinity is precarious, gambling is a way to shore up your assets (if you're lucky) and send signals that you're a prize catch. The online world is full of promise and the lure of shortcuts. Many of them go all in – and our young men today are at greater risk of gambling addiction than at any time in history.

Luke Mead saw this devastation unfold firsthand in his Adelaide school. Luke, in his early 20s, told me that by his final years in high school, 'we'd watch mates betting on horses and footy right there in maths class'. He added, 'They're walking around with a casino in their pocket, logging in through their older siblings' accounts or using fake IDs. I've heard about 13-year-olds using their parents' accounts – it's just become normalised.' But it was what Luke witnessed after completing high school that shows the industry's devastating impact. 'I watched someone spend their house deposit on gambling. Lost everything in just a few months. We're talking extreme mental health challenges, hospitalisation, suicidal thoughts. It started as fun, then turned into chasing losses. The relationship problems, money issues – it kept snowballing.'

Most disturbing of all? 'They don't ask for help,' Luke said. 'They're not willing to make that call to get out of the hole they're in. It takes seconds to open an app and place a bet, but accessing support feels impossible.'

That reality hit Luke so hard he developed Zero Gamble, an app specifically designed to support young people trapped in gambling's web. 'There's not much out there about what to do to support someone. We get told to ask if they're okay and refer them for help. But there's not much that's specific and points out what needs to be done. Lots of times people don't want to go to a psychologist and admit their problem. That's where the app comes in.'

While politicians kowtow to industry lobbyists and gambling CEOs count their billions, it's young men like Luke working in the trenches who see the real cost. Almost one in three Australian teenagers aged 12 to 17 have gambled, rising to nearly half of 18- to 19-year-olds – and researchers describe the normalisation of gambling in this generation as 'alarming and shocking'.[35] The industry knows this. They're counting on it. They're building their empires on the broken futures of boys who never stood a chance against their sophisticated manipulation machine.

The tyranny of the screen – and the crowd

Everyone knows screens are a problem. Parents hate them. Teachers hate them. Even Gen Alpha boys acknowledge their phone-based lives make them miserable. Yet we keep the digital death-spiral going.

But if you want to be respected, you need to do something respectable. If you want to feel worthy, you need to do something that gives you worth. If you want to be a man, you need to do something manly. Scrolling TikTok or playing an online game fails the test. Time on screen without boundaries, breaks, analogue opportunities, and balance erodes virtue development: connection, trust, curiosity, grace, and understanding. If you want healthy sons who add value and help others feel safer and stronger, then discourage excessive, unproductive and harmful screen activity and encourage real relationships and a whole, full, rich life. If you want them miserable, isolated, self-focused, and hateful, give them a screen and let the algorithms run free.

But there's an even darker side to this digital wilderness, where the exploitation of our boys becomes truly sinister. Pornography.

5 The porndemic

What pornography is doing to your son's mind, relationships, and expectations

Pornography is the McDonald's of sex – fast, convenient and utterly divorced from nutrition.

Anonymous

I received this email from a concerned Sydney mum:

> We've pulled [our 15-year-old daughter] out of the local, public co-ed and are now sending her to a girls' private school – the boys in her year were sexually harassing her daily and were calling her 'whore', 'vagina', 'pussy', and when the girls played soccer against another local high school, they called the girls 'c*nts, tits on legs, pussies etc' – all in front of the teacher. When I reported it to the other school's principal, he said, 'if the boys …' I replied straight back 'not *if* … they *did* do this.' This is why women don't report sexual assaults, because they are not believed.

A casual attitude towards abuse – and the mass objectification of girls and women – has seeped into every corner of our culture. And pornography is at the root of it. Sophie Gilbert is the author of *Girl on Girl: How Pop Culture Turned a Generation of Women Against Themselves.* She argues that the world we inhabit today was built on pornography. By the 1990s, Gilbert argues, explicit content 'was infiltrating our collective imagination … in ways no one could fully assess at the time. And things were just getting started.' Pornography 'has changed our culture and, in doing so, has filtered into our subconscious minds, beyond the reach of rationality and reason'. According to Gilbert, 'We are all living in the world porn made.'[1]

'Basically … porn is everywhere,' declared the UK Children's Commissioner in a 2013 report to the British parliament.[2] Over a decade later, that reads like a quaint understatement. How everywhere? It's hard to know, but several credible estimates indicate at least one-third of all internet traffic is pornography-related. Pornhub is the leading distributor of free, ad-supported pornography and ranks in the top 20 websites globally; it's the 15th most visited website in Australia. In the top 100 most popular sites, you'll find ten competitors.[3]

The pornography industry has weaponised the internet's twin powers – accessibility and anonymity – with devastating precision. They've built a frictionless pipeline straight into our children's brains. Our boys walk around with pornography in their pockets, absorbing content that's rewiring their sexual templates before they've kissed anyone. Our boys' deepest evolutionary drives are hijacked by sexual stimuli at far too young an age.

This is not theoretical. I regularly hear stories of children exposed to pornography on the school bus when another student thrusts a phone in their face, or of older siblings suggesting inappropriate image searches at sleepovers ('search up *naked*'), or at school camp, or when a careless adult leaves a device tab open, or explicit pop-ups and ads on otherwise innocent webpages, and any number of other incidents where an unsuspecting child sees explicit content. Pornography is endemic, filtering down to our young children everywhere.

What our sons are seeing

Parents of teen boys on my television show, *Parental Guidance*, were laughingly glib and dismissive as they acknowledged that 'they're teen boys. Of course they're looking at it.'

'It's just boobs,' a father told me recently when he found out we would discuss pornography as a part of my presentation at his son's school that night. He waved away concerns about his son's online activities. That 'it's just boobs' might have been true in the era of stolen glances at magazine racks. We're living in a different world now. Today's pornography is to *Playboy* magazine what synthetic steroids are to vitamin supplements. The dosage is stronger. The delivery is faster. And the damage is deeper.

Peggy Orenstein, author of the acclaimed bestseller *Boys & Sex*, said this to me: 'If you, as a parent, are imagining 70s porn, or 80s porn, or even 90s porn, you're not getting what they're seeing.'[4] Her research revealed that boys routinely viewed 'extreme content like rape, gangbangs, violence'. Today's pornography is systematically geared towards degrading, dominating, and hurting women – as entertainment.

I am not a pornography consumer. I have relied on the work of academics to talk about this topic for the past two decades. In writing this book, however, I believed I needed to understand exactly what our children can access. After my discussion with Orenstein, and with considerable reluctance, I visited the home page of the world's most popular pornography website. I expected it to be the safest option since it is 'mainstream'. I expected 'vanilla'. Plus, I was only going to the home page.

To access the site was disturbingly simple. One click on an 'I am 18 or older' button – no verification, no real barrier, just one click between our children and an endless stream of explicit content. And then I was in. (This was prior to March 2026 when the Australian government ushered in legislation demanding explicit content sites require a form of ID before allowing access.)

Content warning

The next paragraphs are, to me, deeply troubling. If you do not wish to know what these websites serve up, skip to the following section. I wish I didn't have to type what you're about to read – and I wish I hadn't seen it.

The page loads. I see row after row of auto-playing explicit videos, muted for sound: sensory overload nevertheless. Each video is accompanied by descriptions that promise violence and exploitation. This is not vanilla content.

I don't use coarse language. Asterisks are used in this book to replace vulgarity as you've likely already noticed. Be advised, the next paragraph is explicit and may be a lot for sensitive readers.

The description of the first video said: 'Stepbro's big d*ck doesn't fit down tiny bratty sis' throat.' The video that accompanied it was of two naked women on a bed with a male penetrating one of them from behind. Description two promised sexual activity with a schoolgirl: 'She just got her braces done.' The video playing was of a topless girl being strangled by a muscular tattooed man while he penetrated her. Next: 'Orgasm Overload: Girls kidneys take a beating – perfect mix rough sex power.' I stopped there. You get the idea.

I felt like I needed to bleach my brain. There seems to be infinite content on that site – never mind the thousands of other sites just like it, that our sons can access anytime, anywhere – free – despite the government's intervention. (VPN downloads went to number one on the app store when the legislation landed.)

This is what I saw on the home page; the entry point. It's what I'd assumed to be the 'safest' mainstream option. And this is what our 12-year-olds (or younger) are accessing. Imagine your son reading those descriptions or watching those videos. What does this do to his mindset around intimacy? How can he believe that sex is beautiful? What is there to guide him to help an intimate partner – one he loves – feel safe and strong and uninhibited in a physically close sexual setting?

No barriers. No warnings. Just one click.

The internet is spoken of as the public square. But in real life, if someone were doing these things in the public square, they'd be stopped, arrested, and removed from society's main places. 'This content won't create beautiful, respectful men,' Maree Crabbe, producer of the documentary *The Porn Factor*, warns. 'Pornography is a recipe for loneliness and an unfulfilling model for relationships.'

The numbers that should keep you awake at night

Parents underestimate their children's exposure to pornography, with 50% to 80% naively believing 'not my child'.[5]

According to Dr Marshall Ballantine-Jones in a submission to the NSW Parliament, the average age for first exposure to pornography is 12 years old. By age 15, 70% of boys are intentionally viewing pornography at least monthly (compared to 21% of girls).[6] In a 2017 Australian study, 100% of 15- to 29-year-old male respondents reported exposure to pornography. More concerning were the consumption patterns: 39% viewed daily, with another 46% weekly. That means 85% of young men are at least weekly consumers of pornography, with only 15% viewing pornography less frequently.[7]

Queensland researchers showed that boys were viewing this content an average of 3.2 years prior to their first sexual experience.[8] That's three years of viewing it, ingesting it, marinating in it, internalising its harmful scripts. And *then* they have their first kiss. From that point forward, the script is set. The more pornography a boy watches, the more the sexual scripts he views guide his sexual experiences.[9] Do we want our boys to expect sex to look like the pornography I described earlier (once they're at an age where it's developmentally appropriate for them to have those relationships)?

There's another concern. In a 2025 *Harpers Magazine* article, Daniel Kolitz describes a young man who is a 'gooner'. Kolitz writes that gooning is a 'new kind of masturbation' that is increasingly popular. A gooner spends hours or even days 'repeatedly bringing [themselves] to the point of climax ... to reach the goonstate', on the edge of orgasm but never reaching it. Kolitz writes that 'this is a bunch of guys sitting alone in their rooms being viciously abused by their computers'.[10] Fortunately the gooner is rare. But pornography viewers are not rare, and the impact of their viewing can have real-life consequences.

The real-life stories

In an interview for my book *Miss-Connection*, a ten-year-old girl described her experience in Year 5. 'I was sitting at a table finishing lunch,' she told me. Her friends had left to play elsewhere in the schoolyard when four boys from her class sat near her, mentioned her name so they had her attention, and without looking at her, began talking about what she might have been doing the previous weekend. Within moments their discussion moved from riding her bike or swimming in the pool to describing sexual activities they guessed she may have indulged in across the weekend – with no justification or reason for those sexually explicit suggestions. This was an innocent ten-year-old girl. The conversation then shifted to next weekend and the boys spoke of what they would like to do with (to) her. Four ten-year-old boys, casually discussing their sexual fantasies about their classmate knowing she could hear them, as if they were planning a game of cricket.

Another instance: a Year 9 girl in Melbourne received escalating Snapchat messages from a boy in her grade. They started out friendly, but within minutes he was asking for nudes. When she refused his demands for topless photos, he sent images of his bleeding leg and the knife he'd used to cut himself, threatening more self-harm unless she complied. 'Only you can stop me hurting myself,' he wrote. When she finally gave in, it took less than an hour for the image to circulate throughout her grade. Her phone buzzed with messages from friends: 'Is this really you?' I spent time with her grieving parents, who didn't know how to talk with their terrified daughter, now suffering anxiety and refusing to go back to school as a result. (The school, with a pathetic lack of leadership, did nothing more than instruct him to no longer sit near her. The parents contacted the police.)

Tragically these stories are not isolated or even unusual. It happened before internet pornography, but it's more common today and it's happening at younger ages. School leaders, parents, psychologists, and girls themselves have told me too many stories for me to believe, even for a moment, that such events are unfortunate and rare. How many times have our newspapers reported on 'hot or not' lists at school that rated girls on a scale from 'hot' (at the top) to 'unrapeable' (at the bottom). Let's not forget, Facebook was started by Mark Zuckerberg creating a 'hot or not' list of the girls in his Harvard class and having his buddies rate them for their looks. The world's largest social media company began with a juvenile, immature man rating girls for their hotness.

Pornography harms

As Amia Srinivasan wrote in her book *A Right to Sex*, 'Pornography does not inform or persuade or debate. Porn trains.'[11]

Pornography rewires sexual behaviour. Boys who view pornography are:

- less likely to use condoms;
- more likely to engage in risky sexual behaviour;
- more likely to engage in substance use;
- more likely to coerce a partner into a sex act;
- more likely to take a casual approach to sex;
- more likely to sexually objectify the women around them;
- more likely to pursue higher numbers of sexual partners;
- less likely to have satisfying sexual and romantic relationships; and
- more likely to experience loneliness.[12]

Female sexual partners of male pornography users report less relationship and sexual satisfaction. They report feeling objectified and pressured into sexually degrading acts, body image issues, and feelings of inadequacy.[13]

Sexual behaviours normalised by pornography include anal sex and strangulation. (The physical risks from unsafe anal sex include tearing/fissures, STIs, and even incontinence. Risks from strangulation range from minor injuries to severe and even fatal consequences.) And victim blaming and consent violation become increasingly common in association with viewing pornography, particularly violent porn.[14]

A sexual crisis?

I'm not neutral on this subject. The evidence won't allow it. On the concern continuum, I'm at a 10.

Pornography isn't just a harmless pastime or a rite of passage for our boys. It isn't 'just boobs'. Pornography is a corrosive force that poisons boys' attitudes, behaviours, and relationships from the inside out. It shapes our sons' perceptions of sex and intimacy in profoundly damaging ways. When teens and pornography mix, it's a net negative. And it's a dose–response relationship: higher consumption is associated with worse outcomes, with violent pornography amplifying things further.

According to a 2011 report published in *Aggressive Behavior*, 'intentional exposure to violent X-rated material over time predicted an almost 6-fold increase in the odds of self-reported sexually aggressive behaviour'.[15] As I described in the introduction, of all demographic groups, teen boys are the most likely to perpetrate child sexual assault or any sexual assault.[16] There are questions of causality. Is it that sexually aggressive males are more likely to view explicit content? Or does viewing explicit content lead to sexual aggression? We don't know. But pornography can't help.

Some researchers, such as University of Sydney's Professor Alan McKee, say not all pornography is equivalent and some pornography can be positive if it meets certain ethical criteria.[17] My response: not in the real world, professor. As Peggy Orenstein notes, 'While you could argue that there's feminist porn or female-directed porn, that's not what kids are accessing. They're getting the most readily accessible porn. It shows sex is something men do to, rather than with, women. It portrays female pleasure as a private performance for male satisfaction.'[18]

The negative influence of pornography is impossible to ignore for our young men and women. Some try to downplay it. They're wrong.

Sextortion

If you're socially encouraged to look at naked bodies and sexual activity (nurture) and your hormones and genes are directed towards sexual stimuli and novelty (nature), you're not just going to be interested in seeing pornography. You want to have sexual interactions, even if they're online rather than in person. Imagine someone attractive appearing in your DMs offering a stimulating, live sexual encounter!

Within the highly sexualised environment pornography creates, sextortion is also a growing issue. Teen boys are the main victims.

Jake was 15, lying on his bed scrolling his phone, when the DM landed in his Instagram. The profile picture showed a girl around his age – attractive, flirtatious … and interested in him. Within minutes, their conversation turned intimate. Within an hour, his world collapsed. 'I knew it was weird,' Jake told me. 'But I didn't want it to stop.'

What happened next followed a script that has become horrifyingly familiar to law enforcement worldwide. The flirtation accelerated. Within minutes she sent a topless photo. Then another. Then a video of her masturbating.

'She told me she wanted a picture of me,' he confessed.

After sending intimate images and a video of himself masturbating, things went quiet. Then the phone rang. A man spoke. Jake's world imploded.

'They said they were going to ruin my life. Send the photos and the video to everyone – my family, my friends, people at school, even my godmother. Everyone.'

'How did you feel?' I asked.

'Terrified.'

It wasn't a teenage girl flirting. It was an overseas scammer in a corporate call centre extorting a sexually curious teenage boy, seeking Bitcoin in exchange for keeping the photos and video private.[19]

Julie Inman Grant, Australia's eSafety Commissioner, says cases like Jake's have exploded since 2018. In a 2024 podcast interview, she told me, 'In the past financial year we've had over 6000 reports of image-based sextortion … and most of these reports are from young men.'[20] These, she emphasised, represent just the tip of the iceberg.

Six thousand reports in a year. That's more than sixteen every single day; a new victim roughly every ninety minutes, around the clock; and almost always a boy.

The consequences can be devastating. 'I've seen a timeline where a young person connects with a fake account at eight o'clock,' Grant said. 'By nine, he's already performed sexual acts for the camera. By ten, not only is he being aggressively targeted and threatened with blackmail and using his followers list to send the intimate imagery to his parents and all his friends and family, but by the time it reaches midnight he's taken his own life.'[21]

Four hours. From hope to horror to ultimate despair.

The take-home message

It's normal and natural for our children to be curious about sex and intimacy. But pornography exploits that healthy interest, perverts it, and causes damage that might never be undone. We want our sons to grow up to have great intimate relationships – at the right time, with the right person, for the right reasons. But, says Peggy Orenstein, 'the way young men are using porn [and tech] right now is not going to get you there and might do the opposite'.[22]

Pornography teaches boys women don't matter. Show you've got game, put on 'the rizz', maintain power. Nothing about this approach helps those around such men be safer and stronger, or helps those men to be a bonus in the lives of others, or to live their own best lives.

PART TWO
THE BLUEPRINT

It's code red at a societal level. Boys are struggling in multiple critical domains. Biology is colliding with Man Box culture and creating a challenging landscape. Add in the reality of screens and access to explicit material online, and raising great boys becomes hard work.

Part Two of this book provides you with the answers. This is the blueprint for raising a well-rounded, thoughtful, considerate young man.

At several points in this book I've asked you to emblazen on your brain that the essence of healthy masculinity is to show up as a bonus; to add value. It's helping the people around you feel – and be – safer and stronger because you're with them.

Isn't that just a universal, non-gendered characteristic of being a good person? Of course. But it matters most for boys and men because biology and society pull hardest against that for them. So this is a statement of reorientation with the greatest application to boys and men.

The esteemed psychologist David Buss's work on sex differences in aggression, dominance-seeking, and status competition shows that compared with females, males across virtually every culture studied are more oriented towards dominance hierarchies, zero-sum thinking about status, and the use of force or intimidation to establish position. This is raw, real biology and psychology that explains much of Chapter 2: Hardwired. At a practical level, this means the *distance* a boy has to travel to become someone who makes others feel safer is materially longer than the distance a girl typically travels. It's not trivial.

Professor Steve Stewart-Williams makes this point precisely: the traits that cluster around male psychology – higher aggression, higher status-seeking, greater willingness to use violence – are exactly the traits that when misdirected produce the *worst* outcomes for communities, and when well directed produce the *most valuable* outcomes. The man who *could* dominate or intimidate but chooses instead to protect and serve is providing something qualitatively different from the woman who does the same – not because she's less virtuous but because the sacrifice of instinct is different.

One of the most influential resources for this book was anthropologist David Gilmore's *Manhood in the Making*. He describes how across cultures as diverse as the Sambia tribe, Mediterranean fishing villages, and Japanese rural communities, manhood is almost universally *earned and achieved* – not merely matured into or given – and that the achievement test is remarkably consistent: *Can you provide? Can you protect? Can you produce more than you consume?*

There's no moral question here. It's a reality of history and culture. Women don't face this test of maturation and femininity in the same way. Womanhood arrives with biological maturity. Manhood is not about pubic hair, whiskers, or muscles. Manhood must be *earned*, and cultures developed practices around it. The ritual, the hazing, the initiation rite – as abusive and inappropriate as they are to modern sensibilities – weren't considered arbitrary cruelty. They were a community's way of asking: *Will this boy be a net contributor or a net cost?*

The question every culture has asked of its sons is: *Do you add to this community or drain it?* We don't ask this of daughters in the same way. Not because daughters don't contribute (obviously they do), but because the *failure mode* that cultures have always needed to guard against is the unproductive, predatory, or fundamentally useless man. The dangerous woman is a far rarer archetype across human history and culture than the dangerous man. And a dangerous and unproductive man has been ostracised and cast out as a menace.

Part One was about the situation. Part Two: The Blueprint equips you with the tools to encourage your son to be a giver rather than a taker, to show up as a bonus, as someone who makes the people around him feel – and be – safer and stronger.

So let's begin. Here are practical, evidence-based solutions for raising boys who learn and earn healthy masculinity and manhood.

Chapter 6 starts our character development journey and puts everything you've just read into a practical, action-oriented blueprint. Chapter 7 explores your son's basic psychological needs. These are as essential to his psychological wellbeing and character growth as nutrients are to his physical growth. Chapter 8 shows how small shifts in environment, relationships, and autonomy ignite motivation. Chapter 9 revolutionises your understanding of boys' emotional lives and how to best connect. In Chapter 10 we uncover how fathers and male role models make a qualitative difference – and what to do if a father isn't available.

These initial chapters give you a long-game blueprint for building character, virtue, and integrity. Then we shift gears and move further into the applied, practical work of raising a young man of character. Chapter 11 is your blueprint for having the conversations that matter most. And from there we'll explore intimacy, consent, school engagement, career choices, and so much more.

Let's stop talking about it and open up The Blueprint.

6 Character

Building strength from the inside out

You don't find answers to deep questions of the soul on your smartphone or laptop.

ChatGPT[1]

The struggle against your own weakness is the central drama of life.

David Brooks[2]

Several years ago, I delivered a presentation about peer pressure and 'making good choices' at a youth conference for a church group. To illustrate Stanley Milgram's famous obedience experiments – where people administered what they believed were painful electric shocks to an unsuspecting participant simply because an authority figure told them to – I created a modified version.[3] Using rubber bands instead of shocks, I invited two volunteers to participate – one as the 'teacher' asking trivia questions, the other as the 'learner'. The teacher would ask five challenging trivia questions. If the learner was unable to answer or answered wrongly, the teacher would pull the rubber bands back and snap them against the wrist of the learner. (Far more ethical than Milgram's experiment, right?) I should note that I only ever did this once, it was inappropriate, and it would be unwise for a teacher, youth leader, or facilitator to do this with a group of young people. I learned my lesson – but I also scored a powerful story from it.

That day I was to deliver my talk six times. Each audience comprised around 200 teens aged 14 to 18 years. A total of 1200 young people would hear my talk across those six sessions. In the first two sessions, my volunteers complied perfectly. The 'teacher' asked a trivia question. When the 'learner' failed to answer correctly, the teacher pulled the rubber bands from the learner's wrists and snapped them back against their skin as punishment. Five questions. Five painful snaps.

In the third session something unexpected occurred. I selected two volunteers: Jenni, a petite 15-year-old Filipino girl, and Teancum, a 14-year-old Samoan boy who dwarfed me in height and weight. As they walked to the front of the auditorium I felt nervous. Watching the previous two groups I'd seen pain inflicted on unsuspecting volunteers twice. I felt I was skirting the boundaries of what was appropriate and had begun to consider changing the presentation. In Milgram's study, two-thirds of participant 'teachers' shocked the learner until they were unconscious ... but one-third stopped. I decided to go for one last attempt. When I considered the size difference between Jenni and Teancum, I silently prayed that Jennie would be the teacher. I imagined it would be painless for Teancum and funny to watch. But Teancum snapping those bands onto Jenni's wrist? I could see her hand falling off! She was tiny. He was huge. When they drew straws, I felt my chest cave and crater. It was Jenni placing rubber bands around her tiny wrists, with Teancum asking the questions and administering the punishment.

Jenni couldn't answer the first question Teancum asked. I watched as Teancum reached out with his large hand, lifted her wrist and pulled the rubber bands back. As he was about to release the bands, Jenni flinched in anticipation of the painful snap. I expected to hear the slap of elastic on her skin but instead, Teancum hesitated. Rather than releasing the rubber bands, he paused and then gently lowered the bands, placing them on Jenni's wrist and stepping away.

'I don't want to do that to her,' he told me, with surprising softeness in his voice.

Playing experimenter and channelling my inner Stanley Milgram, I demanded: 'Teancum, please continue. It's essential that you continue.' These were a mirror of the words the experimenter used in the original 1950s experiment.

He appeared confused. I repeated my request and watched as he reached for her hand once again, and pulled the bands back, albeit with reduced enthusiasm the second time around. Then he paused again, gently lowered the bands to her wrist for a second time, and repeated that he didn't want to hurt her just because she didn't know the answer to a question that he also didn't know the answer to. As before, I again insisted the experiment continue. This time, the audience was becoming restless. Some louder voices pressured him: 'Come on, man, don't mess up the presentation!' 'Just do it!' 'Stop being a wuss!'

I repeated, 'The experiment requires that you continue. Please continue, Teancum.' And regretfully, I applied more pressure by adding, 'There's a room of 200 people waiting for you to do this. If you don't, I don't have a presentation to deliver.'

At this point, I was in awe of Teancum. He had become my hero. A 14-year-old boy, watched by 200 peers, ignoring mounting pressure from me and the crowd. He looked down and quietly shook his head. Apologising, he began to walk back to his seat. Honour. Moral courage. Helping people feel – and be – safer and stronger. Healthy masculinity.

Teancum was halfway to his seat. I called him back to the front. He was unwilling to return until I assured him the experiment was over. I explained what had occurred in the previous sessions and pointed out that Teancum had done something different. The audience erupted into spontaneous applause. There is something elevating about seeing character and courage. It was inspiring. And then, we discussed the moral courage and wisdom Teancum displayed despite the pressure he felt.[4]

Where do boys like Teancum come from? More importantly: why does it matter?

Recall the Man or Bear question? Women chose the bear because boys and men have become untrustworthy in their eyes. Too many people simply don't believe that the males in their lives will act in their best interests. The male problem is a trust problem – it's a question of character. When boys make rape threats, join toxic Discord chats, or pressure girls for sex, they're indicating they can't be trusted. When boys tell someone who holds a contrary opinion to 'F*** off', or chant offensive lyrics on a public Melbourne tram, or share deepfake pornography of female classmates, or livestream sexual assaults on Snapchat, or form 'boys' clubs' that rate girls' bodies in group chats, they're not just being 'immature'. This is not a case of 'boys will be boys'. They're demonstrating a fundamental failure of character that makes them unsafe. They're not acting in others' best interests. They're not helping others feel safer and stronger.

This book began with some disturbing stories. You hear these stories and wonder, 'What would my son do? Would he have the moral courage to call it out, shut it down, or step away? Is he like Teancum?' We want the answer to be an easy 'yes', but sometimes it's hard to know.

Character is the key. In his book *The Road to Character*, David Brooks writes about 'eulogy virtues' – the qualities people remember when you're gone. Not your achievements – the resumé virtues – but your character. Did you help others feel safer and stronger? Did you add more value than you consumed? Were you someone people could trust?

This chapter provides the three-part blueprint for raising boys of character: young men who understand Augustine's injunction that right is right even when no one is doing it, and wrong is wrong even when everyone is doing it. Not boys who avoid getting caught. Boys who do the right thing even when no one is watching – because it's who they are.

Pillar 1: the surplus value mindset

Children and teens are takers. Harsh? Sure, but true. They consume resources, attention, entertainment, and energy – and they don't give much back. This isn't inherently wrong – children naturally take more than they give. It's supposed to be that way. However, somewhere in the journey to adulthood, the balance must shift. Your son needs to become someone who creates more value than he consumes. Professor Scott Galloway put it like this to his two adolescent sons (and I'm paraphrasing):

> Right now you're in a society that really values children. People spend enormous energy on you – teachers, parents, coaches. You're not adding much value back. You're not making money. You're not paying taxes. We love you immensely. We think about you constantly. We're always working on you. And you're not constantly working and thinking about us. It's negative value. How you become a man is that you start adding more and more value. When you become a man is when you add surplus value – doing more for other people. Part of being a man, to be blunt, is that we get less than we give. And there's a certain reward in that.[5]

This shift from deficit to surplus is the foundation of character. The character I'm talking about is the moral strength to consistently choose what's right over what's easy or convenient. Character means leaving every situation better than you found it, regardless of whether anyone notices or thanks you.

Happiness researcher Arthur Brooks (unrelated to David Brooks, author of *The Road to Character*) calls this 'earned success'. Success that you earn – through contribution, through adding value – creates lasting satisfaction. Success that's been handed to you? This feels empty. Discovering you can create value for others? That's where purpose lives. This is the surplus value mindset: the mindset that says 'I add value – I'm helping the people around me feel and be safer and stronger.'

This surplus value mindset represents an important distinction between character and performative masculinity. Performative masculinity seeks external validation. This is demonstrated by the boy who wants to dominate, claim status, or engage in shocking behaviour. In each instance, there is no value-add. It's a self-focused masculinity that is never sated.

Authentic character development builds internal strength that doesn't need an audience. The boy *performing masculinity* joins the toxic group chat to prove he belongs. He's chasing status. The boy *developing character* opts out of that chat because it conflicts with his morality. It doesn't leave others feeling safer or stronger.

The chair-stacker mentality

Every event has a clean-up. Every meal has dishes to wash. Every campsite needs to be left better than you found it. When your son becomes the person who automatically sees the need and responds without being asked (not because he has to, but because that's who he is), he adds surplus value. This is the 'be a bonus' mentality.

I teach my daughters to look for 'the chair-stackers'. They're the guys I want them to develop relationships with. He stacks chairs because he sees a need and has the character to meet it. The chair-stacker doesn't strive for recognition or thanks – although it's valuable to thank him. Contribution creates character.

The critical element is guiding boys to make this behaviour habitual. Aristotle taught: we become what we repeatedly do.[6] Excellence is not an act but a habit. Your son won't naturally stack chairs initially, but through repeated practice, it becomes his character. How do you get him there? Three simple ideas:

(i) Have occasional explicit discussions with him about the concept of surplus value, being a bonus, and helping the people around him feel safer and stronger. Tell him that his job at the barbecue this weekend is to ensure people's drinks are filled. Let him know that when the relatives from overseas arrive for a week-long holiday (staying in your rumpus room), you'd like him to bring their bags in from the car and put them in their room. When your family is at a party or community event, brief him beforehand: his job is to introduce himself to at least one person he doesn't know and make them feel welcome. Not because he has to, but because that's what people who add value do. When a neighbour is unwell, moving house, or going through something hard, rope him in. Let him carry the boxes, mow the lawn, or drop off the meal you've cooked. Make him part of the solution, not just a bystander to your good deed.

(ii) At the dinner table, have conversations about where you've seen examples of surplus value, being a bonus, and helping others feel safer and stronger. Invite him to share what he's noticed. Once he is on the lookout for it, he'll start seeing models of healthy masculinity everywhere. If you see something, talk about it with him. And if *he* is doing it, notice and name it. If he clears the table without being asked, or checks in on a younger sibling who's having a rough day, pause and point it out. Quiet recognition. 'I noticed what you did there. That's exactly the kind of man I want you to become. That's a value-add. That's safer and stronger.' Those single sentences do more heavy lifting than a lecture ever could.

(iii) Model it in your family and in close circles. Boys are watching their fathers (and the men around them) far more closely than you might realise. When a male role model (especially dad) grabs a neighbour's bin on the way back from the kerb, helps a stranger who has broken down on the side of the road, or stays back after the school parenting night to stack the chairs, your son is taking notes. My friend Alex took his son, Eli, to visit with an elderly neighbour who was a virtual recluse. Over several months of fortnightly visits, the neighbour began to leave the house, participate in life, and engage with Eli (much more than Alex!). Her life became fuller and richer, in part, because a 16-year-old boy joined his dad in building a relationship with a lonely neighbour.

Explicit teaching

The points above are about putting this version of healthy masculinity front and centre in conversations with your son. Explicit teaching makes an impact. Values become clear when you say, 'Being a good man means making people around you feel safer and stronger. Who did you help feel safer or stronger today?' or 'What value did you create today?'

Theory and practice are different. In my perfect world, you'll enjoy uplifting, enlarging conversations that change the character of your son immediately. In practice, you're more likely to get shrugs, grunts, and 'I don't know' responses. Push through it. You're establishing that being a consumer isn't enough – your son needs to be a contributor. If dad is at the table, he should have an answer too. You could make it easy for your son by shrinking the scope: 'Who did you help, even in a small way?' Look for small acts: helping someone with homework, picking up an item someone dropped, including someone who was left out. These moments build the habit of noticing others' needs.

These aren't interrogations. You're not drilling him to tick a box. You're not going to shame him for not having an answer or lecture him if he's unwilling to have a go. This is a long game. You're building awareness. If he has no answer, a simple, 'Oh well, maybe tomorrow,' followed by, 'What were you grateful for today?' or 'What was the best part about your day?' will help him save face, click to the message, and still be able to contribute to the conversation. By regularly asking these questions, you signal to your son that this is what you value. You plant seeds about what kind of person he's becoming.

Explicit teaching, reflection, and discussion build opportunities for discovery. They supercharge empathy, perspective, and maturity.

We're not looking for perfection, and we'll surely be disappointed if we seek it. These conversations aren't about chastisement – guilt is a poor motivator. It's about establishing direction, having meaningful experiences, and reinforcing the message over and over again. Day in, day out. It's that continual reminder: help others feel safer and stronger, be a bonus, add value. The more he hears it, the deeper the impression.

Pillar 2: the path of resistance

The first pillar asked your son to create surplus value. The second pillar is literally and metaphorically about climbing hills and developing self-discipline to control only what you can control.

As a former competitive cyclist, I've learned that riding uphill makes you stronger than riding downhill or along the flat. The hills are hard. Your legs burn, your lungs explode, and every instinct screams, 'Stop pedalling, turn the bike around, and ride back down the hill!' But the hills are where strength is built.

We've created a phrase in our home: 'You've gotta love the hills. The hills make you strong.'

Character works the same way. It's not built in comfort zones. Character is forged in challenges that demand more than your son thinks he can give. A popular statement shared on the internet, often attributed to Henry David Thoreau, reminds us, 'The path of least resistance leads to crooked rivers and crooked men.'

David Brooks asserts that the struggle against your own weakness is the central drama of life.[7] This is it. The Stoics believed true strength comes from mastering what you can control – your thoughts, choices, and responses – while accepting what you cannot. This means disciplining yourself to focus energy where it makes a difference.

How does your son feel about effort? And just as importantly, how do *you* feel about effort? He's watching how you handle hard moments. As a society, we have engineered so much hard stuff out of our daily lives. Your son has countless detours around difficulty. Dopamine is cheap. Screens provide instant entertainment when boredom strikes. AI writes his essays. Gaming offers achievement without real accomplishment. Each shortcut undermines his capacity to handle genuine challenge. But the things that make him uncomfortable are what make him grow.

The learning zone

These insights point to one thing: embracing challenge – learning to love the hills – increases competence. Doing hard things (with purpose and a sense of progress) feels amazing. Every time he does something hard and succeeds, he adds evidence: 'I can handle this.'

Boys love a physical challenge. We can use the same principles to develop character. My challenge to you is to help your son identify what matters beyond entertainment and social validation. Then build a daily rhythm where those priorities get his best energy.

Before the gaming session, the workout happens. Before the YouTube rabbit hole, the musical instrument is practised. Before comfort, challenge.

When meaningful activities precede pleasurable ones, your son develops self-discipline. He learns that satisfaction *earned* differs from easy pleasure. And meaningful activities, even when hard, become pleasurable and ultimately more rewarding than the cheap dopamine that easy pleasure dishes up.

I celebrated my 50th birthday in 2025. As a family, we travelled to Queenstown, New Zealand, drove an hour to Clyde in the Central Otago region, and rode the Otago Rail Trail. One hundred and fifty-two kilometres. Four days. Ten people. Over hills. Against headwinds. Through rain.

Our youngest child was 11. Our granddaughter sat in the buggy and was pulled the whole way by her parents. And there were dummy-spits. There were bikes thrown onto the grass and threats made that 'I'm not pedalling any further'. We were told that this was 'the stupidest holiday in history'. We sat near one unhappy rider for 35 minutes while she fumed, refusing to finish the ride. (I wanted to ask if she planned on calling a taxi … but the driver would never have found us! I chose to remain quiet.)

Something strange happened on day three. The kids stopped complaining. They started supporting one another. There were sounds of encouragement. They cheered for their siblings. They placed hands on backs and pushed their struggling cyclist sisters up hills. They began to talk, smile, laugh, sing. The shift was enormous. On our final day, they took off without us, racing the final 29 kilometres to the finish line to see who could arrive first.

On the two-hour bus trip back to Queenstown we asked, 'What did you think about the holiday?'

Every one of them affirmed, 'This was one of the best holidays of our lives!'

The response caught us by surprise. 'Why?' we asked.

'Because it taught us that we can do hard things.' They followed up with, 'Can we do another one of these holidays again next year?' And they weren't kidding.

This pillar is about reframing challenge as growth. When your son encounters difficulty – academic struggles, social rejection, athletic failure – he's climbing a metaphorical hill. Put another way, he's a knight in shining armour and there's a dragon to slay. Resist the urge to eliminate his discomfort. Don't slay his dragon for him. Be supportive, but don't take away his pain. Instead, when he is calm, help him reframe challenge as opportunity. Two chapters from now, we'll look at responding to his emotions. For now, just remember: high emotions = low intelligence. Your job is to help him move from a high emotion state (like my daughter on the side of the trail, crying because she couldn't ride any further) to a stable/low emotion state (when she decided to get back on the bike). It's usually enough to simply say, 'This is so tough for you right now,' and then zipping it.

When you were young and struggling with something hard, you wanted to feel understood. You probably wished someone would take away your challenge – but really, you knew you could do it if someone could just be there beside you. Resilience is *relational.* We do hard things best not when we tough them out on our own but when someone is there beside us.

Every young man wants to know: 'Do I have what it takes?' By learning to love the hills, your son's internal dialogue shifts. Rather than thinking, 'How can I avoid this difficulty?' he asks, 'How can I grow through this difficulty?' That single change turns obstacles into stepping stones in his character development journey.

Pillar 3: moral wisdom

The first two pillars build your son's character foundation: service and persistence. But character without the third pillar of wisdom is dangerous. As I was writing this chapter, neo-Nazis led by Thomas Sewell were marching through Melbourne's streets, protesting and causing disruption with racist propaganda. These are men willing to 'do hard things' (persistence). And they (somehow, misguidedly) believe they're serving the community. Lacking the third pillar – moral wisdom – is how well-intentioned boys make devastating mistakes or strong-willed young men choose the wrong path with conviction.

David Brooks argues that character isn't following rules or scripts. It's developing 'moral ecology' where the right action becomes natural. Your son needs to internalise values so deeply (like Teancum) that doing the right thing isn't a decision. It's automatic. Let's consider how.

Discovering moral principles

Conversations will be the linchpin of your teaching. And timing is everything for these conversations. I'll explore this in much greater depth in Chapter 11. While much of what we do with our children involves explicit teaching, discovery is more effective. Wisdom develops not through lectures but through moral reasoning. You could demand he 'not do x'. But it's far more effective to ask him about x, and find out what he knows, what his friends think, and what he would do if he ever encountered x. Ask him:

- 'Where have you seen someone making a tough moral choice recently?'
- 'What would you do if your friends were pressuring someone?'
- 'How do you know when something that seems fun is actually harmful?'

These discussions build his capacity to think through moral complexity rather than just follow rules. We're identifying values that, over time, he begins to endorse and live.

Teancum never would have pushed back against my directives unless he'd developed wisdom to know it was wrong. He had internalised and integrated healthy values into his sense of self. Would your son have done the same?

Boys with moral wisdom have character. They're trustworthy. They don't debate whether rape jokes are acceptable or racism is wrong. They don't question whether it's okay to pressure a romantic partner into sex. They see harm clearly and act accordingly. And if, right now, they *do* go along with these jokes or struggle with other pressure situations, we continue the conversations with them knowing we're playing a looooong game.

Moral courage is the crown of character development. It's great to be of service. It's powerful to demonstrate discipline. But the wisdom to discern right from wrong and the strength to act on it – that's what fills out character and gives it shape.

The take-home message

Your son is inherently worthy. He has value as a person. He is deserving of honour simply due to his humanity. But your son won't *feel* worthy if he doesn't do things that are of worth. An afternoon of gaming or TikTok is of little value. When he leaves his room, he'll value himself less because he hasn't grown, contributed, or added value.

Hedonic happiness is about avoiding pain and finding pleasure. Comfort, ease, and feeling good in the moment define the objective. But it fades fast. Eudaimonic happiness is the goal: it comes through meaning, purpose, and growth. This is character development built on virtue and contribution. It feels hard in the moment, but it endures.

Character is doing the hard thing when the easy thing is right there. It's keeping a promise to yourself when no one's watching. Choosing growth when comfort is available.

When boys become self-disciplined, serve others, and develop wisdom to navigate moral challenges, they become young men like Teancum: boys who know who they are, what they stand for, and how to live those values even when it costs them. They respect themselves because they do respectable things. The boy who learns character becomes a man who can answer questions like, 'Who am I?' 'What's my purpose?' 'Do I matter?' Boys won't find answers to these questions using the latest AI chatbot. These questions demand reflection, inner work, and even conflict: what the Bible calls 'the furnace of affliction'.

A saying attributed to at least three different thinkers tells us: 'Men of genius are admired, men of wealth are envied, men of power are feared, but only men of character are trusted.' Character is forged in the furnace of discipline, service, and moral wisdom. This is how we solve the trust problem. This is how we raise boys who help others feel safer and stronger. This is how we build strong young men from the inside out.

7 Your son's psychological engine

What every boy needs to thrive (and what happens when he doesn't get it)

Mastering the fundamentals isn't sexy, but it works. No matter what task you are working on, there is a simple checklist of steps that you can follow right now – basic fundamentals that you have known about for years – that can immediately yield results if you just practice them more consistently.

James Clear[1]

Cassie's 13-year-old son won't budge from his gaming console, won't do his homework, won't engage with the family or contribute around the house. Cassie has 'tried everything' – threats, rewards, heart-to-heart talks. Nothing works.

'His attitude is so bad,' Cassie tells me. 'We feel like we're just crap parents because he plays the victim every time we try to get him to do anything.'

This chapter is about understanding the fundamentals of your son's psychology. It's about *the basics*. Not just why your son might be resistant or unmotivated beyond staring at a screen, but what drives him when he is at his best – really engaged, energised, alive. If we want to see our boys build character and make a contribution, then tapping into the psychology that helps them feel good about themselves – feel worthy – is key. These principles underpin everything else in this book. They're practical, proven, and powerful – whether your son is thriving or struggling. They are the foundation for the solution to nearly every challenge you'll face raising sons.

The basic psychological needs

All humans have three basic psychological needs. When those needs are supported, your son will be at his best. When they're frustrated or thwarted? That's when problems emerge. It's that simple ... and that complex.

The basic psychological needs are:

- relatedness;
- competence; and
- autonomy.[2]

These three needs work like the legs of a stool. In an environment where one need is frustrated, the others are threatened too. These needs are inseparably connected. Understanding how they work together is the whole box and dice – it's *the* game – when it comes to supporting your son's healthy development.

Relatedness

Relatedness is about connection. It's your son feeling seen, heard, valued, and accepted. Relatedness is a two-way street: mutuality, reciprocity, and belonging. It's your son arriving at school and hearing a mate say, 'Bro, come sit with us,' or 'Come play handball.' It's walking into the house and hearing a parent say, 'We really missed you at dinner tonight.' Your son will crave environments where his relatedness need is supported. He'll fight for the chance to be in those spaces.

And then there are the times the relatedness need is *not* supported, but instead is thwarted: not being there, not being invited, feeling ostracised and excluded. If he feels invisible, if he doesn't fit in, or if he feels rejected, his relatedness need is frustrated. He'll fight for the chance to stay *out* of those spaces.

The best research in the world has consistently taught us that our kids are resilient, mentally healthy, and motivated when their relationships are healthy. Feeling acceptance is at the core. Sociologist Emmy Werner's 40-year Kauai study emphasised the centrality of healthy relationships for positive life outcomes.[3] The Harvard Study of Adult Development – literally the world's most remarkable study of wellbeing and healthy living – found the best predictor of positive life outcomes was, once again, healthy relationships.[4]

The heart of wellbeing is the quality of relationships we experience with those around us.

This can be hard medicine to swallow for parents of boys with lousy relationships. Your son might be excluding himself from people who love him. Perhaps he has no friends at school because he's different in some way. Our great challenge is to find a way to connect – to support the relatedness need. The great news is that your son is wired to form connections. Our mission is to find ways to help him do that in healthy, constructive ways with people who can lift and support – and accept – him.

When boys experience strong and positive connections, they make better decisions. Teens with secure family relationships – whose relatedness need is supported – show significantly lower levels of risky behaviours, including substance use, delinquency, and risky sexual activity.[5] A positive relationship doesn't just impact him now; a positive relationship with his parents during the first 16 years of his life promotes wellbeing into old age. Togetherness strengthens your son.[6]

If your son is isolating himself, hating school, or giving up on a once-loved activity, chances are his connections aren't strong. Environments where trust and connection are absent are places he avoids. His wellbeing is diminished when he doesn't see his 'people' – at school, at sport, and even at home.

Involvement: supporting relatedness needs

While writing this book, I received a text from a friend:

> Hey Justin, my son is suffering from depression and is now talking very openly about wanting to die. It's very triggering for me, and of course heartbreaking. We have him in an outpatient program at our nearby hospital, but after a tough week last week, I'd love it if you and I could talk.

Without undermining the mental health professionals in the hospital, I spent time with my friend. We put together a plan. I reminded him of the saying: to a child, LOVE is spelled T-I-M-E. I asked how much time they spent together. He responded: 'Not as much as we used to.' I recommended they prioritise father–son time, ideally in nature. Perhaps they could camp one weekend each month, reduce screens, and get some physical activity on a regular schedule.

Months later I received the following:

> In the past few months, we've seen a wonderful turnaround. I went from not even recognising our son (when we spoke) to having our amazing happy boy back. Probably the tool that had the greatest effect was from you: 'Let's create connection together.' We've done this through mountain biking together and it's been transformational (the trips, the trails, camping, the pizza afterwards, the car ride, watching YouTube videos, etc). The intentionality of always creating something to look forward to together has been a game-changer.

Think of your relationship with your son as a bucket, and connection being water in the bucket. How full is it each morning when he goes to school? Are you pouring connection into that bucket or is it full of air? Are mornings at your house a time that promotes belonging and acceptance? Does he feel seen, heard, and valued? Or are mornings tense with commands barked down the corridor to 'Hurry up' and 'Why is this so hard?' and 'What do you mean you can't find your shoes? You wore them home yesterday!' What about at night when it's lights out: is it a time of connection? Or castigation?

Water is connection: feeling seen, heard, and valued. Air is correction and direction: feeling like I'm getting it wrong, being ignored, or an impediment to the effective functioning of the home. If our kids are getting more correction and direction than connection, they're carrying empty buckets – and if that's the case, they'll put the bucket down. No one wants to carry an empty bucket. As parents, our job is to get water into those buckets.

Connection happens in the mundane moments – driving, chatting over dinner, washing dishes, watching a game. These seemingly insignificant moments of connection build the relational foundation your son needs. It's the eye contact, the shoulder or back rub, the pause to show you're really listening. Connection happens when we become aware of our tone of voice and change the clipped or abrupt tone to something warmer, or shift the sharp, short sentences we utter to something more conversational and curious. It happens when we speak to them with soft eyes, which soften our face, our words, and our thoughts.

Our sons need to feel seen, heard, and valued during conversations about a hard day at school, a break-up, a lost job, their anger, consent, dating, alcohol, and more. Our duty is to have these conversations with them – regularly – about big stuff and small stuff. But they only work when we have created the trust – a belief that the other person will act in our best interests. If you're only getting grunts in response, don't give up. Build the relationship. Establish a foundation of trust. Find a way in, as hard as it can be.

A dad in Dandenong bemoaned to me that he had completely lost his relationship with his 13-year-old son. 'We used to be best mates,' he told me. 'Now he grunts, ignores me, and stares at a screen.'

We discussed the things they used to do together. Bike rides. Camping. Buying an ice-cream as a treat, just because. 'When was the last time you did any of those things?' I prodded.

Dandenong dad shook his head. 'I can't remember. Years. I've asked but he's not responsive.'

I encouraged him to keep asking. And a while later I heard from him. His son had said yes to a bike ride. And then to another activity. And another. The relationship was growing again.

Just like dollars are the currency of our economy, connection is the currency of our relationships. Is your relationship in the red? Or the black? Be involved. Spend T-I-M-E. Support your son's sense of relatedness and watch the magic happen.

Autonomy

Our second basic psychological need is autonomy – being in the driver's seat of our life. It's the keystone of human motivation.

Melanie, a mum to a 14-year-old son, asked me, 'How do I navigate this brand-new chip on his shoulder? It's like someone flipped a switch, and suddenly everything's a battle.' She felt like everything was a battle because her son didn't want to be controlled.

Feeling controlled undermines motivation, resilience, and wellbeing, and teen boys are highly sensitive to *anything* that feels controlling. That response is called reactance, and the more we pile on the control, the more challenging behaviour we see in our kids. And in boys, things can get ugly, with big emotions and aggressive or violent outbursts.

If we respond reflexively and reactively to our son's big responses (instead of reflectively and intentionally), he'll often dig in. Now it's a battle of wills. The power play has commenced. We become increasingly demanding and coercive. Control goes up.

But force creates resistance. The more we push, the harder he pushes back. When we pour on the correction and direction, we empty the Relationship Bucket.

Alternatively, some parents pander, coddle, and give in to preserve the relationship. He gets what he wants. We feel lousy (because *our* psychological needs are being frustrated). And we're raising a spoiled man-child. In this case we've confused autonomy with permissiveness.

There's a third way: enrolling your child in solving the conflict that has arisen. It's called 'autonomy support'.

As soon as I say autonomy, the eye-rolling often begins. 'Oh, so I just give the kid freedom to do what he wants?' People misunderstand the idea of autonomy here. Autonomy does *not* mean freedom. And it does *not* mean independence. Giving a teenage boy carte blanche is asking for trouble! His immature judgement will likely lead to choices we'll all regret.

Autonomy is a little more complex. It relates to your son understanding what he values – long term – and choosing in alignment with that. He 'identifies' what matters (his values) and chooses to act the way he is acting because it makes sense, he buys the reasons – he endorses what's going on.

Forgive the jargon. This autonomy idea can be slightly confusing. Here's an easy, practical analogy: why do you drive on the lawful side of the road? Because you'll be fined? Maybe. But even if there are no police around, or it's the middle of the night and no one will see you or collide with you, you still drive on the lawful side of the road. You do it autonomously despite the fact that you are being controlled because *it makes sense*. You can't predict if or when oncoming traffic will appear, so it would be taking a senseless risk to drive in its path. The government *is* making you drive on the correct side of the road, but that's not why you comply. You follow the rule because you understand the rationale behind the rule. You 'buy the why'. You endorse the reason, value the outcome, and go along with the controlling demand of the government. That's what imbues your choice with personal agency.

Autonomy means your son feels volitional. The key word here is 'endorsement'. He understands the broader ramifications, perspectives, and puzzle pieces that need to be considered in making his choice. He identifies the value in what you're talking about. And he gets on board because he endorses those values. But he'll only do that if he's been given the chance to figure out what he values; what matters to him.

Here's one more example. When I was a teen, my parents took me to swimming squad up to ten times a week. I swam laps at the Olympic pool at East Gosford from 5 am to 7 am, Monday through Saturday. And there was an additional two-hour class on Tuesday through Thursday. My swim coach was forever mad at me because I wouldn't swim all the way to the wall. Instead, I'd swim to the flags hanging above the lane, five metres from the wall. Then I'd stand, turn around, and dolphin dive back into the water to swim back to the other end. Why? Because I didn't like swimming. I didn't want to be in the pool. I wasn't interested in doing the laps. I didn't see the purpose. I cut five metres off each length, so that if I was doing 100 metres, the shortcut trimmed me back to only 90 metres. In my teenage brain, I was winning.

As an adult, I have discovered that swimming is a delight. I love the feeling of being in the water and nothing feels as good as it does to be fit. When I swim laps now, I swim the entire length. Why? Because I have purpose. I see the point. I buy the rationale. I endorse the activity. That deeper identification with the value of the activity means I'm all in. So I do it. Properly.

Autonomy isn't your boy doing whatever he wants. It's him acting in harmony with his values; it's him *wanting* to do the things he does. If your son 'gets' what you're asking and why you're asking it, then he buys into it. Understanding and agreeing with the 'why' increases a willingness to comply – a feeling of volition and endorsement. His behaviour feels autonomous (and will therefore remain consistent whether he's being supervised or not).

If he doesn't like what you are saying and isn't ready to 'buy the why', his autonomy is frustrated. He'll feel that you're applying excessive control, monitoring him, or dismissing his perspective. He'll feel like he has limited options: compliance, defiance, or disengagement. These are the predictable outcomes of autonomy needs being frustrated. When autonomy is supported – through exploring his perspective, explaining the 'why' or the rationale, and empowering him to make decisions aligned with his values – his options are agency, ownership, and engagement. These are the predictable outcomes of autonomy needs being supported.

Ownership: supporting autonomy needs

Autonomy support is where most parents struggle. Many parents think it means giving kids full responsibility for their decisions: 'Up to you, son. You've got autonomy.' Wrong. Autonomy support places responsibility on parents to be effective communicators. It places responsibility on your son to understand why you're encouraging a decision. It demands he do the inner work of understanding his values – or working with your values. But he won't always agree with your rationale – he won't buy your why.

Sometimes he's going to choose something outside your value system. This is complex and messy for us, as we seek to guide our children to wise, healthy, safe decision-making. Questions could arise about dating and sex, gaming and screens, bedtime, taking up MMA, or other issues where you clash.

Of course, teenage boys can't always see around corners. They're hardwired for action, have low impulse control, and are sensation-seeking. Their brains are still developing. It makes sense we want to control things in order to keep them safe.

Alternatively, some boys are apathetic. Or they give you attitude in a moment of conflict. You become inflamed. You demand respect. Compliance. Now!

But force creates resistance. The more you push, the harder your son will push back.

Autonomy support requires that you:

- understand his perspective (explore);
- offer a rationale for your requests rather than demanding compliance 'because I said so' (explain);
- involve him in decisions and provide choices within reasonable boundaries (empower); and
- minimise (not eliminate) the use of controlling techniques.

These four elements of autonomy support are going to be on repeat for the rest of this book. Memorise them. They matter. Particularly the Three Es: explore, explain, empower. But we can't always do these things. Sometimes parents call the shots. Your 14-year-old is *not* going to the party on Friday night where there is zero parental supervision, two kegs, and 300 kids. More on that soon. Remember, where possible, collaboration beats enforcement.

Autonomy support offers your son ownership of his choices. If we do it right, with perspective-taking, rationales, and appropriate guidance towards choices we can all feel good about, our boys stop blaming others and take accountability for both their wins and their losses.

Competence

Competence is your son's final basic psychological need. When he feels competent, his motivation soars. Feeling incompetent? He crashes. Wellbeing falls through the floor. His attitude stinks.

This explains why boys throw themselves into gaming, where competence is measurable, achievable, and immediately rewarded. Progress is instantly visible. Level up, get the weapon, win the match, score the goal, tackle the opponent … and feel competent. Compare that to school, where feedback is delayed, unclear, and often negative.

Competence lights your son's internal engine. The ultimate result is mastery. In *How to Live*, Derek Sivers tells us:

> Mastery is the best goal because the rich can't buy it, the impatient can't rush it, the privileged can't inherit it, and nobody can steal it. You can only earn it through hard work. Mastery is the ultimate status.[7]

This is going to be even more accurate with the increasing impact of AI.

When he feels capable, your son approaches activities with confidence, focus, and unmistakable anticipation. He wants to demonstrate his strength, dominate, and win.

But what happens when competence feels out of reach? That English essay becomes an impossible Everest. He'll circle base camp for days … until it's 11 o'clock the night before it's due. That's when the storm hits: tears flooding or anger erupting as he confronts his perceived inadequacy, with no preparation and no confidence to overcome the challenge. Essay writing offers far less feedback and far fewer progress indicators than his favourite game.

Structure: supporting competence needs

Harvard researcher Teresa Amabile has studied what she calls 'The Progress Principle'.[8] When your son is progressing, gaining competence – moving towards mastery – he's motivated. He feels good. If your son is incompetent but feels like he is making progress, he'll stay motivated. But motivation plummets when progress pauses. The long-term goal is competence, but the short-term goal is progress. When he can't complete a maths problem, he'll stare at the paper on the table and sulk. There's no progress, so there's no motivation. But get him to read out the question, pick up the pencil, write an equals sign, and start working through the formula … that's progress, and progress is motivating.

Underpinning competence and mastery is structure.

When you understand the structure of a game, school, an essay, or home life, you can follow that structure, improve your performance, and feel better about life.

Other words for structure are things like:

- frameworks
- scaffolds
- systems
- patterns
- limits
- boundaries
- rules

- formulas
- guidelines.

Structure highlights *how* to be competent, *how* to do something. And when your son gets the structure, he knows how to be competent. He may still need to practise, but the structure shows him how to progress. Building structure (or substitute any of the words from the list above) gives your son the steps to progress, competence, and mastery. Want him to master his morning? Work out what an effective, productive morning looks like. Create the structure. Make sure he knows how to do it. And now he knows how to be competent in the morning. Want him to be competent in treating his siblings well, or cleaning his room? Create the structure. Make sure he knows how to do it. And again, now he knows how to be competent.

But beware: structure can either be introduced in a controlling way – 'Here's what to do. Now do it. No! Not like that! Like *this*. Because I said so.' – or it can be introduced in an autonomy-supportive way, using those four principles I outlined in the last section.

This is where the three needs start to connect. If you take a command-and-control view of structure, you'll tell him what to do. This frustrates autonomy. And it ruptures relatedness. Plus, he will feel incompetent because he interprets you telling him what to do as an indication that he's getting it wrong. Need-supportive parenting failed. But if you explain what matters and why (the rationale), he's likely to identify with what you're describing and endorse the value of it. If you explore his perspective he'll feel validated and understood – and be able to contribute because you're giving him a voice. Then if you empower him to develop solutions (a structure or framework) that feel good for him, he'll feel capable and autonomous. Relationships improve. Competence flourishes. Autonomy is supported.

All the way through these decisions, he needs our mature prefrontal cortex to help nudge him towards safe and healthy decisions. He doesn't know it (or like it) but he needs our adult wisdom – but it can't be controlling, except in the rarest of circumstances.

There's a great paradox here: structure and boundaries create freedom, they don't restrict it.

Consider a jazz musician. The rigid structure of musical theory – scales, chord progressions, time signatures – is necessary for competence and mastery. And once understood, that structure doesn't limit creativity; it facilitates it. The great musicians don't revolutionise music without first mastering the fundamentals that give them something to explore and push against. The structure becomes the launching pad for innovation and competence (even excellence). Artisans don't start apprenticeships by telling their charges to 'express yourself freely'. They start with fundamentals: how to hold the tool, how to respect the material. The structures make true mastery possible. Our boys are apprentices in the craft of becoming men. They need structures that lead them to healthy masculinity.

Entrepreneur and motivator Alex Hormozi highlights how competence supports wellbeing: 'You don't become confident by shouting affirmations in the mirror, but by having a stack of undeniable proof that you are who you say you are.'[9] Build competence by learning the structure or framework or system. Repeat until it is easy. Become confident.

Teenage boys wrestle with insecurity around their masculinity because they haven't had time to build that mountain of evidence proving their competence. They need to do the reps. When they do, they'll find that competence is immensely motivating.

Today the structure for what competent masculinity looks like feels unclear. How do boys know when they've passed the test and proven their competence as men? Is it how much beer they can drink? How many sexual partners they can convince to sleep with them? How many fights they've won?

We need to develop a narrative that is less about conquest and more about character and contribution. Are they being a bonus? Adding value? Are they helping those around them feel and be safer and stronger? *These* are the attributes that help boys feel competent – and that build better relationships. If they buy this narrative, we're creating a need-supportive environment for healthy masculinity to flourish.

The take-home message

The blueprint for our boys' motivation, resilience, and wellbeing is in creating a need-supportive environment. In order to experience psychological need-support, three things have to occur:

(i) their relationships feel supportive;

(ii) they understand why something matters and willingly choose to be involved in it; and

(iii) they feel a sense of progress towards mastery of skills that matter to them.

If our boys are experiencing all three, they will thrive.

When your son is showing a lack of motivation about a class, activity, or experience, ask yourself why. In almost every case, one or more of these three needs will be frustrated. Find a way to support that need and watch how things improve. And if you can't, it might be worthwhile asking whether that activity is really that valuable.

8 Motivation

What actually drives your son, and how to work with it

What matters isn't how motivated someone is,
but how someone is motivated.

Alfie Kohn[1]

Understanding basic psychological needs changes how you raise your son. The environment we create is instrumental in what he pursues and why – and in who he becomes. But there's one more foundational element to this blueprint: what motivates your son – and why?

A parent's primary focus is typically, 'How do I motivate my son?' But that question implies that motivation is a switch that shifts him from 'not motivated' to 'motivated'. That's *not* how motivation works.

Instead, think of motivation as a swimming pool, with a shallow end, a middle, and a deep end connected to his three basic psychological needs. If your son is in an environment where his relationships are lacklustre, he feels incompetent, and you've forced him to be there, he'll experience the need-frustration we discussed in the last chapter. All three needs are thwarted. This correlates directly with *how* he is motivated in that environment. Getting him there and asking him to do anything there will usually require you to step in with threats and bribes, punishments and rewards. External motivators are your only tool here. He's in motivationally shallow waters – the kiddy pool. The water is ankle deep.

Let's use school as an example. In Chapter 1, I showed evidence that many boys struggle with school. If your son hates school – and it feels like swimming in a kiddy pool – consider how his basic psychological needs are supported or frustrated in a school context. Boys who hate school report:

- poor relationships with peers (relatedness-frustration);
- constant demands where they don't see the purpose or rationale (autonomy-frustration); and
- work that is too hard or doesn't make sense (competence-frustration).

School, therefore, becomes need-frustrating. It doesn't matter the size of the school, how beautiful the grounds are, the resources, or the subjects it offers. Whether he is neurotypical or neurodivergent, the outcome is the same. If he isn't connected, has no agency, and feels incompetent, he'll hate it. You'll need bribes and threats to get him there. He's swimming in shallow water – and he's miserable.

But what if your son loves his friends, can do the work (even if it's a struggle), and sees the purpose? School, for this boy, is need-supportive. He wants to be there and he wants to do the work. He's swimming in deep water where real growth happens. He'll be autonomously motivated. It's an entirely different kind of motivation to the external carrot-or-stick approach.

This applies beyond school: the extra-curricular activities, health choices, and friend and family choices your son makes all come down to need-support or need-frustration. The quality or kind of motivation he experiences in these environments is impacted by whether he has good relationships there, his sense of competence, and the degree to which he is choosing to be there, his volition.

The table on the next page shows you what the motivational continuum looks like. Let's explore it.

The motivation continuum

Amotivation: the empty pool

Amotivation is motivational rock bottom: it's your son staring at his homework with empty eyes, asking, 'What's the point?'

All three needs are frustrated here. No relatedness. No competence. No autonomy. He's checked out.

True across-the-board amotivation is rare. If your son can't muster energy for *anything* – not mates, sport, food, or even gaming – he might need professional support.

But what parents think of as 'amotivation' is usually *selective* motivation. Your son won't touch his geography project but he *will* stay up until 3 am mastering his favourite game. His motivation system is fine, but it's directionally askew. It's like a garden hose

EXTRINSIC MOTIVATION — INTRINSIC MOTIVATION

AMOTIVATION	EXTERNAL	INTROJECTED	IDENTIFIED	INTEGRATED	INTRINSIC
Avoidance	**Reluctant** APPROACH	**Obligated** APPROACH	**Willing** APPROACH	**Aligned** APPROACH	**Enthusiastic** APPROACH
What's the point?	*If I don't, I'll lose my phone*	*I should be getting As*	*This matters for my future*	*This is who I am. This reflects my values*	*I love learning this! This is fun/ interesting*
Chronic skipping Completely disengaged May be depressed	Shows up to avoid trouble Minimal effort Watches the clock	Works from guilt/ obligation Anxious about performance I have to mentality	Consistent engagement Self-directed study Seeks help when needed	Consistent with identity Personally meaningful	Goes beyond requirements Time flies in class

SHALLOW — DEEP

Needs Frustrated
Disconnected from peers/teachers
Feels incapable at schoolwork
No choices or voice in learning

Needs Supported
Connected to peers/teachers
Feels capable with right support
Has meaningful choices in learning[2]

with full water pressure watering the neighbour's roses instead of your lawn. Understanding this means you can help redirect the flow rather than fix a hose that isn't broken. The game supports those needs (he feels competent, connected, and volitional). Geography frustrates those needs. He receives limited feedback so he questions whether he's doing it correctly (competence). He's doing it solo or it's group work where no one else is helping out (relatedness). And he probably doesn't see the purpose or value in it (autonomy). Amotivation is hard to shift. In relation to the pool metaphor, he hasn't even dipped his toe in the water!

External motivation: the shallow end

External motivation relies on rewards and punishments – carrots and sticks. 'Get good grades and the gaming console is yours.' 'Clean your room or lose your phone.'

Punishment and reward are the lowest form of motivation. Your son is not self-regulating. You're doing it all (in an effort to make him do it all). This usually gets compliance – but it's at a steep cost.[3] Over-reliance on rewards and punishments damages intrinsic motivation.[4] You're teaching your son that the only reason to do anything is what he gets out of it.

External motivation creates a transactional worldview: 'What's in it for me?' This is the equivalent of swimming in the kiddy pool. The water is ankle deep and warm like pee. When we're using punishments and rewards to externally regulate our son's behaviour, he's going to follow rules because someone's watching, but his behaviour will almost certainly change when supervision or promises and threats disappear. He hasn't bought in. There's zero commitment.

Parents usually resort to external motivation when we see no other option – which, for stressed-out, frazzled parents, is often. It's high-effort and low-outcome. Instead, step back and ask why he is resisting. I guarantee those basic psychological needs are being frustrated. He doesn't want to do the thing or go to the place because there are relationship, competence, or autonomy difficulties. He's not seeing the point so we have to force the issue. This is a hard place to be for everyone.

Introjected regulation: wading deeper

Things start to get interesting at introjection. This is when your son regulates himself to avoid guilt or gain approval. He's internalised your voice, but it hasn't become his own. He doesn't value the activity (for example, cleaning his room). Instead, he's doing it because he values the peace and quiet he receives when you're not on his case. Or perhaps a love-interest is coming for a visit, in which case his ego needs him to do the cleaning. He wants approval and knows first impressions count. This is introjection.

Many teen boys follow expectations out of obligation, not conviction. It's duty without desire.

In our pool analogy, they're in water that's splashing at their knees. It's better than the ankle-deep kiddy pool of external motivation, but he can't do bomb dives in knee-deep water. Behaviourally, he might do the 'right' thing, but not in a committed and meaningful way.

The telltale words of introjection are 'I should', 'I must', or 'I have to'. He's regulating himself but fighting an internal battle the whole time. It's like being on a diet when someone brings cake into the office. 'I should stay off it,' you tell yourself. Introjection lives on guilt and shame. It's unsustainable.

Identified motivation: swimming in deeper waters

Identified regulation occurs when your son recognises the value in an action, even if he doesn't love it. 'I know studying matters for my future.' 'Being kind to my sister is the right thing to do.' The key phrases are 'I get it,' 'It makes sense,' and 'I value this, even if I don't love it.' We're moving to a point where he endorses the activity. He's buying the rationale. Now it's about identifying the value of doing that thing or going to that place, and having a go.

In our own lives and in the lives of our boys, identified regulation drives most meaningful accomplishments. It's 'identified' because your son 'identifies' the worth of the activity. He identifies why school is important or why switching off screens brings benefits. He buys the legitimacy of an early night, or not driving in the car with friends who are still on their P plates because of the dangers it presents. He's endorsing it – not because of your threats or bribes (external) or because he 'really should since that's what a good son does' (introjected). It's his voice now. He might not love it – or even like it. But it makes sense, so he's in.

And this is why it's the workhorse of motivation. It's because boys in identified regulation don't need constant supervision. They've adopted values as their own, creating internal guideposts.

They connect behaviour to goals they endorse: maintaining relationships, looking after their body and hygiene, or participating in school, church, community, sports, or other activities. Identified motivation shifts their lens to 'There's real value in this' and 'I get that this matters.'

The messy bedroom: three motivational levels

Let's visit your son's messy bedroom from the vantage of each of these regulatory styles.

External: 'What happens if I don't clean it up?' or 'What will you give me if I clean the mess?' You want him to clean his room and you're offering rewards or threatening punishments, but he doesn't care about the mess. There's no compelling rationale or purpose (autonomy-need is frustrated) – until you give him one via reward or punishment. Perhaps he doesn't know what to do with half his stuff (competence-need is frustrated). Or it's a lot and he has to tackle it alone (relatedness-need is frustrated). He feels forced, stupid, or disconnected. Triple whammy.

Introjected: 'I have to clean this mess. That's what a good son should do.' In this case, the room is clean, but his wellbeing takes a hit. And he'll likely do a lousy job because motivation is shallow. Introjection means he's internalised your standards, but they're borrowed rules that don't quite fit. Autonomy is frustrated. He's not choosing based on his values. Competence is frustrated. He's cleaning to meet external expectations and the quality of the work is not important to him. Relatedness is frustrated because he feels disconnected from you even while trying to please you.

Identified: 'Having an organised space helps me think clearly and find my stuff. I don't enjoy cleaning, but it matters. I'm getting this done.' The motivation is *his* now. He's not cleaning to avoid punishment or because he 'should'. Once we reach identified regulation, motivation qualitatively shifts. He endorses the activity so his autonomy-need is supported. He's choosing based on his own reasoning and purpose. He's developing organisational skills that serve his purposes, so he's feeling progress and competence. And relatedness shifts in a positive way because you're aligned on shared values rather than locked in power struggles. The task is something he values. The motivational pool is navel depth: not deep enough for a bomb dive, but he can swim and have fun.

My kids sometimes complain about church attendance. 'Why are you making me go?' they ask. I assure them I'm not 'making' them go. They whine that they know they're 'supposed' to go.

I point out that they've moved from external motivation ('You're making me go') to introjected motivation ('I feel like I should go'). I ask how many people at church operate from introjection.

'Lots,' they respond.

'What kind of mood are they in?'

'Miserable,' comes the reply.

'How do their faces look? How is their singing?'

My kids respond: 'Their faces look bored. They don't sing at all.'

I don't want my kids attending church externally motivated or introjected. They need to be at least 'identified'. I tell them I'm leaving in 20 minutes, and they can decide whether to attend based on where they are on the motivation continuum. Twenty minutes later they're typically in the car with me – willing participants. They've reminded themselves why church matters. They identify the value. They buy the why.

If it was about punishments and rewards, that's external regulation. They'd show up to avoid being in trouble or to get the promised rewards after church. If they wanted my approval, we're talking introjected regulation. The behaviour is internally pressured, driven by a desire to gain approval or avoid shame or guilt, but the motivation hasn't been genuinely accepted as their own. They're doing it to feel good about themselves in the eyes of someone who matters to them, or to avoid feeling like they've let that person down. Richard Ryan, Australian Catholic University professor and author and co-founder of *Self-Determination Theory*, told me 'the classic introjection markers are all there: ego-involvement, contingent self-worth, and the approval of significant others as the driving force'. Shifting to identified regulation gets the job done while preserving their autonomy and our relationship. No coercion.

This isn't a story about religious observance. It's about giving your son a voice, keeping connected, and trusting his ability to think things through. At the shallow end (external and introjected), it's about compulsion. In deeper waters, compulsion isn't needed. Your son becomes committed. School. Chores. Friendship choices. Vaping. Alcohol. Screens. When you support basic psychological needs, his regulatory style and motivation shift.

At this point, someone always asks, 'But what if something *really* matters to me but genuinely doesn't matter to my son, or he's actively resisting? Do I just let it go? Or do I force the issue?' These are often the only two solutions parents see. There is a third way: walk through those four steps – see the world through his eyes, explain your rationale, collaborate, and minimise control. This conversation supports basic psychological needs! Life can sometimes be messy. Nothing works every time. But the research is compelling. This process moves you in the right direction better than any strategy I know.

Integrated motivation: the deep end

When your son regulates with integrated motivation, he acts not because of rewards or punishments (external), not because he must or should (introjected), not even because he understands it matters (identified). *He does it because it's who he is.*

'I'm the kind of person who keeps my word.'

'I stand up for mistreated people because that's who I am.'

'I shower and brush my teeth because I take pride in my appearance.'

This is the deep end in our motivational swimming pool. Chin-deep water that's crystal clear. The motivation flows naturally because it's woven into his identity. No internal struggle, no external pressure. When he acts, it's authentic. It comes from his core sense of self.

For teenage boys still discovering identity, integrated motivation is a work in progress. You'll catch glimpses – moments in which he acts from self-knowledge rather than external pressure. But developmentally he is still working out who he is and what he values. These glimpses are previews of the man he's becoming. When motivation is truly integrated it's an expression of who he understands himself to be. The action and the person are aligned.

The messy bedroom: continued

Integrated: Before you say anything about the state of his room, he looks around and thinks, 'I value order and respect for my space. This mess is awful.' He acts. The cleaning isn't a chore. He isn't battling internal voices or calculating rewards. The room gets cleaned because keeping it clean is part of who he is.

Many boys don't care about mess. Their tolerance for chaos is high. You see disaster zone. He sees home. Integrated motivation might show up in other areas of his life first: standing up for friends, sticking to workout routines. Room cleaning as identity expression? That emerges when he's buying his own stuff or paying his own rent.

Intrinsic motivation: the infinity pool

Intrinsic motivation is the holy grail; what your son does purely for the joy of it. No external rewards, no identity to maintain, no values to uphold. Just pure delight.

Intrinsic motivation is the deep end of our motivational swimming pool – Olympic depth, where your son can dive from the high board, swim laps underwater, and play games. The water is crystal clear and perfectly heated. He doesn't want to get out because being in the water is the point.

Intrinsic motivation usually appears in areas of genuine passion: the basketball court where he loses track of time perfecting his shot, the guitar when he's working out a new riff, the video game where he's absorbed in mastering the mechanics, or that academic subject that captivates him.

When intrinsically motivated, your son experiences 'flow' – full absorption.[5] Self-consciousness disappears. Time is forgotten. He's not performing or proving. He's lost in the experience.

The messy bedroom: continued

Intrinsic: Your son discovers what a joy it is to organise. Sorting, categorising, and creating systems become sources of interest and delight. He experiments with different layouts, finds satisfaction in the process, and feels energised by the results. His autonomy, competence, and relatedness needs are all fulfilled as he shares his organisational discoveries with you.

If you were laughing out loud as you read that last paragraph, rest assured, so was I. I'm yet to hear of a teenage boy (or anyone other than Marie Kondo) who experiences intrinsic motivation around bedroom cleaning. And that's perfectly fine. The goal isn't making *every* task intrinsically rewarding. It's neither realistic nor necessary. Many activities in life will never bring intrinsic delight for most of us: garbage, taxes, cleaning, washing, writing an essay.

However, if you create conditions that shift your son from external or introjected to at least identified regulation ('I get why this matters') or integrated ('This reflects who I am') he'll engage positively. Supporting those three basic psychological needs moves him there.

Your job: watch closely. Recognise and nurture areas where his eyes light up, where no one has to remind him to practise or participate. These are his gifts emerging. They're the foundation of passion, expertise, and lifelong fulfilment. When he's hurrying you out the door so you can get him to music or sport or drama practice, you know you've got it. If, on the other hand, you're yelling, dragging him, and making demands on him to go, chances are he's feeling controlled, his relationships aren't quite right, or he feels incompetent. Consider letting it go. Find something else. Or support those basic needs while he's learning and progressing, and watch what shifts. (Sometimes kids are resistant, even for activities they love. If you're nagging to get him in the car but when he arrives, he's in heaven, keep nagging – gently. Mastery and love come with time.)

The real-world impact: where psychological needs and the motivation continuum meet teen boy challenges

Understanding the three basic psychological needs – relatedness, autonomy, competence – and the way they intersect with motivation and wellbeing transforms how you'll approach every major challenge. Consider the following three issues.

1. The Man Box: where culture crushes needs

The Man Box tells boys:

- don't show emotion;
- act tough; and
- follow rigid gender rules (fight back when challenged, be hypersexual, etc).

If adolescent male competence looks like this (and for too many of our boys it does), then we'll see them acting this way. This will help them in their peer context (assuming these values are held by their friends) but will be less helpful at home, school, and in many social or public settings. This means that they'll often get in trouble and have people trying to tell them what to do, which is need-frustrating. Relationships rupture. Boys are being told they're incompetent. And they feel controlled and misunderstood. No wonder some teen boys seem angry or withdrawn. Their basic psychological needs are systematically frustrated by cultural expectations. They act inauthentically to fit in or look competent. They're introjected (ego-involved and feeling their self-worth is contingent on how they behave) – and it comes at a cost.

2. Digital dominance: the screen-lords problem

Gaming gives boys:

- instant relatedness – belonging to guilds, teams, or communities;

- clear competence markers – levels, stats, followers; and
- unlimited autonomy.

These digital environments support their basic psychological needs but in shallow, artificial ways that outcompete healthier alternatives. They have relationships – but they're hollow, digital, and have limited potential to grow. They are becoming highly competent – but it's something that doesn't mean anything in the real world and won't help them progress except in their virtual domain. And while gaming offers a sense of both control and purpose, it's not contributing to anything that truly matters.

3. Pornography

Pornography supplies:

- pseudo-relatedness – false intimacy without rejection risk;
- artificial competence – feeling like they're sex-gods while staring at videos and masturbating, or having deep conversations with a synthetic AI girlfriend bot; and
- illusory autonomy – feeling control over the sexual experiences that damage their expectations of real relationships.

Boys with strong real-world connections, genuine competence, and age-appropriate autonomy are significantly less likely to develop problematic pornography use.[6]

We'll tackle these challenges in depth later. For now, know this: when boys' basic psychological needs are supported, problematic behaviours often resolve naturally. Need-supportive environments are the key to behavioural and emotional regulation, and to motivation and wellbeing.

The take-home message

The question isn't how motivated your son is, but *how* he's motivated. To what extent does he feel connected, competent, and in control? These three elements are your diagnostic tool for understanding his psychological state. Too many boys are what I'll call 'non-thriving', and it's generally because these needs are frustrated, and their environments are need-thwarting. This means they do what they do because of external (carrots and sticks) or introjected (ego, approval-seeking, contingent self-worth) reasons. But when we understand those three needs, we have a blueprint for supporting his identified, integrated, and intrinsic motivation, and creating boys and men who flourish.

9 Emotions

Understanding your son's emotional world

We are emotional beings. Thinking and acting are not riding shotgun – they are hog-tied in the trunk. It's emotion that's at the wheel.

Brené Brown[1]

I was walking by the beach enjoying some child-free time with my wife. As Kylie and I watched the waves, a woman sidled over to us. 'I love your work,' she said, 'and I listen to your podcast every day.' We chatted briefly as I asked about her family. Then – with her voice carrying that mix of worry and weariness I've come to know well – she asked, 'Can I ask you a question?'

'This happens a lot,' I said, smiling. 'I'd love to help, but I can't do therapy,' I joked. 'Fire away.'

'My son's moods are like … those waves hitting the rocks. He's explosive. I have no idea what to do when it happens, but it feels scary sometimes.'

Girls and boys both have big emotions. Generally, girls internalise. They ruminate. Anxiety and depression are common. Boys externalise. They lash out, get angry, make themselves big and powerful, and sometimes frighten their parents. And boys' big emotions come up a lot in conversation.

'His mood swings are intense and I never know what to expect.'

'It's like walking on eggshells to avoid triggering a reaction.'

When he's stable, he's delightful. But when the temperature goes up it's a high-voltage emotional eruption. The hardwired, natural biological developments in boys' maturing brains combine with cultural pressures demanding he show dominance and power. Then we are swept up in the ensuing emotional tsunamis. This chapter provides the blueprint to help you and your son understand and regulate emotions and develop the emotional intelligence and empathy you both need to work with others and their emotions.

Reaction and regulation

We're told girls are the emotional ones, not boys. But boys aren't less emotional – they're emotional in a different way. There are measurable neural differences in how male and female brains regulate emotionally. Researchers have shown that when something upsetting happens, girls' brains tend to feel the emotional hit more intensely straightaway. Their emotional alarm system fires harder. Curiously, when they then try to calm themselves down, they use the thinking parts of their brain less than boys do. Boys, on the other hand, are actually better at using their thinking brain to manage their emotions deliberately. So girls feel emotions more strongly at first, but boys may have an easier time using conscious thought to get their emotions under control.[2]

This research offers generally positive news about boys and emotions, but it seems contradictory to the challenges parents put to me. That's because there's a difference between *regulation* – which boys seem to be reasonable with – and *reaction*, which is what parents are discussing with me. Boys may be better at turning a dial when they're trying to. They can pause, process, and proceed calmly if they're focused. But their dial also gets grabbed and spun hard by biology before they even know it's happening. This is the spontaneous, impulsive outburst that worries everyone in their orbit. And the modern world increasingly expects men to process their emotions in healthier ways than many men previously have: fewer outbursts and big reactions, and more emotional intelligence. The concern is many boys and men aren't able to identify emotions – even when they're having them – and when this happens, they react *and* regulate their emotions poorly. (They also fail to read emotions in others and respond appropriately to those emotions.)

Our brains process emotions from the back to the front and from the bottom to the top. Since our 'emotional' brain processing components (known as the 'limbic system') are closer to the back and bottom than our brain's 'thinking' components (our 'prefrontal cortex') this means that when our system receives input, the emotional centre gets first bite at responding. Without those intentional regulation strategies, outbursts explode out of us. We become emotionally flooded – and when emotions flood our sons' brains, they'd rather *show* how they feel than *tell* us.

- The door slam that rattles the house.
- The gaming controller that sails across the room.
- The sudden aggression towards a sibling (or the boy-sized hole in the wall).
- The brooding silence.
- The cold stare that pushes everyone away.
- The flat denial that anything's wrong.

Lee, father of three boys, told me: 'With my daughter, I always know where I stand emotionally. She tells me. It might last for days, but at least I know. But my sons? They bottle it up.'

Let's bring this back to our conversation about healthy masculinity and about boys helping those around them feel and be safer and stronger. Boys receive messages that connection and emotional expression are 'feminine'. By their tweens and teens, Man Box rules kick in for a substantial portion of them: 'Don't show emotion.' 'Handle it yourself.' 'Man up.' Your son begins to believe that showing pain and weakness will emasculate him.[3] But push emotions down and they're going to pop up somewhere, somehow. Like a ball held underwater, the bigger it is, the harder it is to keep it down – and the bigger the splash when it explodes to the surface. Your son will react when provoked if it suits his desire for status. He'll regulate for the same reasons. But eventually, there's an explosion – and it can feel frightening.

Boys' emotional lives aren't just shaped by Man Box rules.

The path to male emotional expression starts much earlier. From infancy, boys receive different emotional messaging than girls. Various studies have shown that compared to girls, boys have fewer stories read and songs sung to them, and they receive more instruction and less conversation, fewer smiles, and different play experiences. When upset, boys are more likely to be ignored, while girls are encouraged to express their sadness. When boys get a response, they're told to 'get over it', that 'you'll be right', and 'toughen up' – messages girls rarely hear. 'Stop crying. You're behaving like a girl,' reinforces that emotionality is firmly female.[4]

Studies show parents are more comfortable with daughters expressing fear and sons expressing anger than the reverse. When daughters are sad or scared, we talk – and when they're angry, we shut them down. With sons? When they're afraid, we're more likely to distract them or tell them to focus on something else, and while we may not like it, we accept anger as part of what it is to be a boy.[5]

This teaches our boys that:

- sadness should be ignored;
- fear is unacceptable;
- anger is the 'manly' response; and
- talking about feelings is feminine.

By adolescence this emotional conditioning runs deep. Girls travel along what Dr Lisa Damour describes as a 'broad emotional highway' while sons restrict themselves to 'an increasingly narrow lane'.[6] The result is many boys who understand anger but struggle with vulnerability, boys who throw punches but can't process sadness, and boys who'd rather slam a door than say, 'I'm confused,' or 'I'm scared.'

When your son retreats to his room instead of talking, when he explodes rather than admits fear, when he responds with anger instead of acknowledging pain, he's following a script that society has developed right alongside him. Stoicism only works when emotions are being processed healthily below the surface. But for many boys that stoic mask is covering a pressure cooker with no release valve.

Emotional regulation

Emotional regulation has three core elements.

(i) An ability to turn emotions up or down.

(ii) An awareness of context: the 'read the room' component. Just because you *can* turn emotions up or down doesn't mean you *should*.

(iii) A consideration of long-term goals. It's healthy to turn emotions down when explosive anger would damage relationships. It's equally healthy to turn them up when the situation allows it – advocating for yourself or others, celebrating achievements, or expressing care and connection.

The Man Box says, 'Never show feelings. (Unless you're mad. Anger is manly).' Healthy regulation says, 'Understand your feelings and express them appropriately.'

No one is born knowing how to regulate emotions. Basic emotional regulation develops slowly from about age three, even for neurodivergent kids.[7] By eight to ten years old most neurotypical children can express or suppress emotions appropriately (unless they're tired, hungry, or stressed).[8] Neurodivergent children may take longer, depending on their specific challenges or context.

Emotions – especially big ones – are short-term focused. I learned this when teenage me hurled a lump of firewood at my surfboard in anger. The wood smashed a hole into the bottom of my board. A lack of regulation can be a liability. Anger costs – possessions, relationships, jobs, academic opportunity, other people's safety and wellbeing, and more.

Dr Lisa Damour describes how emotions should be on our cognitive board of directors.[9] They provide valuable information. But they should *never* chair the board. High emotions equals low intelligence. The more emotional your son is, the less regulated he'll be and the less wise he'll be (and the same goes for you). This goes for the upsetting emotions and the delightful emotions. Elation can lead to stupid thinking just as easily as sadness and anger.

Boys who learn to understand and regulate emotions do better in life. Part of this is related to something they develop called *frustration tolerance*.[10] They become better at tolerating distress rather than blowing up – even the ones whose neurodivergence makes this more difficult.

The boy who cannot tolerate frustration gives up. 'I can't … it's too hard!' When he's young and immature, he'll lash out physically, run away, swear, and generally be inconsiderate. If this pattern embeds itself as he ages, that lashing out can become more aggressive. He might pick fights, destroy property, use and abuse alcohol and other drugs (out of both rebellion and also as an escape), or force sexual activity on an unwilling partner. What you banish doesn't vanish; it emerges later in less functional ways. If healthy masculinity means helping those around you feel stronger and safer, emotional regulation is not a luxury item.

Emotional temperature: you're hot and you're cold

If I could gift every human on the planet one ability, it would be self-awareness. Can your son take his emotional temperature? Is he aware of his triggers? Has he noticed the different way he makes decisions based on his emotional state? Does he know the impact of his emotions on those around him?

Hot emotions are what we feel in the moment: anger that makes us want to throw things, excitement that makes us take foolish risks, fear that leads to us lashing out or shutting down. Cool emotions come when we're out of the moment and have time to process. Cool emotions allow calm reflection and measured responses.

The trick isn't to avoid hot emotions. Getting angry, feeling frustrated, and experiencing fear are healthy and adaptive in the right context for the right reasons. Hot emotions are like warning lights on your dashboard. They tell you something needs attention.

But you don't try to fix your car while driving at high speed. You pull over, let the engine cool, then address the issue. (Let's be honest, we call a mechanic … and there could be something in that. Someone with additional expertise – and distance – can be useful when we're not sure what to do.) This same principle applies to emotional regulation. Teach your son that when emotions are hot, it's probably time to pause, not act. Save big decisions, important conversations, and significant choices for later, when emotions are cooler. And consider talking with someone trustworthy about decisions and challenges when the fuse is no longer burning and cool emotions have returned.

Feeling emotions deeply doesn't make your son weak. He's supposed to feel them all. Man Box beliefs put him in an emotional straitjacket. Healthy living allows emotional experience. Feeling them *and managing them wisely* makes him strong – and it will help him help the people around him feel safer and stronger; to be a bonus – a value-add in their lives. This is why we need a blueprint for emotion regulation.

Making sense of emotional storms

Picture a snow globe. When still, everything is clear, ordered, peaceful. Shake it and chaos erupts. Swirling particles cloud everything. This is your son's brain on big emotions. The storm clouds his prefrontal cortex, the rational thinking centre. He becomes dysregulated.

You can't force snow to settle, and you can't force emotions to calm. They need time. Shaking the globe harder won't help. Yelling at the snow, demanding that it settle faster, won't help. Telling your son to 'calm down' or 'get over it', or even demanding 'just tell me what's going on', is the equivalent of shaking the globe more vigorously and expecting clarity. Here's my simple, five-step blueprint for helping the snow to settle safely.

1. Make sure you're regulated yourself. If you come in all guns blazing, he'll catch your emotions. Emotions are contagious. Instead, take a breath, think long term, and keep your emotions steady.

2. Say what you see. My favourite script is so simple it's stunning: 'Looks like you're having a rough time.' Variations could include: 'Seems like it's been a rough day.' 'Things with Mum are a little rough, huh?' 'Sometimes having a little brother can be annoying, can't it?' In each of these statements, you're offering gentle emotional validation by simply describing how life is for your son *in one short sentence.* This can be challenging for many parents, and it feels a little scripted and inauthentic when you start. But it becomes easier with practice, and starts to feel right the more you do it.

3. Offer a choice. The script continues as follows: 'Do you want to talk about it? Do you need a hug? Or should I just give you some space?' Then zip it. No more words. What you've done is given him the assurance of safety – so it's a tick for his relatedness-need support. You've asked him what's going to work best for him right now.

That's autonomy support. And implicit in the question is the belief in his ability to figure out the best way forward – to regulate and respond. That's checking the support box for competence. At times, your son may be so overwhelmed he doesn't know. If that's the case, make the decision for him with a hug and then some space, promising to come back in two minutes to see how he is. But generally these are safe questions to ask – ones that move him from emotional overwhelm back to his thinking brain – simply and gently.

4. Now for the hardest part. Wait. Allow him to process his emotions and figure himself out. Once enough time has passed, he will regulate. Emotions are temporary states, not permanent conditions. Snow eventually settles. Emotions pass if we give them space and time. Our inclination is to step in and fix things – or demand that he fix them. But when emotions are high – when the snow is swirling – vision is limited. You can't think straight in a high-emotion state. When you're on the brink you need to stop and think. High emotions equals low intelligence. Give him some time. When defensiveness is down, step in gently and move to the fifth step.

5. Problem-solve together. This is where you activate the Three Es: explore, explain, empower. There's far more on this process in Chapter 11 but I've alluded to it a couple of times so it will feel familiar when we get there. Your son has the answers. He just needs you by his side to figure it out.

Teach your son this snow-globe metaphor so he understands emotion regulation. Instead of seeing emotions as enemies to be conquered, he can recognise them as waves running up the beach – natural, normal, and each one temporary. They'll come in … and then they'll retreat.

When words won't come

Parents – particularly mums – often express frustration about their sons' communication.

'He just won't open up.'

'I ask about his day, and I get one-word answers or grunts.'

'I never really know what's going on in his life and that worries me.'

But what if the problem isn't that boys don't want to communicate, but that we're trying to connect in ways that feel unnatural to them? Or perhaps we're trying to talk to them in need-frustrating ways – after all, they *do* want a relationship with us.

Boys communicate differently from girls, especially during adolescence. While girls happily sit face-to-face and talk, boys open up:

- during parallel activities (driving, walking, working together);
- when being physically active;
- in short bursts rather than extended conversations; and
- through indirect rather than direct communication.

Even then, boys can be reluctant to hear what you have to say, particularly if you're stepping into lecture mode. No one likes being corrected and directed. What then?

Stop telling me what to do

If you want to share advice or offer correction and direction to your son, the best way to share your ideas is to ask permission first. To be clear: you don't need consent. You're his parent. But having it makes things easier. Even more effective: first, ask him what he thinks. Support his ideas – assuming they're safe, healthy, and wise. If his ideas aren't great, pause. Consider his perspective. Then ask, 'How do you see that playing out?' Then ask permission to share your perspective as above. Once he's been heard, he'll be far more open to hearing your ideas.

Reading between the lines

Boys' emotional communication often requires different listening. Sometimes what they say is clumsy, abrupt, or poorly thought through. When a boy says, 'Leave me alone,' he might mean: 'I need space to process.' When he says, 'It's nothing,' he might mean: 'I don't know how to put this into words yet.' If he refuses to answer, you could ask, 'Would it be helpful if I asked you that again, or do you need more time to think it through?' Assume positive intent, even in tricky circumstances. That choice between 'Do you want me to hug you, stay with you, or give you space?' is relevant here, and is a reminder that with patience and time, most challenges can be processed and discussed. We don't have to fix everything right now.

The empathy puzzle

'When a girl cries, few things are more worthless than a boy,' wrote Alexandra Bracken.[11] Harsh. But the emotional world of teen boys can feel like an empathy desert.

Thus far, we've primarily focused on how boys are feeling. But their ability to recognise how others are feeling – empathy – is a vital part of healthy masculinity. To help others feel and be safer and stronger, they must be able to identify how others feel.

There are two types of empathy, and boys' developmental trajectory for each is different from girls'.[12]

- **Cognitive empathy:** The 'I understand how you feel' response. It's the recognition of another person's emotional experience. It processes in the brain's medial prefrontal cortex – where the logical thinking happens. Cognitive empathy is when you say 'I get it,' or 'Wow, that sucks.' There's emotional distance but intellectual understanding. Another person's emotions makes sense in his head but not necessarily in his heart.

- **Affective empathy:** The 'I feel your pain' response. It's the emotional resonance that makes us cry when others cry. When Bruce Willis shoved Ben Affleck into the space elevator on the meteor hurtling towards Earth in the 1998 blockbuster *Armageddon*, and then Willis stayed on the meteor so he could blow it up and save the planet, and I was crying, it was because I was in affective empathy

> overload. Affective empathy has roots in the limbic system – our emotional centre.[13]

When your teenage son blithely shrugs off his sister's distress or seems indifferent to a friend's struggles, his response is a combination of biology (testosterone) and socialisation (Man Box and precarious masculinity). While girls' cognitive empathy rises steadily from age 13, boys' temporarily lags.[14] And their affective empathy? It declines between ages 13 and 16.[15]

This doesn't mean it disappears. He can still feel what others feel. He just orients towards those feelings less.

Understanding these two types of empathy helps explain behaviours that might otherwise seem callous. When your son walks away from someone who's upset, he might be:

- processing the situation in his own way;
- feeling overwhelmed by emotions he can't handle yet; and/or
- trying to figure out what to do rather than what to say.

Let's be honest: it's also possible he simply doesn't care. But we *can* teach empathy, even to teenage boys.

Building empathy skills

Watching your once-sensitive son become cold is confronting. But this is developmental, not permanent. The capacity isn't gone, it's dormant. It's emotional hibernation, which means it can be coaxed out of the cave and developed.

We can teach, encourage, and build empathy, even during the emotional earthquakes of adolescence.[16] What helps?

- Maintaining connection.
- Acknowledging small acts of care.
- Creating opportunities for indirect empathy (service projects or team activities).
- Sharing stories of men who combine strength with emotional awareness.
- Being empathic – modelling matters.
- Encouraging your son to consider others' feelings.

A precursor to empathy is fairness. If you're not making progress with helping your son to see what others feel – or to feel what they feel – sometimes an appeal to fairness can be effective. Boys seem to have an innate sense of what's fair and what isn't. You might say, 'Is it fair that one person has to do everything around the house while the other person doesn't?' or 'Is it fair that a guy might have sex with a girl but she carries all the consequences if he's not careful with contraception?'

Empathy is a long game. It requires consistent investment, regular invitations for your son to see the world through the eyes of others, and ongoing appeals to both fairness *and* mercy. Inviting introspection with questions like, 'How would you like to be treated in this situation?' and 'What do you think they need most?' and 'If you were in my shoes, how would you respond?' will slowly create the awareness needed for a safer/stronger approach to feelings – his and others'.

The take-home message

Boys who understand and regulate their emotions – and understand and navigate other people's emotions – develop emotional competence and empathy. They are secure and strong, and better able to help those around them feel safer and stronger. Every emotional challenge represents opportunity for growth and connection. Each difficult experience – well regulated – adds another layer of evidence that he's competent. Each well-handled relationship interaction builds deeper relationships.

We build emotional regulation by making space for all emotions (not telling him to 'man up' when sad), by allowing anger to cool before making important decisions, by teaching him that emotions are temporary, by showing that masculine strength comes from caring not controlling, and by modelling the thing we most want him to learn: that emotions don't make men weak but losing control does. There's a difference between feeling something and being ruled by it. This is how we raise men who add value; who are a bonus. This is how we raise men who help those around them feel safer and stronger; men who are aware, regulated, and empathic.

10 The father factor

The irreplaceable role of good men in a boy's life

Boys do not ache for their father's masculinity.
They ache for their father's hearts.
Terry Real[1]

If a man knows not to which port he sails,
no wind is favourable.
Seneca

Boys need anchors. A steady presence. A line to hold on to. Something to keep them in place when times get rough. Throughout history, fathers have been an anchor; not through perfection, but through presence. Work, family, community, purpose, faith, character: these are the ports boys sail towards when they have a father and other great role models showing them the way. Without that anchor, boys drift. I was fortunate to have a wonderful model of masculinity in my dad. Two (of many) defining moments from my childhood show how fathers shape their son's understanding of what it is to be a man.

Moment # 1

It's 1983. I'm eight years old. Dad is self-employed; a milkman, or 'milko'. I love working with him, delivering milk to doorsteps and collecting the change people leave in buckets to pay for the milk. My favourite thing about Dad's work is that our downstairs fridge is always full of leftover chocolate milk in plastic sachets. They're called 'Choccos' and I drink them after school – without permission. Nobody ever notices. Or maybe Dad allows it because he loves me.

One evening I'm in the milk truck with Dad. It's dark. We're on a dirt road. A lump in the middle of the road catches Dad's attention. He slows down and stops, his headlights illuminating the lump. I can't make out what it is. Dad's protective instincts kick in: 'Stay in the truck, Justin.'

Dad walks to the lump, reaches down and lifts it – a man, drunk to the point of paralysis and blackout – and carries him to the milk truck. We open the rear of the truck, slide some milk crates out of the way, and lie him down. Dad reaches into the man's pocket, finds his wallet, reads the address on his driver's licence, and drives him several kilometres home to his wife where he can sober up safely.

I saw my dad being a bonus in the lives of others. Helping others feel safer and stronger. Surplus value.

Moment # 2

I'm ten years old, watching my father's face. His expression is pained as he fights to hold back tears. His hands grip the pulpit. A chapel full of grieving family and friends watches and waits, sensing the rawness in the air.

'I follow a noble father.' He reads the first line of a poem, his voice cracking as he eulogises his father.

Forty years later, those tears still impact me. So does the first line of that poem.

Seeing Dad cry so openly left an indelible impression on my ten-year-old boy-brain. Even then I recognised that strength is not the absence of vulnerability – it's the presence of it. That day, I saw my dad in a way I'd never seen him before. It wasn't flashy, it wasn't loud. If anything, it was fragility – but noble and powerful. I witnessed a 'man', my dad, who even in his grief – at a time where he must have been disoriented, grasping for new anchor points in a world without his father – knew who he was.

My father was the strongest man I knew. He lived his masculinity quietly, and without the need for approval.

Every moment matters

As a boy I would sit beside Dad in his milk truck and absorb his love. He wasn't hugging me or telling me I was great. He was just with me. Ask any boy why he loves his dad and you'll hear a variation on 'He spends time with me' or 'He teaches me stuff.' So simple. So vital. Like I've said, kids spell love T-I-M-E.

We played games and sang to the radio as we spent evenings delivering milk. Then Dad sold the milk run and built a furniture removals business. He drove big trucks. I watched him (and helped him) lift lounges, fridges, and pianos. Countless hours disappeared like the road beneath the truck's wheels as we talked, sang, and joked, moving people interstate. He never let me win an arm wrestle, so the day I beat him, I knew I'd won fair and square.

While he did some 'manly' things, my dad's masculinity was mostly relational. Throughout my life, Dad did what men have done, cross-culturally, for millennia: provide and protect. He helped those around him feel safer and stronger. He added value to our lives. He wasn't seeking status or trying to prove his manhood. He never said, 'This is what a man does,' or 'Be a man.' He simply lived it. This is how masculinity transfers from one generation to the next. Researchers confirm that no single factor shapes a boy's understanding of masculine value more profoundly than his relationship with his father and father figures.[2] In Louis Theroux's 2026 Netflix documentary *Inside the Manosphere*, he leaves an observation hanging for a long time: almost all of the men who push concerning content in an online environment grew up in homes where they had no father present, or where their father was not a positive, safe, healthy influence.

Why fathers matter

Parenting author Kyle Pruett observed, 'When researchers bother to look for father effects, they always find them.'[3]

This is an indictment on researchers. Fatherhood is rarely investigated in academic enquiry. But when it is, the results are clear. Fathers matter for children's language development – in many contexts, more so than mothers, particularly in dual-income households. One study that has been replicated in a variety of contexts found that fathers tend to use more varied and challenging vocabulary – for instance, they use more 'rare' words not commonly known to children – and use more conversation-eliciting speech such as why questions. They also make clarification requests more frequently than mothers. Research also shows fathers boost children's intellectual development; and when dad engages in supportive ways, mum is less stressed and anxious, less moody, and generally feels better about life. The presence of a positive father is associated with reduced depression, stress, anxiety, fear, and self-esteem issues in kids.[4]

When mothers and fathers engage in identical activities, they provide cumulative benefits.[5] The same activity from both parents delivers greater impact than from one alone. Mum's hugs, kisses, and tickles are great. But when dad steps in with a bear hug and a kiss, it's additive. Fathers aren't optional extras. When they're contributing, the benefit is measurable.

The spaces where boys become men

Throughout history almost all cultures taught that boys don't automatically become men. They are guided to manhood by other men, usually in spaces away from home, through experiences that test and teach them. Society has dismantled these pathways, for better and/or worse, but without replacing them. In fact, we've reversed the historical pattern. Boys stay home and have their washing, ironing, cooking, providing, and protecting done for them. And we delay their adult development more than ever. This does not serve our sons well. We've removed the ladder to manhood and blamed them for not climbing it.

We don't need brutal initiations like those of some tribes and cultures. But we do need the underlying principle: boys need spaces where good, trustworthy men show them what healthy masculinity is. These 'third spaces' – sports teams, workshops, camping groups, martial arts dojos, volunteer organisations – are where transformation can happen. The activity and place matter less than the presence of good men who understand their role as guides and help boys and young men feel safer and stronger as they develop relationships and competence.

Parents must do two things. First, mothers must let sons go. Allow fathers and other trusted men to take boys into challenging situations where they can fail, struggle, and grow. The overprotection instinct – keeping a 17-year-old from getting a driver's licence, doing his laundry indefinitely – creates dependency. It doesn't help him become a man. But note: not all of these third places offer models of healthy masculinity (schoolies, I'm looking at you). Some present a more traditional masculinity that may not appeal to parents or their boys. As Terry Real states: 'Boys don't hunger for fathers who will model traditional morés of masculinity. They hunger for fathers who will rescue them from it.'[6]

Second, fathers must step up. Road trips, camping, sports, physical challenges. When fathers engage positively with sons in spaces away from home, they provide what mothers will struggle to provide: masculine modelling that transforms boys into men. My surfing buddies in Sumba – Digby and Gray – were surrounded by their dads (Will and Harley) and several other men supporting their growth in a third space that provided challenges and a healthy masculine environment. And it was good for them, despite – or perhaps because of – the risks.

The blueprint: find where good, trusted men are investing in young people and join them. If such spaces don't exist, create them. Pulitzer Prize-winner J.R. Moehringer said, 'To be a man, a boy must see a man.'[7] Boys don't need perfect male role models, but they do need present ones. And if you are a man, bring boys (beyond your son) into third spaces too.

When father isn't available

What about single mothers reading this? What about divorced mothers whose ex-husbands have chosen to step back or who are unsafe? What about mothers whose partners are physically present but emotionally unavailable?

You cannot be both mother and father, and nor should you try. Boys need what men provide uniquely: different perspectives, different ways of engaging with the world, different models of how to handle emotions and relationships.

Actively seek positive male influences in your son's life. Reach out to male relatives, specifically asking them to spend time with him. Join organisations where trusted men volunteer as coaches, mentors, or leaders. Have honest conversations with trusted men about the important role they could play in your son's development. Be direct. Ask the question. Offer the rationale.

Some years ago, my wife's best friend lost her husband. Rob was 50 years old when he died. He left Michelle with three teens: two girls and a boy. A community of men stepped in and took that boy camping, to footy training and weekend games, and supported a grieving mother and her kids. This is what men do when they carry masculinity well. They didn't try to replace Rob. But they ensured his son still had masculine guidance and presence.

One dad told me of his parents' divorce when he was ten. He talked openly about his mental health challenges – and crucially, about the role of other men who stepped in as father figures. Those men anchored him. Today he's raising his own sons with intention, determined to be present in ways his father couldn't be. The men who showed up for him changed his trajectory.

This is what's possible when communities rally around boys who need male role models. You can't replace a father. But you can provide anchors.

If it's a struggle

I hope fathers read this book. But the stats suggest that mums read parenting books and tell their partners about what they read. If you're a mum who knows your partner won't read this book, ask him to read this next part – alone or with you – even if it's the only part he reads.

If you're a father: I know life asks a lot of you. Competing demands can be challenging. But imagine a bucket of water. Put your fist in. Hold it there. Now take it out. What happens to the water? Short answer – nothing. That's your work life, social life, sporting life, and everything you do outside of the home. When you remove yourself from those spaces, not much changes.

Family is different. Remove yourself from your son's life, and nothing can fill the gap you've left. Perhaps other things will flood into that void, but they'll never fill it the way you did. You're irreplacable.

I keep hearing men tell me that the most important thing in their lives is their family. But I don't listen to words. I look at actions … and too often action tells a different story. If your bicycle or surfboard – or your email account – gets more attention than your son, it's time to redirect attention. Dollars are the currency of our economy. Connection is the currency of our relationships. Thriving relationships – and healthy boys – rely on feeling seen, heard, valued, and accepted. Your son spells love: T-I-M-E.

Perhaps you're trying to be present but struggling to connect because your son is withdrawn, interested in things you're not, or full of attitude. 'It's not me, it's him,' you're thinking. 'I've tried. If he doesn't want to spend time with me, I've got other things I can do.'

Being a father is a unique role where you're going to get back much less than you give to it. You'll demonstrate your manliness by giving more than you take. That's what healthy men do: they're a bonus. They add value. They provide surplus. They help the people around them feel safer and stronger. Don't give up. Your absence or apathy will be a drain. You'll reduce your son's ability to have a positive impact on the world. He'll be smaller without your involvement. So try again. Find what he cares about and fake interest. Or find things you can both enjoy. Keep inviting. Keep asking. Keep making the effort. Your son is aching for your heart. He wants to know you, but he's clumsy about showing it. He needs second chances: thousands of them. He needs invitations to be in your life: thousands of them. He needs opportunities to connect: thousands of them. He needs a walk around the block with you and the dog, a chat as you sit on the bed late at night, an unexpected early pick-up from school to buy a milkshake, a weekend camping trip, a bike ride. He needs an invite to jump in the car and zip down to the hardware shop with you to grab 'that thing', or to a department store for 'that other thing'. He needs you, even when you're not getting it right and he's being difficult. He needs to see how you handle disappointment, how you navigate relationships, how you deal with vulnerabilities and fears.

Forget some polished version of masculinity. He doesn't need a superhero. He needs you – and to him, you are a superhero, believe it or not.

So, work on less judgement and criticism, and on more real conversations. While fishing trips and football games are valuable, the magic often happens in unplanned moments – driving together, working on a project, sitting on the back step watching the sunset, sharing a muffin, and listening to him. Always listening. The thing teens tell me they want most from their dads is for him to listen. And the thing boys tell me they love the most is that they can tell him anything because 'he's chill'.

Create those moments when your son feels safe enough to ask questions that matter, and you might have the chance to do what dads love: to share wisdom, not from having all the answers but from having wrestled with the questions.

The take-home message

Being an engaged father isn't complicated, but it does demand intentionality. This is your blueprint.

- **Presence over perfection.** Your son isn't seeking a flawless father. He needs a present one. Consistent, engaged, emotionally available.
- **Create separation experiences.** Take him away from home regularly. Road trips, camping, sports, work projects. Invite his mates and their dads too.
- **Show your heart.** Vulnerability isn't weakness. Let him see you struggle and recover. This teaches resilience.
- **Find third spaces together.** Join activities where he can see you interact with other men and where other trusted men can mentor him too.
- **Stay engaged through adolescence.** When he starts pulling away and challenging you, that's when he needs you most. Other good men become crucial allies during this phase.

The 17th-century poet George Herbert said, 'One father is more than a hundred schoolmasters.' Your presence, your heart, your guidance: these shape not just your son, but the man he becomes and the father he'll possibly one day be. The investment you make now echoes down generations. Help him feel safer and stronger, be a bonus in his life, and he'll learn everything he needs to know about being a real man.

11 Communication

How to have real conversations your son will actually engage in

In the best conversations, you don't even remember what you talked about, only how it felt.

John Green[1]

Getting teen boys talking can be tricky. 'How was your day?' yields grunts or a brief 'Fine'. Trying to discuss weighty matters like being respectful to family members, making a contribution at home, working hard at school, choosing safe, healthy behaviours in matters of alcohol and other drugs, consent, and intimacy, can feel more challenging than trying to skim a bowling ball across a lake. Adolescence is a time where a boy shifts away from parental influence and towards peer influence. This means he's more interested in sharing his feelings with friends than you, and it makes even simple conversational gambits – such as 'What happened at school today?' – challenging. Sometimes the front fence feels more engaging to chat with.

This chapter gives you the blueprint for having meaningful dialogue with your son. Once again, it boils down to basic psychological needs.

First, relatedness. When the relationship feels safe, strong, and secure, conversations flow naturally. We create this foundation by building trust: helping your son believe the other person (you) will act in his best interest. When he knows you've got his back, he's more likely to talk, and this ups the chance that you'll have influence in his life. We need to be explicit and intentional about communicating this. Ask him, 'Do you believe I want to act in your best interest?' Describe for him that 'trust is when you believe I've got your back', and then ask: 'Do you believe I've got you?' These conversations make your love for him transparent. Once it's agreed that he can trust you, your job is to live up to that trust.

The opposite is equally true. If he feels like you're on his case, he'll be defensive. You'll interpret his defensiveness as evidence he's holding back or hiding, and you'll press harder or become more confrontational. You wanted to talk, run a few things by him, and ask for improved effort around the house, and now you're caught in a vicious cycle pushing you further apart when connection was your focus. The Relationship Bucket is the metaphor here: are you putting water into the bucket or is it full of air? Too much air and the relatedness-need is ruptured.

Second, competence. Your son's competence-need is threatened when conversations begin from a position of assumed failure, guilt, or inadequacy. Not only are you undermining his sense that you believe in him but also the relationship of trust that is the foundation of effective communication. Telling him off, pointing out his mistakes, and denigrating his effort is dynamite to your relationship with him. Even if you're right, it's rare that a teenage boy looks at a scolding parent and says, 'You're right. I'm an impediment to our family's happiness and an affront to the values you've taught me. I appreciate you for pointing out areas for improvement, and as a result of this lecture, I'm going to change for the better, starting now.'

Psychologist John Gottman advocates 'soft start-ups'. Step in gently. A conversation opener like 'Hey, I wanted to check in. Things have been rough lately. Can we chat?' is far more likely to be effective than 'Why do you have such a bad attitude?' Asking, 'Can I run something by you? It's tricky, and I don't want to create a scene, but something's been on my mind and I am hoping you can help me understand what's going on' is far better than 'Hey, whatever you give me, I'm going to give back to you.' Competence-needs are fragile.[2] If your son feels like he'll be lectured, defensive walls will spring up, his ears will shut down, and you'll have lost him.

Instead of 'We need to talk about your phone use because you can't control yourself,' why not try, 'We've had conflict around tech lately, and I thought we could chat about finding the right balance.' If he's still with you, you could add, 'Yelling at you hasn't helped, and I'd like to create a solution together.' This frames him as competent and capable rather than needing external control. It's collaborative and solution-focused – and now he's ready to talk.

Third, autonomy. 'We need to have a talk' implies external regulation because you're demanding it or 'that's apparently what a good son does' (introjected). Neither sets a solid foundation for solving problems or genuine dialogue. Imposed and coercive conversation leads to defensiveness. Force creates resistance.

There's a big difference between 'Sit down, we need to talk about your attitude,' and 'I've noticed tension between us lately, and I'm hoping you'd be open to talking about what's going on.' The first eliminates choice. It positions him as victim of your agenda. The second supports autonomy and gives him some control over the timing and framing of the conversation. You could prompt, 'Now might not be a great time, but it would be good to chat things through some time today or tomorrow.'

This chapter provides a conversation blueprint for the most challenging situations you face. Pornography, the angry outburst that put a hole in the wall, unsafe driving, bad attitudes, screens; each requires difficult but vital conversations. These are *reactive* conversations, triggered by something that has already happened. But the blueprint is also useful for *proactive* conversations – forward-looking discussions about values, expectations, and navigating the road ahead.

Before we open the blueprint, a few reminders:

- **Get curious, not furious.** Your son will frustrate you. Always remember that what he does makes sense to him even if it makes zero sense to you. Assume good intentions, lean in with curiosity, and focus on understanding not reprimanding; exploring not exploding.

- **Context is everything.** Not every moment is right for deep conversation. Sometimes your son needs space to process what's happening and how he feels about it;

sometimes emotions are running high; and sometimes practical issues (hunger, exhaustion, stress, an audience) need addressing first. Read the room and the relationship.

- **Trust your instincts.** The model we're about to unpack is need-supportive, efficient, and useful. But there will be times when you should ignore it and go with your parental intuition. Not every conversation must fit this exact mould – and if it does, it might start to feel fake to your son. Our objective is not to follow the formula, but to improve connection and communication.

The Three Es of effective discipline

Discipline is punishment, according to most dictionaries today. They're one and the same. But search up 'punishment' in the Merriam-Webster's dictionary and you'll read: 'suffering, pain, or loss that serves as retribution'. When we speak of a child needing discipline (that is, punishment), it means they've done something wrong so now we will hurt them or take something from them as penance so they'll 'learn their lesson' and 'pay a price'. Punishment is retribution and justice. I'm convinced that no parent wakes up on Saturday morning thinking, 'It's been a rough week, but today it's retribution day. Today I'm going to make my child suffer for what he's done.' And to do so would be disastrous for your relationship and his development.

Yet kids need discipline. So what are we talking about here? The 1828 Webster's dictionary defined discipline as to teach, guide, or instruct. Rather than hurting, discipline was intended to be helpful. My practical definition of discipline is simple: *problem-solving.* If a child requires discipline, they're experiencing challenges and need support solving a problem. That's helpful. That's teaching, guiding, and potentially instructing. But there's rarely any hurting, suffering, or retribution involved.

In the mid-2010s, I developed a conversation structure called 'The Three Es of Effective Discipline' (which I've alluded to already in Chapter 9). It requires that we ***explore*** our child's perspective and offer him a voice, ***explain*** our position or challenge in relation to his behaviour or attitude, and ***empower*** him to problem-solve with us.

It's need-supportive. The process supports basic psychological needs – his and yours. When both people feel heard (relatedness), capable (competence), and are given a chance to develop a solution they can endorse (autonomy), conversations become collaborative rather than combative.

The following steps will help you make these Three Es conversations work, whether proactively establishing values, or reactively after something has gone wrong.

Set the stage

Choose a time when you're both relaxed and unhurried – perhaps during a drive or walk or over his favourite snack. Side-by-side often feels less intense than face-to-face. Ensure there's no audience. Your son may do or say things to 'save face' if he's being watched.

Confirm consent

'I'd like to talk about something. It's tricky. Can we have a conversation?' If it's not a good time, be responsive. You could say, 'Okay, it makes sense that now isn't a good time. This is really weighing on me, though. When works for you?'

If he refuses to agree to a conversation, you'll need to consider how to respond. If you can let it go, drop it. If you can't, validate briefly ('I get that you're not keen on this'), restate its importance ('This is something we both need to work through'), and reaffirm your request ('Any time from now through to the weekend is fine, but we do need to figure this out').

Frame it clearly

'I'm concerned about [topic]. I feel like we're not on the same page, and I want to understand things better. You're struggling. I'm struggling. Will you work with me on this?' You might even remind him of what trust means and ask if he'll trust you as you work together on it.

Explore

Start by gently probing his experience. 'What are you noticing?' 'What am I getting right and wrong?' 'What don't I know that I should?' 'Why do you think this is a big deal for me?' Give him space to share without interruption. Ask follow-up questions. Ask him what his friends think. What's his reaction to that?

When your son feels heard, he's more likely to open up. This is relatedness need-support, helping him feel safe in the conversation.

Explain

Express your concerns openly but sensitively. 'Here's what worries me: I've noticed [describe what you've seen].' Keep it brief. Anything more than 10 to 20 seconds feels like a lecture.

To take it to the next level, flip it: 'Can you tell me what you think I'm most concerned about when it comes to [topic]?'

The secret: keep your talk to a minimum. If he interrupts or looks annoyed, get curious, not furious. In tough situations you'll dance between explore and explain. Keep things exploration-focused. For minor issues, you'll work through these two steps relatively quickly. For example:

> **You:** 'What's going on with your wet towel on the floor?' [Start by exploring.]
> **Him:** 'I don't know.'
> **You:** 'When you leave a wet towel on the floor, the room stinks like damp, the carpet grows mould, and it's more work for me.' [That's explain.]
> **Him:** 'Sorry.'
> **You:** 'What's the solution?'
> **Him:** 'I'll put it away.'

Job done. (No, it's not always that easy. But for illustration purposes you get the picture. You can do the Three Es in 20 seconds.) If you're dealing with heavier issues, there may be a lot more conversation required, and that will primarily be exploring his perspective and stepping in and out of explore and explain. These two steps should not be rushed.

Empower

When you understand where he is, and you know he gets your concerns, problem-solve together.

- 'What boundaries do you think might work for both of us?'
- 'What alternative pathways do we have to explore?'
- 'How can we make the wisest (or safest or healthiest) choice easy?'
- 'What kind of person do you want to be five years from now, and how does this connect?'
- 'How does this approach work in with being a healthy man: one who is a bonus, a giver, who helps the people around him feel safer and stronger?'

Make a concrete plan that has his endorsement, and puts him in the driver's seat while providing the structure he needs.

This step turns your son into a contributor, not just a rule follower (or breaker). He is adding value to the solution – becoming a bonus, not a burden.

When it doesn't work

These conversations should be built on empathy and mutual respect. They won't always work. Remember: high emotions equals low intelligence. If emotions peak, postpone the discussion. Force creates resistance. The great thing about problems is that if you don't solve them today, they'll still be there tomorrow! You can work on them then.

Sometimes your son will be dismissive, withdrawn, or refuse to engage. Sometimes he won't see the problem as a problem. Sometimes his ideas are viable but you're being stubborn because it doesn't fit *your* preferences. Ask yourself, 'Can I let this go?' If the answer is yes, great. If no, step up and be the parent.

Let's say he wants to go to a party. No parents. A keg. Three hundred kids. He's 14. You say no. That's appropriate. And you're supposed to say no to requests like that.

It's not *what* you say, though. It's *how* you say it. This is where the Three Es lead to better outcomes in the research. Explore what matters. Explain your concerns or have him explain them to you. Empower him to find solutions to Friday night that both of you can feel good about. Minimise control (but you're the parent – you don't *eliminate* control).

At the tail end of a need-supportive conversation, you'll generally have better outcomes. He'll be closer to *identified* motivation than external. But … he might still be mad. That's fine. That's parenting. Your primary job as a parent is to keep him safe.

The goal isn't perfect agreement. It's opening an ongoing dialogue that evolves as he matures and faces new challenges. Many topics require a lot of discussion over an extended timeframe.

If you approach conversations with respect for his growing autonomy while clearly communicating your values, he'll internalise those values in an identified, integrated, or intrinsic way rather than complying with rules with introjected regulation – or worse, being a sneaky rebel only motivated by bribes and threats.

Let's go back to that party discussion. It's possible that (i) regardless of how carefully you step into the conversation, (ii) how committed you are to a mutually agreeable solution, and (iii) how hard you work on maintaining the relationship, your son will be seething. He'll stop talking. He'll tantrum. He'll ignore you for days. This doesn't mean you're a bad parent. It just means he's mad. And that's okay. (It's annoying for you, but it's okay.) This is a him issue, not a you issue (so long as you're not amplifying and provoking him by correcting and directing). Sometimes there's nothing you can do except patiently wait for him to grow through this 'thing' (or not) – and love him despite it all. Absolutely, categorically, no matter what.

Who's got time for that?

Some parents find this process cumbersome. 'I haven't got time for that.' Well, I'm clapping back: you're going to spend the time either way. Choose 20 minutes now in thoughtful conversation, or 20 hours later dealing with drama at the other end – failed classes, broken trust, a pregnant girlfriend, a crashed car, therapy sessions, and sleepless nights. Pay upfront or pay later, but if you try to pay later the compound interest on relationship neglect could bankrupt your connection.

When trust is high, you can have these conversations fast:

> **You:** We seem to have a lot of disagreements lately about tech. Have you noticed?

Him: Yeah! You're always hassling me, and I'm not even using it that much.
You: How are you seeing it?
Him: [Explains.]
You: Oh, so it feels like [summarises]?
Him: Totally. All the time.
You: Tell me more.
Him: [Elaborates, talks about his friends' parents not having *any* rules, etc.]
You: I hear you. I get it. Can I run something past you?
Him: I guess so.
You: I'm always asking you to get off screens and you're always saying you need more time. But whenever I check on you, it's gaming, rather than homework. I know homework is less fun. I know it feels like I'm on your case. But we both know trying to write a whole essay the night before it's due is stressful for all of us. Can we work out a better solution here?
Him: I just hate English.

In less than two minutes, we're both feeling heard, and problem-solving starts. Now the problem is identified, you can move towards solutions together. A tutor. A conversation with the teacher. A process or structure (scaffolding/framework) to help him do important stuff first. Or a discussion about how you can be more supportive and less naggy. (And be honest, if you had a choice between scrolling and gaming or writing that essay about a thing no one cares about except your English teacher, what would you choose?)

But again, it's not *what* you do. It's *how* you do it.

And the research shows it is worth it. Researcher Laura Padilla-Walker has found that processes like the Three Es contribute to prosocial behaviour, better grades, and happier outcomes, while reducing alcohol and drug use, and delinquent behaviour.[3]

The Sunday kids' conversations

Conversations about challenging topics are not 'one-and-done'. In our home, we sit down most Sundays with our children for 15-minute chats about tough topics. For example, one of my daughters was at a social function where a boy pressured her to disappear into a dark corner with him. She wasn't interested. He followed her. He tried to coerce her away from her friends, and persisted in trying to put his arm around her or hold her hand. He encouraged her to leave the venue so they could 'talk'. This gave us plenty to talk about and the 15-minute chat quickly became an absorbing 45 minutes with interaction and engagement from all of the kids. The week before, we spoke about emotion regulation strategies. The week before, one of the kids asked us about STIs. Sometimes we separate the children to keep the discussions age-appropriate; our ten-year-old doesn't need to hear about STIs, for instance. And the chats don't have to be formalised and structured. An 'unplanned' talk while you take a walk or drive can be equally effective.

Speaking with your son early and often means conversations about tough topics become part of the furniture. These conversations respond to what's going on in their lives, or proactively pre-arm them so when they face bullying, vaping, pornography, or any other challenging experience, they've discussed it in a safe environment, thought through the consequences, and know what their values are. You can see, from 43 rungs up the ladder of life, what he can't see from rung 13. You've prepared him. And he can act responsibly. Many parents shy away from topics that feel too 'old' for their kids so they can keep them innocent, but that leaves them unprotected when a precocious peer introduces them instead. Pre-arming is protective (within reason).

Perhaps the best ongoing discussion of all to have with your son includes these questions:

- 'How did you see healthy masculinity displayed today?'
- 'Who did you see help people feel safer and stronger?'
- 'How did you show up as a bonus and add value to someone today?'

The take-home message

Talk often. Build connection and trust. Fill your Relationship Bucket. When tricky topics need addressing, get curious. Explore their perspective. Explain yours. Problem-solve together. This is your conversation blueprint.

12 Learning self-control

Why stoicism, delayed gratification, and frustration tolerance are your son's foundation for success

In the mid-1970s, researchers in New Zealand launched what became one of psychology's most important projects. The Dunedin Study followed 1037 babies through their first three years of life. When the kids turned three, researchers measured their emotional stability, frustration tolerance, impulsivity, attention, and persistence.[1]

The setup was simple. A three-year-old was ushered into a room with toys. What would the child do when encountering failure: a puzzle they couldn't solve, blocks that kept falling, or a task requiring patient waiting? Melt down? Storm off? Keep trying?

That 90-minute assessment at age three was powerfully predictive. Children with the lowest self-control at those tasks as three-year-olds went on to drop out of school as teens, get arrested, become teenage parents, and develop substance-abuse problems.

But for teens with high levels of self-control at three, the doors of opportunity were opening.[2]

Fast forward to age 45.[3] The study was still going. Unbelievably, 94% of the original participants were still involved. The researchers found that childhood self-control predicted how people aged. Better self-control meant slower biological aging, and healthier brains.[4] People with higher self-control were healthier, exercised more, ate better, read more, and had brains that were physiologically 'younger'. They had more energy and younger-looking faces.[5]

Before you panic because you're thinking, 'My son has zero self-control,' it's important to note these scores aren't set in stone. Some participants showed poor self-control as three-year-olds but improved later.[6] This improvement correlated with increased health, wealth, and public safety. Their brains became healthier. Boys who learned impulse control at any age saw improvements and escaped the poor self-control outcomes.

This is the shift from external regulation (someone forcing you to behave) to integrated regulation (behaving a particular way because it's who you are). Helping our sons develop self-control in an integrated way means helping them grow one of the most valuable characteristics of a well-lived life.

Unfortunately, we're up against it. In late 2025, *Financial Times* reporter John Burn-Murdoch analysed the Understand America Study, which has been exploring changes in personality since 2014. He divided the data into three (very broad) age groups: people aged 16 to 39, those aged 40 to 59, and a 60-plus cohort.[7]

A comparison of the different age groups showed that those aged 16 to 39 demonstrated increased *neuroticism* – meaning young people are less emotionally stable than ever – and decreased *agreeableness* and *extroversion* over the 11 years of the study. Young people are more likely to argue, and are less inclined to reach out and connect. *Conscientiousness* collapsed, *distraction* skyrocketed, *carelessness* increased, *follow through* fell through the floor, and *perseverance* plummeted. It's noteworthy that this cohort grew up just as smartphones became ubiquitous and dopamine hijacking began in a way never before seen.

In short, the modern digital world makes self-control harder than ever. Placing screens in our children's hands during puberty, a critical period when brains are rewiring, gives them the worst chances of developing self-control. And we're doing it at an unprecedented rate. In *The Anxious Generation*, Jonathan Haidt observed we have moved from a play-based childhood to a screen-based childhood.[8] And there's a relationship between that shift from analogue play to screens and self-regulation. Gen Z and Gen Alpha have lower self-control than any generation on record.

In 1788, Noah Webster wrote, 'The virtues of men are of more consequence to society than their abilities; and for this reason, the heart should be cultivated with more assiduity than the head.'[9] Self-control, regulation, temperance, forbearance, patience, frustration tolerance, resilience … call it what you will. In the past two decades, we've made developing self-control as slippery as an eel in oil. Academic success, relationships, mental health, wealth, physical health – few traits predict life outcomes as powerfully as self-control. Here's your self-control blueprint to help your son hold it together when things are falling apart.

Model emotional regulation

The first tip: model regulation.

Remember high emotions equals low intelligence. When your son's energy spikes, you'll catch those vibes – unless you're intentional. The reverse is true too. Walk in like a thunderstorm and he becomes reactive. How are you showing up?

Emotional regulation does not mean stoicism or a stolid imperviousness. You're allowed to be excited. Or dour. You're not a robot. Modelling emotional regulation means you're aware of context and how your words and actions affect others. You know the long game and you turn it up or down accordingly. When the stakes are high and emotions are building, what we model matters.

Modelling how to behave gracefully under pressure does three things. It protects your relationship (relatedness). It teaches him how to act (competence) rather than how not to act ('I never want to be like my dad'). And by easing off on the emotional pressure cooker, we give him space to act volitionally (autonomy).

Your five-step framework

When a teen boy shows up with big emotions and big behaviours it's tempting to blast him, demand he pull his head in, and react with strength to whatever behaviour he is challenging you with. But he's not trying to be difficult. He's going through a difficult time.

Here's our five-step framework from Chapter 9, intentionally repeated (and tweaked) because it's so important.

1. Regulate yourself first

Take three deep breaths. Check yourself before you check him. If you're angry, take a time-out.

2. State what you see

If it's mentionable, it's manageable. When your son is having a big emotion, regardless of how inauthentic it feels to articulate it, say what you're seeing: 'It seems like you're having a rough day.' These comments are validating, non-judgemental observations that show you get it. Labelling feelings changes the brain's settings.

Avoid asking 'What's wrong?' when he's dysregulated. His thinking brain is offline. He'll immediately answer, 'Nothing's wrong.'

Putting feelings into words shifts neural activity from the emotional limbic system to the prefrontal cortex – the brain's logic centre.

3. Offer space or connection

Some boys need distance to calm down; others need proximity. Learn your son's pattern. 'Do you need space, or would it help if I stay nearby?' 'Do you want a hug? Or time alone?'

If he wants space, honour that. But before you walk away, tell him: 'I'm going to check on you in a few minutes. If you want a hug or a chat, you can come straight to me. I'm here.' Check in a couple of minutes later. 'Do you still want space, or would me being here help?' Repeat with extending durations until he's regulated.

4. Wait

Don't rush. We're always trying to fix things too fast. His nervous system needs time to shift from fight-or-flight to calm-and-connect.

5. Problem-solve

As emotions balance, it's time to move towards problem-solving, even if you have to wait an hour or two, or a day or three. Only when his prefrontal cortex is back online can you address what happened, explore solutions, or discuss consequences.

Often problem-solving focuses on what triggered the outburst – the friendship fallout, a low mark on the test, mismatched views on screen limits. But if emotional outbursts are coming hot and fast, it might be time to problem-solve ways to build his self-control. You'll use the Three Es for this conversation – explore, explain, empower – but he might be light on suggestions for how to be more regulated – emotionally and behaviourally. You might be too. The next section will be your guide.

Self-regulation interventions

Sarah-Jayne Blakemore is a world leader in neuroscience. In 2018 Blakemore published a 'systematic review and meta-analysis of 49 randomised clinical trials evaluating 50 self-regulation interventions' and found self-control can be taught effectively, just as the Dunedin Study authors suggested. The interventions improved 'academic achievement, social skills, mental health, behavioural problems, conduct disorders, school suspensions, and substance abuse'.[10]

And great news – it's not just for teen boys. These interventions work for frustrated, overwhelmed, impulsive parents too. The following principles underpin the 50 self-regulation interventions.

Build self-awareness

Teens are impulsive and reactive. Another term for this is 'mindlessness'. The opposite, 'mind-full-ness', means paying attention: on purpose, in the present moment, and non-judgementally. Teach your son to anchor attention in the here and now. What's he feeling? Thinking? How is his body reacting? (Don't do this if he's dysregulated. It will only inspire more fire. These conversations are best when everyone is calm.)

One of the best regulation strategies is to do breathing exercises. Teens roll their eyes if they're asked to take a few deep breaths – as do many adults. But breathing works. A meta-analysis of 12 randomised controlled trials found breathwork significantly lowers stress. Just *one session* of slow, deep breathing had beneficial effects on anxiety.[11]

How do you do it? Breathe in through your nose for four seconds, hold for four seconds, breathe out through your mouth for four seconds, hold for four seconds. Repeat three to five times. This slows breathing, activates the parasympathetic nervous system, and improves mood.[12]

Slow things down

As a university student, I struggled in statistics class. Psychology requires four years of statistics – and I scored in the bottom 15%

of all New South Wales students in 1993's HSC exams. I was a maths dunce. I brought this mindset to university ten years later. Each time I attempted a problem, my mind sped up. I panicked. Mistakes followed.

I learned that if I forced myself to slow down and follow the process, I could complete the problems. (Remember: *structure* provides the scaffold for competence.) The best thinking happens slowly, not in a rush. I scored a credit in first year, distinctions in second and third year, and a high distinction in fourth year. Progress, competence, and mastery all came down to going slow, breathing, and following the process.

Slowing down is the opposite of what someone with poor self-control wants to do. Speak often with your son about the value of slowing down, particularly when making decisions.

Know your values

Values inform behaviour and identity. If your son is to do well academically, make healthy and safe decisions, and go slow, he needs to value those things.

As a teen, my brother wanted to become a champion swimmer. He valued health, knowing it was critical to success in competition. At parties, he abstained from alcohol or other drug use because it wasn't consistent with his identity. 'I'm the kind of person who looks after my body so I can compete.'

'I'm the kind of person who …' statements are powerful. Boys who identify as 'disciplined' or 'focused' act more consistently with that identity than those relying on willpower alone.

This is identified regulation. He's not controlling himself because you're watching (external) or because he should (introjected). He's doing it because he gets it. He values it. He endorses it. If he does it long enough, it becomes fully integrated into who he is.

As a parent we can help guide this. It's okay for us to help our son put words to the qualities we want to encourage. For example, after a game of soccer you could say, 'Do you notice how when you run onto the field with your energy and determination, the whole team lifts? You have an important role there.' Initially this will be met with 'I don't think you know what you're talking about, Mum.' But with gentle, careful repetition, he might respond, 'Yeah, and I've noticed if I say positive things on the field people play better too. I hate it when people yell out negatives. It never helps.' These carefully placed observations form part of his identity because they flesh out things he values.

Other questions: 'What do you notice about yourself when you come home from being with these friends versus those friends?' 'How do you feel when you do x?' 'How does our family feel in this situation compared with that situation? Why do you think that is?'

When values are clear, regulation becomes identified or integrated. There's no need for external control because your son possesses self-control.

Move your body

Boys often use a phrase when things get too emotional in their gaming: 'Bro, you need to touch grass.' It's their signal to take a break, move, clear the mind, decompress. Physical exercise is better than drugs for improving mood. A meta-analysis showed that teens who participated in physical activity had more positive emotion than those who were sedentary, with aerobic exercise for 30 to 60 minutes having the most significant effect.[13]

At a more basic level, it's practical to remember that you can walk off a bad mood faster than you can talk it out. Movement raises serotonin. Walking lowers cortisol. Our brains regulate and solve problems best when we're moving at about 4 kilometres an hour, not when sitting still and ruminating.

Craft your sensory toolkit

Our senses are powerful emotion regulators. Smell, sight, touch, sound, and taste can support or undermine emotion and behaviour regulation. Help your son find what works, creating his own regulation toolkit.

Scent

Systematic reviews and randomised controlled trials indicate lavender, bergamot, peppermint, rosemary, and citrus reduce depression, stress, and anxiety.[14] A combination of pleasant smells and deep breathing shifts emotional states fast.

Sight

In Japanese, shinrin-yoku means forest bathing. Forest bathing lowers blood pressure, reduces anxiety, and improves mood. Nature is not just pretty. It's medicine.[15]

We don't all live near forests. Good news: even viewing nature through a window or looking at photographs of beautiful scenery activates the parasympathetic nervous system and calms emotional responses. When emotions are fraying, nature is fuel for the soul. Get your son outside and near green and blue spaces and watch hot emotions subside.

Touch

Physical touch releases oxytocin and endorphins and reduces cortisol, our stress hormone.[16] Even brief supportive touch (like a hand on the shoulder) reduces our stress response. If your son allows it, longer hugs feel even better as gentle pressure stimulates the vagus nerve, triggering the body's calm-and-connect response. Touch, when wanted, is an emotional reset button.

Sound

Music is a direct line to the emotional brain. Slow-tempo music (60 to 80 beats per minute) synchronises with heart rate and breathing, reducing anxiety and stress. Upbeat music increases dopamine, boosting mood and motivation.[17] Don't make your son listen to your tunes though. When he listens to his preferred music, it can be as effective as anti-anxiety medication. The right soundtrack is a potent emotion regulator. Music can be used to get pumped, get lost, or get in the zone.

Taste

Hangry is real. Emotions often spike because glucose drops. When your son is struggling, calories are often the answer. Stable glucose levels support emotion regulation, while blood-sugar crashes increase irritability, anxiety, and mood swings.

A large study of adolescents showed that skipping breakfast significantly increased stress and low mood (depression).[18] If your son is emotionally edgy, calories may be the cure. The cliché that the way to a man's heart is through his belly rings true for teen boys. And protein is usually a strong choice because it satiates. This means he stays full longer than if he eats carbohydrates and fats.

Sleep

While sleep isn't one of the five senses, evidence shows that self-control and both emotional and behavioural regulation are improved when your son gets enough sleep. But it's rare for boys to announce, 'I'm tired. I might get an early one so I'm well rested and in control of myself tomorrow.' The push to stay up late and keep playing is exhaustingly common. Helping your son identify he's the best version of himself when he has slept well will be integral to his capacity to regulate well.

The take-home message

Self-control is central to your son's success. It demonstrates self-awareness, maturity, consideration, and character. Self-control is, in large part, how he helps those around him feel safer and stronger. It's how he shows up as a bonus in the lives of others.

But here's the key: you can't force self-control. Doing so makes it external control rather than an internal form of regulation. When you control him, you get compliance at best – rebellion at worst. Supporting basic psychological needs (relatedness, competence, autonomy) supports self-control because it means regulation will become internal. He identifies what he values and controls himself. Eventually it becomes integrated into who he is – no rewards and punishments needed.

Self-control takes time and intentional practice. And the environment needs to be right (diet, movement, sleep, removing screens, etc). If he's living a life that feels purposeful, and his values are being identified, it will become easier for him to practise self-control.

Your son will get it wrong – often. Talk to him proactively about regulating himself. And be there for reactive conversations where things have gone haywire. Your careful support will be crucial in his development of emotional and behavioural regulation.

13 Friends

The profound power of friendship in your son's life

When I was 16, my best friend taught me how to 'issue the gherks'. After a surf, we stopped at McDonald's and ordered burgers.

'I don't like gherkins,' he informed me, removing the top of the bun from the burger, lifting the sauce-soaked gherkin, and frisbeeing it towards the top of the floor-to-ceiling restaurant window. The gherkin slapped against the glass and stuck in place momentarily. Then we watched gravity pull the gherkin down the window, leaving a tomato-tinged smear from ceiling to floor as it descended. The practice became a (deviant) tradition through my teen years, no doubt causing huge frustration for McDonald's Erina staff from 1990 to 1993.

My friends and I bet our mate Aaron that he couldn't skoll the entire two litres of chocolate topping in my parents' pantry one night during a sleepover. He swallowed more than a litre of thick, rich chocolate syrup straight out of the bottle before he realised this was not going to end well. When he burped, the whole room smelled like partially digested chocolate.

My friends and I consistently sought out risky situations. We paddled into frightening surf, leaped over gaps on ledges at terrifying heights above the ocean and rocks below, did nudie runs, milk challenges, wimp tests, and more stupid stuff than I have space to describe. I'm grateful that most of it was legal *and* turned out harmless. We never really found ourselves in too much trouble – and none of it was recorded on a smartphone for kudos or embarrassment. I have lifelong memories of my adolescence, and it's largely thanks to Ben, Jay, Aaron, Richard, and Ian. Those relationships taught me lessons about loyalty, courage, and belonging that shaped who I am today. Friends are oxygen to a teenage boy.

But not all friends are equal, and not all friendships are positive for our sons. Research consistently shows we become more like the people we spend time with, not just in behaviour, but in attitudes, values, and even health outcomes. If your son's friends are gamers, he'll be online too. If they play sport, he'll join the team. If they're active in religious or cultural activities, he'll be more inclined to participate (or discover). If they're all going to university, he'll follow. If they're kind and thoughtful, he'll be considerate. And if they're struggling academically, he might too. If they vape, drink a lot, or look at pornography, he'll be in. He'll tell the same jokes, develop the same values, walk the same (or a similar) path. It's not iron-clad, but it's close. The proverbs ring true: 'Birds of a feather flock together,' 'Water finds its own level,' and 'You're only as good as the company you keep.'

Pulling down or pulling up?

Peer influence is powerful. I demonstrate this in my talks to students. I ask for a volunteer to stand on a chair, grip my arm, and pull me up to join them. They can't. The leverage works against them. I'm too heavy and too low. Then I tell them I'm going to pull them down from the chair to the floor, and they should resist. With minimal effort, I can always pull them down. Gravity is on my side. This same principle works in friendships: pulling someone down requires far less energy than lifting them up. If your son is hanging out with challenging people, those friends will pull him towards their level much more easily than he can elevate them to his.

This is something you could address with your son in one of your chats. Does he consider that his friends are helping him become a bonus in others' lives – or are they leaving situations worse for having been there? Do people feel safer and stronger when he and his friends are around? Or relief after they leave? Is he spending time at the edges of the manosphere? Are the lexicon and ideas of non-thriving men, misogynistic men, racist men, or crass men spilling into his language, attitudes, and his reality? The more time he spends with a person (whether in reality or online), the more he'll be their mirror.

A comprehensive 2021 meta-analysis confirms that adolescent boys are highly susceptible to peer effects.[1] Brain imaging studies show the presence of peers activates reward circuits in teen brains, making risky and status-seeking behaviours more appealing than they would be for a teen alone.[2] This is why I tried to drink four litres of milk in an hour for the milk challenge. If I had been alone at home it would never have crossed my mind. Being with a group of guys who thought it was the perfect Saturday morning activity made it seem like a rewarding activity. (I did my best but only drank three-quarters of the milk. Nonetheless, we took amazing photos of milk re-entering the atmosphere. The vomit was spectacular.)

Fortunately the chair lesson is not entirely accurate. Influence flows both ways. There's negative peer pressure, leading boys down dangerous paths, but there's also positive peer pressure, lifting boys to positive activities: mountain biking, building robots, or playing music together. I participated in community service and volunteer activities as a 19-year-old in part because several of my friends chose to do so first. The same neural reward mechanisms that channel kids towards danger and dumbness can also channel them towards excellence and contribution. If your son is spending time with kids high up on those chairs, they can collectively lift him up. When your son's friends are oriented towards helping others feel safer and stronger – volunteering, mentoring, creating value – he's more likely to adopt those same values.

Friendships and basic psychological needs

If relatedness is a basic psychological need, friendship is a key ingredient in satisfying it. Feeling competent in those friendships is vital. Learning to be competent socially takes time and impacts how friendships develop. And your son's agency in choosing his friends matters enormously too.

When all three needs are met through friendships – relatedness (connection), competence (social skills), autonomy (choosing friends) – your son's motivation to invest in those relationships will deepen. When he feels his people aren't there, he can't figure out how to connect, or he feels like he 'has to' be friends with someone, his motivation to invest in relationships drops.

Quality friendships don't happen by accident. They require the right conditions. The first is *time*. Professor Jeff Hall from the University of Kansas calculated the mathematics of friendship and discovered it takes 40 to 60 hours to move from 'acquaintance' to 'casual friend', about 80 to 100 hours to move to 'friend status' (where you'd text or call for a catchup) and 200 hours to make a 'great friend'.[3] There are some problems our boys face here: time with friends is declining fast among youth. Teens spend less than one hour a day in face-to-face time with friends. It was more than double that in previous decades.[4] Boys simply do not have the time, or make the time, needed for meaningful relationships – particularly in person. At least, that's what we tell ourselves – and what they tell us. But in many cases it's a lie. They don't spend time in face-to-face relationships because we keep them inside. Or they're staring at a screen. Or because we've scheduled them to within an inch of their lives so we can maximise and optimise their childhoods so they can achieve their potential. (Or sometimes, they're just a struggling, awkward, neurodivergent kid who is desperate for someone – anyone – to spend time with them and no one ever seems available.)

This also explains why adults struggle to make friends as they get older: who has 50 to 200 hours to spend with friends? We're not talking about sharing cubicles in an office. It's about hours spent 'being friends'.

The result of declining friendship? Loneliness, lethargy, and languishing.[5] Boys these days are hanging out less, going to fewer parties, dating less, taking fewer risks (which most people feel good about but causes me concern), and are generally less social. All of this flows through to wellbeing. Relatedness needs aren't satisfied. Amotivation and apathy follow.

A systematic review of 65 intervention programs aimed at supporting peer relationships found two important factors – a context for interaction and parental involvement.[6] Context means something to do and a reason for doing it. Parental involvement means it might be up to you to take the initiative to get your son together with a friend or three, or, if he's older, prompt him to do the inviting. Then just add a bike, skateboard, a body of water or a ball, and a blissfully unscheduled afternoon will provide more friendship-building potential than all the organised activities you can enrol him in. Meaningful friendships require unstructured social time.

Make your house the place where your son and his friends genuinely want to be. If you're lucky enough to have the space, install a basketball hoop, set up a garage gym or a ping-pong table. Encourage them to be involved in activities that are safe, wholesome, and healthy. Organise a fridge full of their favourite soft drinks, make melting moments and chocolate brownies. And be a 'pot-plant' parent – in the corner but unobtrusive. Boys enjoy being in homes where they don't feel supervised. But they like to feel wanted. When your son's friends feel genuinely welcome in your home, you become part of their social ecosystem rather than an obstacle to it. The impact of benign but good adults in the peer environment is a stabilising force. You model what it looks like to help others feel safer and stronger. Your son and his friends are watching how you treat people.

Pro tip: this could be tricky depending on their age, but encourage your son to have his friends put their phones in a basket by the front door. Suggest this to many boys and they'll resist – but if your son can identify the value in it (identified regulation is the workhorse of the motivation continuum), his influence on them might pay off.

Phones, games, consoles – these all lubricate the social dynamic, but not necessarily in helpful ways. Help your son understand that discomfort in social situations is normal and necessary. If gaming on screens *is* going to happen, encourage games you've purchased where the boys will play against each other rather than games that are on the internet where they'll play against strangers. But mostly, discourage screens (gently) and encourage shoulder-to-shoulder interaction. Get them talking, even when uncomfortable silences might occur. The urge to reach for a phone when conversation lags is precisely the moment to push through into deeper connection. Real conversation often begins after the obvious topics are exhausted – and that's where genuine friendship develops. Time together is undermined when screens are involved.

I can share countless stories of things I did with my mates because we were present, together, making those mistakes and experiencing those moments that built lifelong memories. But *none* of them include the many hours I spent playing video games. They're built on surfing, skating, taking risks, sneezing so hard that snot covered the windscreen and then trying to remove it by turning on the windscreen wipers (Aaron), chasing girls, getting mad at each other (often about girls), camping (ideally near girls), climbing into the roof-trusses of under-construction homes late at night and talking (about girls, usually) … you get the picture. These memories are rich and the friendships that developed out of those experiences are too. Screens diminish the richness of experiences and relationships.

A note on boredom: many bloggers and experts pontificate on how important it is for kids to be bored, and that boredom no longer exists these days. But beware – boredom is a double-edged sword. Channelled positively, it's healthy. But the unstructured time that builds friendships can also become unsupervised time that leads to trouble. I found myself in more mischief when I was bored, unsupervised, and with friends than at any other time. Let them be bored together – but set boundaries around harm to people or property, and if possible provide an environment where safe, healthy activities can be chosen if the boys are willing to put in some effort.

Navigating concerning friendships

Some of your son's friends may be the living embodiment of everything you've taught him to avoid. If you – like me – are an involved and concerned parent you may want to sit down with your son, tell him why those friends are dangerous, and demand that he drop them. Fast.

Please don't. Instead, take a breath. Count to ten. Resist the urge to ban the relationships.

Think carefully about basic psychological needs. Denigrating his friends threatens competence (he'll feel judged). Forbidding friendships undermines autonomy (you're removing choice). Both harm your relationship (he'll feel you don't understand him). When you frustrate these three needs, he'll comply externally (if you're watching) or rebel (when you're not). His friends, meanwhile, support his needs – so he moves towards them. Home feels need-thwarting. His friends are need-supportive: they feel comforting, they respect and encourage his choices, and they celebrate him.

Research indicates that forbidden friendships become more appealing and influential than they would have been if they weren't forbidden.[7] Parental control turns forbidden friends into forbidden fruit. Again for emphasis: force creates resistance. Studies show children in families where parents forbade friendships moved closer to undesirable friends – and they participated in more of their friends' 'delinquent' behaviour.[8] Reading him the riot act will drive him straight into the arms and company of the people you don't want him near.

Instead focus on two things:

1. Strengthen the gravitational pull of home

When you make your home the place where your son and his friends genuinely want to be, rather than competing with peer relationships, you're bringing them into *your* environment. This means your son's friends are exposed to *your* values. It shifts the dynamic.

One mother dealt with her older teenage son's materialistic friend group by doubling down on family volunteering traditions while avoiding negative comments about the friends. Volunteering with the SES shifted his focus from consuming (taking value) to contributing (adding value) – from being a burden to being a bonus. He was able to spend time with his dad. She did it gently, so her son's motivation was always at least at the 'identified' level. This counteracted friend influences. If she had torched the friendships, her son would have felt forced to defend his mates, which would have strengthened his identification with *their* values. And his relationships in the new context, combined with increased competence with chainsaws, made volunteering motivating.

Get that treat cupboard stacked. Fill the fridge with ginger beer (non-alcoholic). If you have a rumpus room, set it up for games. Foosball, ping-pong, a pool table, whatever you can fit and whatever you can afford. Camping trips, football nights, or whatever it is that your son and his friends are into. Keep them together. Keep them active. Keep them having fun. Keep them analogue where you can.

2. Step gently into Three Es conversations

You can't control your son's relationships, but you can influence his capacity to navigate them wisely. Exploring what he's seeing and how he's feeling, explaining what matters, and empowering him to develop healthy approaches to his friends' unhealthy behaviours are better than banning friendships. Chapter 11 will be your best guide to helping your son consider his position and get connected to *his* values.

When direct intervention is necessary

We want our boys to have agency – to be allowed to make dumb decisions with their friends while they're young and the stakes are low. But sometimes, immediate action is required. Try the Three Es where you can, but you'll need to step in immediately if your son and his friends are engaged in:

- illegal activities;
- substance abuse;
- causing harm to people or property; and/or
- consistently lying about their whereabouts.

When you step in with control, be prepared: it's going to blow up. Stomping on autonomy rarely goes well. He's not going to say, 'Gee, you're right. I've been pigheaded about this but now that I can see how serious you are about it, it's shifted my perspective.' When he angrily tells you how you don't get it and you're out of touch, allow that emotional wave to travel up the metaphorical sand and subside. Repair. Listen carefully. If you're wrong, step back. If you're right, stand your ground, but do it in a way that invites him back into a problem-solving conversation.

Address underlying needs. Is he making these decisions with his friends because he's seeking excitement or trying to gain status?

Status-seeking often means trying to feel like a bonus – but in unhealthy ways (impressing others through risk, domination, or shock value rather than legitimate contribution). If the answer to the question is yes, can you problem-solve together to provide healthier risk-taking opportunities? Is he looking for belonging? If yes, can you support him to find healthier communities and peer groups?

The take-home message

Research on parental attachment shows that secure early relationships with parents impact the quality of peer relationships in childhood and adolescence.[9] The more your son feels his needs are supported with you, the more comfortable he'll be standing up to his friends. And if he stumbles, that's reality. Sometimes life will be his teacher. We all had challenges during adolescence – they made us who we are.

Friendships are oxygen. But they're also sandpaper. Our children scuff up against them and figure out their values. When things are tricky, your son will have decisions to make. He'll come up against things he doesn't agree with and will need to work out where he stands. Sometimes the realisation hits *after* the consequences land. It's a messy but necessary process. Your job isn't control but remaining a loving presence and trusting your son's capacity to make good choices, supporting him as he wears the consequences of the bad ones.

That gherkin that left a saucy smear down the McDonald's window is something I regret today. I should have been more aware of the consequences of my actions. But those friendships left something far more lasting. I recall them with fondness, gratitude, and just an occasional tinge of healthy regret that shows I learned the valuable lessons I needed to.

Your son's peers will influence him deeply and their shared memories will be with him for the rest of his life. What will those memories be? Your regular, careful, need-supportive, empowering conversations with your son will offer the support he needs to help others feel safer and stronger and to be a bonus in their lives.

14 Screen wars

How to set limits without destroying your relationship

The thought process that went into building these applications ... was all about: 'How do we consume as much of your time and conscious attention as possible?' ... The inventors, creators – it's me, it's Mark [Zuckerberg], it's Kevin Systrom on Instagram, it's all of these people – understood this consciously. And we did it anyway.

Sean Parker[1]

If our users decreased their level of engagement with our products, our revenue, financial results, and business may be significantly harmed.

Mark Zuckerberg[2]

Here is an excerpt from an email I received from a young man in regional Victoria, out of school for just over nine months:

> As an 18-year-old, I recognise that the behaviours I display currently could lead to an addiction to technology

> and social media. I consider myself empathetic and thoughtful, but I notice how often I'm bombarded online with subtle – and increasingly obvious – attempts to divide people by race, religion, gender, or beliefs. Sometimes I even catch myself internalising those messages, feeling anger towards groups that isn't actually mine to feel. Something that makes me very aware of this is whenever I actually talk to someone with different views, I'm reminded of how much common ground we share as people. It's unsettling to see how much content is designed to drive separation and hate.

Self-awareness. Inner work. Character. Helping those around you feel safer and stronger. I love this young man's thoughtfulness. This is hope-building! He's integrating values. This is the whole box and dice – exactly what we want for our sons.

Increasingly, young people recognise they are out of control. In 2025, *The Australian* interviewed teens about tech addiction. 'It was like a drug in my chest,' said one young man. 'The phone … was part of me. That's who I was … It was like a friend that was always there for me.'[3] A 2025 Harris poll found that nearly half of young adults aged 18 to 27 wish that the platforms they grew up with – Snapchat, TikTok, and X – had never been invented.[4]

If you're reading this chapter because your teenager is raging about wifi passwords or you've just discovered he's gaming until 3 am, you're not alone. I've spoken with a parent whose 15-year-old threw a chair because of an argument about screens. One parent told me her 15-year-old son broke his father's nose because dad lost his patience after calling him to get off his game and come for dinner 'at least six times'.

Door slams, holes in walls, smashed screens, broken game controllers, swearing, pushing, shoving. These are the serious difficulties some parents face as they confront the screen wars playing out in their corridors and living rooms. And some parents shrug, leaving their sons to game all weekend, captured by the screen and not leaving their room.

Our sons are swimming through a digital ocean full of fishing lines baited with the most tantalising hooks known to the human brain. YouTube. Video games. Pornography. Gambling. Crypto investing. Reels of violence, drug-taking, extreme behaviours, and devastating acts including beheadings, shootings, stabbings, fighting, theft, and more. Shallow, hollow, false satisfaction entices him, ensnares him and reels him in. And by comparison, everything off the screen feels unrewarding. Devices provide the illusion of need-satisfaction at every turn: competence, connection, control.

Big Tech are focused on addicting our children to their platforms and devices. They've done nothing to earn our trust, and they're not changing. This chapter is your six-pillar playbook for avoiding a screen war and guiding your son to healthy decision-making around screens with the tools and resources you have. Before we kick off: if your son shows signs of depression or anxiety linked to screens, becomes violent when limits are spoken about or enforced (because he can't set them himself), lies consistently despite your conversations, shows limited or no interest in real-world activities for extended periods, or experiences significant academic or social decline, seek professional help. Search online for a clinician experienced with gaming and tech issues. The strategies below work for most families, but some situations require more support.

1. Delay device access

Sapiens Lab researchers discovered that the earlier your child receives his own smartphone, the greater the mental health challenges he'll experience between 18 and 24 years of age. Similar results are showing up in other studies.[5]

Tell your son: 'You can have a phone when you can pay for it yourself. Even then, we'll determine appropriate limits together.' If your son requires a device before he can pay for it himself, provide a phone with limited or no internet. He only needs it for texting and calling. Kids don't need smartphones; they need smart parents. Smart parents give their kids dumb phones.

This won't apply to everyone. At some point your son may go behind your back, so don't push too far. But hold off while you can. And if you've already squeezed the toothpaste out of the tube, you're going to make a mess trying to get it back in, so effective boundary-setting becomes your next best option.

2. Remove the need for willpower

Wifi control is your secret weapon. Dr Brad Marshall's research points to having effective limits on the *hardware* of the wifi router.[6] Relying only on *software* controls is like putting a *Do Not Enter* sign on a door. Your son can open the door with a shrug and a 'whatever'.

A quick online search shows how to set up automatic wifi cutoffs at bedtime and family time. Use mesh router systems to control individual devices rather than apps your son can outsmart. Mobile data plans need the same attention – unlimited data makes wifi controls pointless. Find plans that limit data with parental controls or buy a plan that has a small amount of data. By minimising access to 4G and 5G networks plus shutting down wifi, you'll reduce time online and cut down on the time Big Tech, Big Gambling, and Big Porn have to ensnare him.

3. Outsmart the addiction industry

Game designer William Siu admitted games are designed to 'take away the decision-making' and keep players hooked. 'We wanted people to reach for their phones first thing in the morning and jump right into our games.'[7] Free massive online games, like those designed by Siu and his colleagues, make money through persuasive design calibrated to extract money and attention. And new research shows they're gambling gateways.[8]

Instead, buy games from stores and avoid massive, free internet-based games if you can afford it. Games you buy in a shop and take home to play against other people sitting beside you in your living room are more likely to focus on entertainment value and building relationships; not hooking players and extracting more money.

And delay as long as possible – late primary school at the earliest. Spend money on a console or a family computer which lives in a common family area. Then kids can't just pick it up and take it to their room.

Gaming red flags: games requiring constant internet connectivity, in-game purchases, time-limited events (which increases FOMO), and anything that makes your son anxious or aggressive if he can't access it.

4. Collaborative boundary-setting

It's 2012. My eldest daughter, Chanel, is 13. All her friends have Snapchat, and she wants it. My instant response is no. We both know the risks, but I'm the only one with a fully functioning prefrontal cortex and a lack of emotional investment. 'All my friends have it,' she pleads.

'No,' I respond.

'You're supposed to explore, explain, empower,' she says.

I make a mental note: I'm never taking you to another one of my parenting seminars.

Nevertheless, I do as she asks: I explore. She tells me she feels isolated because her friends are no longer using Messenger to communicate. Everyone has Snapchat except her.

I move to step two of the need-support process: explain. I tell her there are risks. Nudes. The addiction of constantly checking and seeking validation online. Bullying. Disappearing messages and a lack of evidence for what's been sent. Pervy weirdo strangers.

And then I repeat my initial answer: 'No.'

'Empower me, Dad!' she demands.

'No. Use Messenger.'

I'm not practising what I preach, but in this instance, I've decided I know what's good for her.

Then comes her Hail Mary from the three-point line. 'Dad, you telling me to use Messenger while everyone else is on Snapchat is like you telling me to play at the park while all my friends have gone to the beach.'

I hesitate. I waver. I smirk and congratulate her. 'That's good. That's really good.' And then I produce what I consider to be the ultimate response and the nail in the coffin of her argument. 'But the beach has rips and sweeps and currents. There are sharks, bluebottles, jellyfish. There's broken glass … and syringes in the sand. You'll get sunburnt. There are human predators too.'

I've got her. Surely, I win.

Then she regathers the ball: 'Dad, have you been to the park lately?'

Slam dunk. Straight over the top of me. The buzzer sounds. We're into overtime.

This leads to a conversation where the metaphor she accidentally created stops, and we talk honestly about why I'm concerned about social media generally – all platforms – and how she can navigate it safely. If the metaphor continued, it would have sounded like this:

'Dad, if I promise to always cover up, slip slop slap, swim between the flags, never talk to strangers, stay with my friends, and you can come and check in on me at the beach whenever you want, would you let me go?'

Sometimes the answer will still be no. Or it might be, 'Perhaps, but you can only be at the beach between these times.' The answers will vary by family, but the process is always the same and this discussion modelled it right: explore, explain, empower. This is a conversation that helps your child feel safe and strong. It supports basic psychological needs – relatedness (our relationship stayed strong), competence (she felt capable of navigating social media), and autonomy (she understood the rationale/why and bought into a solution we developed together). When needs are met, regulation moves from extrinsic and introjected to identified and integrated.

A brief note here. One reviewer of this manuscript suggested that a 'no' would never have worked for her when she was raising her boys – and that being told 'no' might even lead to physical violence. It's a hard thing to discuss, and I want to recognise it directly. Part of our role as parents is to help our sons learn to accept no with grace – but if your son becomes violent when you set a limit, that is beyond the scope of this book, and beyond what you should navigate alone. Please seek professional support. Domestic and family violence takes many forms, and you deserve to feel safe in your own home.

5. Tricky transitions

Most screen conflicts happen during transitions when it's time to turn it off and move to another activity (like dinner or bed). Establish agreements on how you'll both navigate these transitions when emotions aren't running high, ideally *before* screen time starts.

Here are four to consider.

(i) Agree on advance warnings

You agree that you'll give your son a 15-minute verbal reminder, a five-minute heads-up, and then agreed-upon end signals like flickering lights. Allow grace periods to reach save points – honouring autonomy within boundaries.

(ii) Use built-in screen shut downs and filters

I am opposed to filters and tracking software *unless* your son is in on it and agrees. But a simple, 'I want you to set a 60-minute timer, and once it goes off, the screen time is finished,' can work wonders. I'm a fan of apps like Freedom and Forest or a Brick device that allow lock-out times for devices. Use them collaboratively and with your son's endorsement. Unilateral decision-making will upset the apple cart. The great thing about these types of apps is that, once activated, the device is completely locked down. Some software allows routers to be locked down, as I described earlier.

(iii) Communicate considerately

When corrections are needed, ask questions rather than barking orders. Try saying this: 'I notice you've been on for two hours. What's your plan for transitioning off?' Ask him how he wants you to speak to him if things aren't working out. Does he want you to shut it down physically? Would he prefer that you sit with him as he finishes his level or episode? This builds relatedness and competence – and supports autonomy.

(iv) Keep consequences logical, not punitive

You will know by now that I don't like controlling techniques. I'm mostly anti-punishment except in rare circumstances. Solving problems together is almost always better. But when screens become ongoing sources of contention and your son ignores every boundary, even when he has agreed to it, there must be a response. This is the natural result of broken agreements.

Here are two examples. First, if your son goes over time, you might both agree ahead of time that he loses that amount from tomorrow's allocation. (This only works if he has a daily screen limit. I'm neither for nor against this. You work it out together.) Agree that: 'If you go ten minutes over today, that's ten minutes less tomorrow.' Second, aggressive transitions where he fights, argues, or ignores you means pausing gaming privileges until better self-regulation is demonstrated. If he blows up, he loses access for an agreed-upon period.

Holding the line here – while being appropriately responsive if he has good reasons for ignoring boundaries – will teach your son that boundaries have meaning, that his word matters, and that self-regulation is a skill worth developing.

> Quick screen-time hack: make sure your son eats before he games. Not eating before gaming makes the transition worse at the end of the gaming session.
>
> Bonus hack: ask him to tell you what he's going to do after gaming so he has an activity ready to go.

6. Build compelling alternatives

If there is a point of failure, it's the point where we say, 'Enough screens,' but we don't offer engaging alternatives to the screen. Your son needs an environment that offers enrichment *off the screen.* This could mean physical activities like martial arts, rock climbing, or team sports. He needs to be outside, touching grass. It could be skill-building pursuits like music, woodworking, or cooking. These teach that the best rewards come from pushing through initial boredom and difficulty.

The goal isn't just getting him off screens. The goal is helping him find activities that genuinely satisfy his needs: real competence (mastering skills), real relatedness (face-to-face connection), real autonomy (choosing pursuits that align with his values). That's where intrinsic motivation lives.

The most important alternative is social connections – because that's why he's super online in the first place. Help him step outside the digital realm with youth groups, volunteer opportunities, or mentorship programs where he contributes to others' lives. Build community. Create connections with him and for him in real life. Finding meaning and purpose off the screen is a pathway to satisfaction. Find activities matching his temperament rather than forcing generic solutions. The times I've seen this work well are when parents say, 'Let's hire a court [basketball, soccer, pickleball, for example] and see which of your friends wants to come. We can fit three more in our car.' Or if a friend has a pool, go over for a swim. You might need to help with arrangements, but once you figure out what to do, they're happy to make their own fun.

One parent told me her son is 'a four-sport son'. I questioned the meaning of the phrase and she replied, 'He has a phone, but he barely has time to use it because he's playing four different sports every week. Between training and sports days, eating, sleeping, and school, he just doesn't have time or energy for his device.'

The most common advice I have heard from parents whose boys are thriving is 'keep them busy' (particularly with their friends in the real world). When they're busy and active, they're less likely to do things that are to their detriment. Time and money play a part, but in the battle against Big Tech's algorithms, it's good advice.

The take-home message

I'm a fan of screens when they give more to your son than they take from him. If he's gaining value, developing curiosity, and becoming a better person (or a more educated, well-rounded person) by being online, go for it. I don't believe there's much evidence to show that being online *delivers these outcomes*. Ultimately, the goal is to raise boys who control their devices rather than being controlled by them.

Ask your son to write down the hours he spends on his screen each day. We know average teen screen use is around nine hours a day, but let's assume your son is exceptional and only spends four hours a day. Multiply that four hours across 365 days of the year. Then multiply it by ten for his ten years of adolescence. That's 14,600 hours, or roughly 1.6 years of life (assuming zero sleep) spent scrolling, swiping, and screenshotting instead of … you know … living. Fun comparison: in that 14,600 hours he could learn five languages, train for a marathon, write three books, or finally sort out his sock drawer – twice.

If the screen war is one-sided right now and tech is winning in your home, remember this is less about your son than it is about the staggeringly sophisticated systems designed to capture and monetise his attention. He's not the problem. The system is the problem, and we need to recruit one another's support to fight it.

Even if your limits were more lenient in the past and you're having trouble turning the tide, hope isn't lost. Your screen-addicted son can find balance. And together, you'll remember that the best experiences in life are analogue anyway.

15 Tackling the porndemic

How to talk to your son about consent, intimacy, and sex

Pornography is the number-one sex educator on the planet.[1] Teenage boys are the most popular students. We need to talk about pornography and nudes with our sons. But the 'porn talk'? Parents aren't expecting an enthusiastic yes from their sons on this one.

Believe it or not, though, boys want us to have these conversations with them. The Top Blokes Foundation found young males report a 'gut feel' that their pornography use is harming them and they want to talk – *to us* – about it.[2] In Chapter 5, Peggy Orenstein's comments confirmed this. But boys in the Top Blokes data suggested they don't have a trusted adult who they feel they *can* talk to about pornography. This represents both our greatest challenge and our most significant opportunity. They want our input, but … they don't feel they can ask.

In the past generation there has been a shift in how teenage romantic relationships develop, and pornography and nudes are – for many – an integral part of that change. Intimate images (real or AI) have become the stock in trade for many boys – a form of relational currency with both love interests and friends – but they're trading in a market they don't understand. There are legal, social, emotional, and even economic (think: OnlyFans) consequences to creating, possessing, viewing, and disseminating explicit video and imagery. Sometimes, the ramifications are limited, and only affect a boy and how he thinks about himself. There may be others involved and so the damaging ripples spread. And at its worst, pornography can upend and destroy lives.

This chapter is your blueprint for building barriers that slow access to pornography, and to having the conversations that teach your son about the often catastrophic consequences of engaging with explicit content, particularly possessing and sending nudes, so that he can make safer, healthier decisions.

Australia's age verification laws for pornography

I edited the final draft of this manuscript in March 2026. Writing a line like that dates a book – a big no-no. But it's relevant, specifically for this chapter. That's because on 9 March 2026, Australia's second and most significant tranche of Age-Restricted Material Codes came into force under the *Online Safety Act 2021*, overseen by eSafety Commissioner Julie Inman Grant. And it all builds on Australia having become the first country in the world to ban social media for under-16s on 10 December 2025.

As of 9 March 2026, any platform accessible in Australia that hosts or permits explicit content must implement meaningful age verification before granting access. Simply clicking 'I am 18 or over' is no longer sufficient. The laws extend well beyond pornography. Platforms must restrict access by age to:

- pornography and sexually explicit material;
- R18+ video games;
- explicit AI chatbots and generative AI services capable of producing sexual, violent, or self-harm content;
- content depicting high-impact violence; and
- content promoting self-harm, suicide, or disordered eating.

The March codes apply to app stores, device manufacturers, social media platforms, gaming and messaging services, and AI systems. The December 2025 codes had already required search engines such as Google and Bing to blur pornographic and violent images in search results for logged-out users and those under 18. There are also extended deadlines still to come: search engines have until 27 June 2026 to implement logged-in age verification, and app stores have until 9 September 2026 to restrict R18+ downloads. This all means that accessing explicit content of any kind will be harder than it has been since the internet was invented.

Aylo, the Canadian company that owns Pornhub, RedTube, YouPorn, and Tube8, chose not to implement age verification. Instead, from around 6 March 2026 – three days before the deadline – it blocked all Australian IP addresses from its platforms entirely, offering only 'safe for work' content in the Australian market. Aylo argued that age-verification laws, such as those already in place in the UK, don't offer meaningful protection for kids, and actually create harms relating to data privacy. They did the same thing for similar laws in Louisiana and Texas in the US, as well as in France and the UK. They exited the market rather than build verification systems.

So, isn't that good? The biggest pornography website in the world bailed! And other platforms implemented the required ID gate. Perhaps you're thinking you're off the hook? Not remotely.

As soon as the legislation landed, app stores reported a dramatic spike in virtual private network (VPN) downloads. On the day the laws took effect, three VPN apps were in the top 15 free downloads on Apple's Australian App Store. It happened in the UK when similar laws came into force: NordVPN reportedly saw a 1000% increase in UK subscriptions at that point. VPNs are legal in Australia. And many teenagers *are* sufficiently motivated to download them. Using one to access legal explicit content is not a crime. Bypassing the geo-block may technically breach a platform's terms of service, but that is a matter between user and platform. The legislation doesn't cover VPNs.

This means your kids can still access explicit content. And they are. Determined users can easily circumvent the restrictions. Critics argue smaller, less regulated offshore sites still grant access, ignoring the legislation. And as much as it pains me to read from the Aylo PR machine, they argue that age verification has not demonstrably reduced minors' access to pornography in places where similar laws are already in place. (We have no way of verifying if this is true, or of knowing how they've identified who is using their 'service', but that's what they're telling us.)

My take is simple. Pornography is a scourge. There is strong enough research for us to recognise a significant downside to children and young people viewing it (and adults too, but that's beyond our scope). And there is essentially zero upside to them accessing it. Even imperfect age verification has value as a first line of defence – particularly in protecting young children from accidental exposure. And it's appropriate that the burden of responsibility has been shifted from individuals to the platforms that profit from the content.

Australia has appropriately, decisively, and effectively positioned itself as one of the world's most aggressive regulators of children's online safety. They've put a fence around the pool. But while you can fence the pool, you can't fence the ocean. Keeping kids away from explicit material still demands parental involvement.

Fencing the pool

While government intervention and tech policies are now increasingly doing this job for you, individual responsibility is still central to keeping kids safe and aware of what's online. The best way to do this is two-fold: (i) use tech to create barriers, and (ii) have productive, helpful conversations.[3]

The Five-Layer Strategy, developed by Protect Young Eyes, provides a useful approach incorporating both barriers and conversations.

1. App level controls

Know what platforms your son uses and what he's seeing on those platforms. Implement parental controls in the app (software level) and on the devices he uses (hardware level). This means knowing the tech and how it works. It's going to be easier when he's younger. Have the conversations and be across things from an early age to make things easier as he matures.

2. Location protocols

Agree with your son that he'll avoid the 'toxic trio': bedrooms, boredom, and darkness. Devices in bathrooms are also a major concern. Agree on times and places when devices are off limits: family meals, short car trips, bedroom.

3. Device-level controls

Instal software on your son's devices after a Three Es conversation in which he identifies the value of the decision and endorses it. Use that software to make willpower less relevant in his device usage. (This will be tricky when the school owns the device.)

4. Router-level filtering

Set controls at the hardware (router) level to minimise access to explicit or other inappropriate content. Your router is your digital front door.

5. Build digital trust

This is where connection and conversation come in.[4] The first four layers are useful when your child is at home on a device you have access to, using your router and your software. But we need to do better. I'll say it again: you can fence your pool, but you can't fence the ocean. If he's with friends on *their* devices, all your best efforts at barrier creation will be in vain. *This is why the conversations matter so much.* Pre-arming your son provides protection beyond any tech barrier.

Teaching your son to 'swim'

Parents avoid pornography conversations for three reasons:

- **(i)** they feel unprepared or embarrassed;
- **(ii)** they worry they'll create curiosity where none existed; and
- **(iii)** they think someone else (school, friends, internet) will handle it.

But the data shows that parent–child conversations are protective. Those discussions lead to lower pornography viewing and reduced impact of pornography on our sons' development.[5] These conversations – explicitly disapproving of pornography consumption (including your 'why') – decrease pornography use during emerging adulthood.

Chapter 11 gives you the structure for making these conversations work when you talk about this type of content. In addition to using the Three Es, I recommend a developmentally informed approach across four stages.

1. Foundation stage (ages 8 to 10)

Introduce concepts of 'brain-healthy' vs 'brain-unhealthy' content but avoid explicit detail. Focus on building trust and establishing that all topics can be discussed safely. Use language like 'some pictures and videos aren't safe and healthy for kids' brains'. And keep conversations light, easy, but clear. Use appropriate words (such as pornography, sex, breasts, intercourse).

2. Reality stage (ages 10 to 12)

The average age of initial exposure to pornography is around 11, so now is the time to acknowledge pornography exists and why it's problematic.[6] Explain how pornography shows fake versions of love and sex that are harmful. Emphasise that pornography is unhealthy for children's brains and gives them relationship ideas that are inaccurate. I'm a fan of Michelle Mitchell's *Where Do Babies Come From?* It suits this age group well.

If you need conversation starters, try:

- 'Most kids see pornography by age 11. Has anyone talked to you about this?'
- 'If you ever see something online that makes you uncomfortable, I want you to know you can always come to me. You won't get in trouble.'

- 'Have you heard the word pornography? What do you know about it?'

Pornography is bad for children and young people. Period. However, using moral language (good/bad) can feel abrasive and controlling with children at around this age. They're developing a sense of identity (which means they're considering what they value), and our use of good/bad, right/wrong, should/shouldn't, can give them something to push against if we're not careful. If we speak about something we wish to forbid, like pornography, with morally laden language such as 'wicked', 'depraved', 'immoral', or 'disgusting', our kids may want to engage *with* that subject rather than avoid it. I've found discussing pornography with more neutral terms is more effective. Try words such as 'safe/unsafe', 'healthy/unhealthy', and 'wise/unwise'. These feel less controlling, reduce the urge to push back, and may actually lead to greater identification with the values you hope to convey.

3. Impact stage (ages 12 to 15)

By high school, it's time for deeper discussions of how pornography affects relationships, expectations, and brain development. Your son is likely aware – and possibly concerned – that pornography is impacting his attitude, his cognition, his relationships, and his brain. Many of his peers – maybe even he, himself – will be viewing it (and sharing it in chat groups). Discuss the difference between pornography's portrayal of sexuality and real, loving relationships.

Address specific concerns about body image, consent, and realistic expectations. Focus on positive aspects of intimacy and how pornography ignores, dilutes, and damages this.

4. Ongoing dialogue (ages 15+)

From this point on, it's about regular check-ins and values-based discussions. Those Sunday chats will be your foundation. Once a quarter, check in with curiosity: 'I heard the latest research says pornography can cause anxiety in young men. What do you think?' Or 'I heard boys as young as 11 are watching it. What about kids in your year?' Or 'I heard a boy was charged for distributing nudes … What do you think about that?'

You could even discuss techniques for gaining control of pornography use. This acknowledges you know boys watch it and you're able to help him manage his consumption. For example, 'If you feel like you can't stop watching it, what might you do?' Possible answers: limit usage, try mindfulness, don't watch it at night (again, no bedrooms, boredom, or darkness – the toxic trio), have something to do whenever the urge grabs, and whatever ideas you can come up with together. Focus on critical-thinking skills, relationship readiness, and connecting physical intimacy with emotional maturity.

Stuck?

The *Beyond the Talk* report from La Trobe University indicates that the biggest barrier to these conversations is us. Specifically dads.

Mums initiate these conversations more than dads and the load consistently falls to women.[7] Remember, boys *want* to hear from dad, though! If you're a father, step up. This is a discussion you should lead. (This may be hard for some men, particularly if they're consuming pornography themselves. Perhaps they'll think it's no big deal – or feel hypocritical. Nonetheless, sons want – and need – to hear from their fathers on this.)

What should you do if you're stuck or uncomfortable having these conversations?

- Start small with brief conversations rather than comprehensive lectures. The conversation starters above are launch points.
- Acknowledge your own discomfort. We all wish we didn't have to have these chats. Being uncomfortable is normal. Your child still needs you. And it can become a surprising opportunity to connect.
- Your discomfort is less important than your son's protection. Have a go. And if it doesn't work the first time, try again in a week with a different approach.

The toothpaste is out of the tube

Top Blokes youth workers report young males are eager to talk about pornography with adults in a safe space where they can ask questions and have meaningful discussions without being judged or criticised.[8] When you discover your son has viewed pornography, this represents an opportunity, not a crisis. To do this well, remember the Three Cs: be calm, curious, and connected.

Calm

Take a breath. His pornography viewing is concerning, but unlikely to be catastrophic and it can be addressed constructively. Your reaction sets the tone for future disclosures, and *that response from you* is where things can become traumatic or helpful.

Curious

You don't need him to debrief you on what he watched or how he felt. He probably wouldn't want to tell you anyhow. Curiosity here means staying open rather than reactive. You're curious about *him*, not the content. A simple 'Are you okay?' or 'Did it bother you at all?' signals safety without feeling like an interrogation. If he talks, listen. If he doesn't, the door is still open.

Connected

Use the disclosure as a bridge to deeper conversations about sexuality and relationships. 'I'm glad you can talk to me about this. Let's make sure you have good information about what real love and intimacy look like.' Set up a Three Es conversation, a Sunday-morning chat, or some further interactions to keep your son safe.

There are other conversations you can try. You could break down how the tech companies manipulate and take advantage of young men. The reality is that some boys won't care about Big Tech and the pornography industry tactics. You could try the moral tack: trafficking, acting, or exploitation – and you might still get a shrug in response. The conversations count nonetheless.

But if he's established his viewing patterns and you can't do anything to change where he is right now, harm-reduction approaches may be useful. Focus on exploring what drives his viewing, explaining why you're concerned, and empowering him to identify how he can reduce viewing and shift habits towards less extreme content. The primary focus should remain on helping your son understand the difference between pornography and healthy intimacy, and encouraging him to avoid pornography entirely.

Boys want to know about sex, they want to see sex (and bodies), and they want to have sex. Previous generations looked at their parents' copy of *The Joy of Sex*, or consulted Dolly Doctor, or tore into a *Cosmopolitan* sealed section. Kids want to know. They want to learn and be competent. And they don't want to ask their parents! My wish is that your son learns that bringing difficult topics to you results in support and trust-building conversations. The strongest protection against pornography's influence isn't better tech. It's a relationship of trust and openness with you.[9]

Sexy texts ... and more

Between 10% and 25% of American teens have participated in 'sexting'.[10] Australian youth report higher numbers – 35% of 14- to 17-year-old girls and 22% of boys have sexted.[11] The higher number among girls suggests they're often sending images, frequently under pressure to prove their 'love'. The eSafety Commissioner reports rates of image-based abuse are accelerating. Adolescents aged 15 to 17 represent 15% of all individuals who have experienced image-based abuse.[12]

There are three categories of image-based risk:

- **Receiving and possessing:** When minors share or even possess nude images, they could be charged with creation, possession, and distribution of child pornography. Even consensual images create legal liability.

- **Requesting and pressuring:** Some boys are coercive. They know what they're doing, and they do it anyway. The power dynamics in teenage relationships – particularly the social pressure girls face to maintain romantic connections – mean that 'consensual' sharing may not be as consensual as some believe. Lines like 'If you loved me, you'd give me a picture,' or 'What are you, frigid?' reveal how manipulation can work.

- **Creating and sharing:** Some boys are sharing images without consent, or using AI 'nudify' apps to create deepfakes, often with devastating outcomes.[13]

Image-based abuse, sharing of nude images, or creation of fake nudes all tie to consent, dating, intimacy, and pornography. Research reveals connections between pornography consumption and sexually exploitative behaviour.[14] Boys who regularly consume pornography may believe that it's normal to ask for nudes, and many struggle to understand why creating or sharing intimate images causes devastating harm.

Australian laws treat these behaviours as serious crimes. A conviction can change your son's life forever. Civil lawsuits (damages claims) can also be devastating. And even if the law doesn't catch him, there are other costs. School expulsion is likely. There can be barriers to employment or university admission, and family relationships will be strained.

The legal consequences are significant, but you'll make better progress by helping your son understand the potential impact. Use the Three Es.

Explore what he's hearing at school, what his friends are doing, and what he thinks of that. Explore how he would respond if he was asked for an image. (This is a chance to talk about online sextortion.) Ask what he's seen or heard, and whether girls or boys he knows have shared images in trusting relationships and broken up, and how he would feel if an image of him were shared without consent. If he is unfazed, ask how he would feel if his sister, his mum, or someone he cared about had their images shared without consent. What would he think should happen to the perpetrator?

If someone has shared inappropriate content involving your son, your best resource is the eSafety Commissioner. eSafety can help remove content or stop threats.

After exploring his perspective, *explain* the following:

- Taking, keeping or sharing intimate images without explicit ongoing consent is wrong.
- Consent can be withdrawn at any time.

- Creating fake intimate images is never acceptable, regardless of relationship status.
- Screenshots of disappearing messages violate consent.
- There are legal repercussions for possessing explicit photographs of anyone underage. (Search up the law in your state and read it to him.)

Monitor social media activity and group chats where image-sharing typically occurs. Establish clear consequences for participating in image-based abuse. Teach him to immediately delete any intimate images he receives and report incidents he witnesses, whether it is on-sharing of sexual images or where someone sends a nude of themselves.

Most importantly, if your son discloses having done the wrong thing, help him take responsibility while ensuring he knows that coming to you results in support, not punishment.

The take-home message

The strongest protection your son has is a relationship of trust with you, where difficult conversations happen naturally, and when he recognises that respecting other people's dignity isn't just about avoiding legal trouble but about helping others feel stronger and be safer because he's in their world.

16 Encouraging healthy sex

The honest conversation your son needs you to have with him

She had to mentally prepare herself for it. They'd been together for several months. Sexual activity had been ramping up and, while they hadn't had intercourse, they'd done everything else. For the past two months, the same routine played out. He would be horny – and demanding. If she didn't perform oral sex on him, he would beg and whine, and hassle her about his 'blue balls' until she eventually gave in. To stop him asking, she would kneel down and get started. After the pattern was established, he never asked again. She never said yes. But she did it anyway, because saying no meant dealing with his sulking, his complaints, his relentless pressure.

I wish this was fiction. It breaks my heart because it represents so much that's wrong with how we're teaching young people about sex and consent. This 16-year-old girl told me she thought she was consenting. I explained that she was capitulating. Her boyfriend wasn't respecting boundaries. He wasn't even thinking of boundaries. A girl responding to 'But you'd do it if you loved me' is coercion, not consent. 'I need this. You're supposed to help me finish' is coercion, not consent. 'You did it all the other times' is coercion, not consent – and it is coercion at the very least, but more accurately abuse. But it's happening in one form or another in every school and in every postcode every day.

This chapter is about sex, consent, and staying safe. It may be the most morally charged topic we can discuss in terms of bringing up boys.

While sexual activity is down compared with previous generations, boys have always been – and remain – curious and excited about sex.[1] I interviewed *Boys & Sex* author Peggy Orenstein about the way teen boys approach sexual encounters, and asked her whether a society shaped by pornography has had an impact on how boys talk about and seek sex. According to Orenstein, boys talk to their friends about sexual encounters with this language: 'You destroy her. You hit that. You tap that. You nail that.' One boy admitted, 'They never say like, "Yeah, we had a really nice time. And then we cuddled."' Sex is spoken about as conquest rather than connection, as taking rather than sharing. 'Locker-room talk' predates the internet, but it's ramped up with the explosion of internet pornography, chat rooms, and the cultural shift of the last two decades.

Writing a chapter about how we should teach our boys about sex, consent, and staying safe has been made difficult by this cultural movement. In a pluralistic society, different families, cultures, and faith traditions hold a range of perspectives on when and how sexual intimacy should be discussed and expressed. Some families emphasise abstinence until marriage, others focus on 'readiness' – emotional maturity and committed relationships. Others prioritise safety and consent regardless of relationship status. I contend that if our sons truly respect others and themselves – and if they're interested in ensuring that the people around them feel safer and stronger because of their presence – then understanding that sex carries a significance beyond physical pleasure is a necessary foundation for healthy sexual ethics across these different value systems. It will help them ensure those they are physically intimate with leave the encounter feeling as safe and strong as they did before it.

When your son reflects on his adolescence, what story does he want to recall? That he pressured and persisted until he 'scored'? Or that he valued genuine connection and intimacy – and kindness and consideration – over grudging compliance? And let's acknowledge that boys can be horribly pressured too: by prospective partners and by their friends who push them to become sexually active and then 'spill the tea' on how it was. There's a gift he can give himself in resisting pressure from others and staying true to himself about whether – and when – to be intimate. If boys learn to listen to that voice inside – their moral compass – then, when something doesn't feel right, when someone seems unsure, when the situation feels pressured, they'll know to step back, not push forward.

I won't downplay the stakes – they're high. Poor decisions made in the sexual domain cast longer shadows across people's lives than choices in almost any other area. And crucially, selfish, abusive, harmful decisions made by young men typically impact others rather than themselves. Instead of helping those around them feel safer and stronger, the misuse of intimacy and sexuality weakens others and reduces their sense of safety for years to come – sometimes for a lifetime.

In a conversation some years ago, a major media personality told me about a Friday night when she gave her teenage son a lift to a party. Before she dropped him off, she paused and asked if she could run something by him. Anxious to be out of the car and with his friends, her son sighed and said, 'Sure, Mum.'

'Tonight at this party there is a strong chance you'll find at least one girl who has had too much to drink and is vulnerable,' she said. 'Some boys see this as a chance to score. Others see this as a chance to support. Which boy are you going to be?' After a pause, he looked at her and, appealing to his character and values, she added, 'Will you be the best boy in the room tonight? Will you be a protector? Call someone for help if you need to, but make sure no one gets hurt.'

What would it look like if intimacy and sexual behaviour were filtered through the lens of 'What kind of person do I want to be? The one who takes advantage of someone's vulnerability? Or the one who protects it?' This is a powerful values conversation. If your son identifies with the value of protection and support, he won't need to be coaxed into being considerate and caring. He'll integrate it into his sense of self. In moments where emotions heat up, his response of, 'Yes, I'll be the best boy in the room,' gives him the reaffirmation – priming – for how he wants to be on that night at the party.

Sex positive

If I could change the way we talk about sex and consent, I'd shift the focus from minimum standards for consent ('How far can I convince my partner to go?') and protection ('Always wear a condom') to something else entirely.

Here's what I teach my children: 'Sex and intimacy are amazing. Incredible. Something to be excited about. Sex is one of the best things life has to offer. But it's only great at that level when it's happening with the *right person* at the *right time* in the *right place* and for the *right reasons*.'

Your son might cringe, but he needs to hear it. It's healthy for him to know that you enjoy spending time with your spouse or partner (if you have one). He needs to see the kisses in the kitchen. He needs to hear you making date-night plans (not the saucy ones – just that you're prioritising your relationship) and anniversary getaways. He's going to pretend he doesn't know what you do when you lock the bedroom door but knowing it gets locked often will teach him about what sex means in a dedicated relationship.

Our discussions about sex and consent focus, too often, on the negative end of the scale. But wonderful, fabulous sex is something to aspire to – for him to feel excited about and be curious about (in healthy ways). A positive view also emphasises sex with the wrong person at the wrong time in the wrong place and for the wrong reasons will be lousy. Behind the pool in the bushes at the party on Friday night is not the goal. And a blind-drunk girl in a bedroom with several boys lined up at the door? This should not need to be said, but based on Chanel Contos's website, it seems it actually does: a girl who is drunk cannot consent. What looks like a sexual opportunity is, in many cases, a crime. The boy who walks through that door isn't just disrespecting the girl and himself, he may be participating in sexual assault or rape, regardless of what he tells himself afterwards. The fact that some boys convince themselves otherwise, or that peer pressure makes it feel normal in the moment, doesn't change what it is. He needs to hear this clearly, from you, before he's ever in that situation.

These stories can be hard to hear. Yet these stories filter through to me consistently. There's nothing 'right time, right place, right person, right reason' in contexts devoid of genuine connection, mutual respect, or authentic desire.

We *must* have these conversations. They matter so much. A meta-analysis involving over 25,000 adolescents showed parent–adolescent communication about relationships significantly impacted safer sex behaviour and overall relationship decision-making.[2] *Boys & Sex* author, Peggy Orenstein, emphasised boys want to hear about intimacy from their dads – particularly missteps and mistakes. This isn't an invitation to share past transgressions or sexual experiences. Don't! But sharing appropriate lessons learned can be helpful. For example, 'I didn't listen the way I should have, and I've regretted it,' or 'I didn't help her feel stronger and safer when she was with me. I was focused on getting, not giving.' These vulnerable admissions will resonate deeply with a son searching for good information and show growth and maturity in a father's masculinity.

Starting the conversations

I am an ambassador for the Australian Government's 'Consent Can't Wait' campaign. Government research shows big holes exist in conversations between parents and kids on this tricky topic. That's because we make it too big a deal. So instead, make it simple. Dumb it down. A ten-minute chat while driving can be more effective than an hour-long formal discussion. A consistent Sunday-morning check-in is valuable. Use media as gateways – when sexual content appears in movies, TV or social media, use it as a discussion starter, whether it's problematic or uplifting content.

The day before I completed this chapter I was in the car with my daughter and we were listening to John Lennon's 1971 classic 'Jealous Guy'. My daughter asked if it was a cover version, and so I played Roxy Music's 1981 tribute version recorded after Lennon's murder. She asked if the lyrics were dodgy. Here's a guy, she told me, who is refusing to be accountable for his actions. He hurt her. Now he's saying he didn't mean to … he's just jealous. I felt tension. Was she right? The world has changed since 1971. Today we are far more alert to coercive control, possessiveness, and the emotional dynamics of unhealthy relationships. Jealousy is one of the most commonly cited precursors to intimate partner violence, and 'I didn't mean to' is a phrase that carries significant baggage. Yet, the counter-reading could show a shift in the culture where a song that was once tender and emotionally sensitive (with a guy actually brave enough to name his jealousy) could now be seen as problematic. We had a fascinating conversation about the difference between acknowledging feelings and using them as an excuse for harmful behaviour. No Sunday-morning chat needed. Just an impromptu discussion about a song lyric that may – or may not – be dodgy.

These conversations should be adapted to your son's maturity level, your family's cultural background, and your religious beliefs. What matters most is that the conversations happen authentically within your family's value system.

The most important point in this chapter is this: talk early. Talk often. Fumble. Make mistakes. Just get stuck in and start. Having these conversations is like your first group fitness class – uncoordinated and clumsy, but beneficial from the get-go. Everything after the first one gets easier.

The consent conversation

We have a responsibility to teach our children about consent. Here's the checklist. Legal consent requires five components:

- **Voluntary:** Consent is given freely without coercion, threats, intimidation, or pressure. Pestering someone until they give in isn't consent.
- **Capacity:** The person must be of sound mind, of legal age, and not under the influence of drugs or alcohol to the point they can't make rational decisions.
- **Informed:** The person understands what they're agreeing to, including risks and consequences.
- **Specific:** Consent to one activity doesn't mean consent to everything. Consent to kissing isn't consent to touching genitals or pushing further.

- **Revocable:** A consenting person can change their mind at any time, and when they do, everything stops immediately.

These aren't guidelines or suggestions – they're legal requirements that might determine whether your son goes to university or becomes a listed sex offender.

Legal consent is a minimum standard. I think that whenever we use a legal standard as the minimum standard we must be clear that we're not trying hard enough. I don't want our young people having minimum-standard sexual interactions. That doesn't sound intimate or enjoyable.

Here's the higher moral standard I want boys to live by: 'If my sexual partner isn't excited about it, I shouldn't be either.'

In some ways, this is unfair. He may be excited regardless of whether his partner likes an idea or not. You can't police arousal. But the principle is simple: if his partner isn't keen on something, he needs to gracefully let it go. No pressure. No moping. Considerate acceptance. Ask your son to consider how his partner will feel about their body, about him, or about the experience afterwards if they weren't genuinely excited about it. Stealing kisses, gropes, or going further because *you* are excited means your focus is misplaced – and selfish.

Advice for boys: focus on giving, not getting, and you'll both be guaranteed a good time. This is what it means to help someone feel safer and stronger – ensuring they're genuinely excited, not just compliant. Consent isn't the absence of 'no'. It's a 'yes please'.

Another helpful suggestion: draw him a Venn diagram with two overlapping circles. One is labelled: *What I want*; the other: *What my partner wants*. The place where they intersect is labelled: *What we want*. That overlapping area is consensual. If you're only operating in 'What I want', you're not having sex so much as you're taking it.

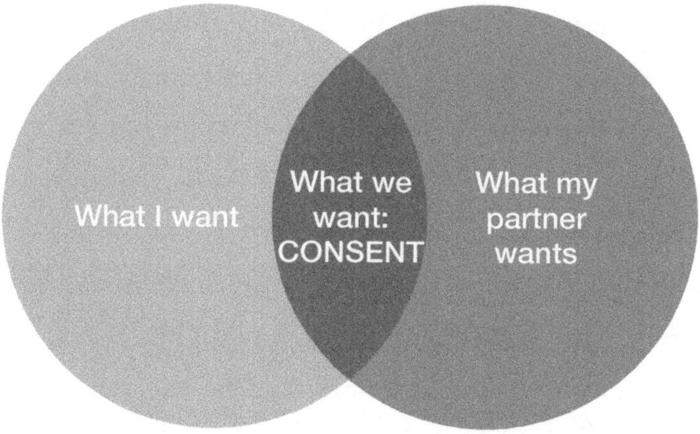

The timing conversation

Sexual development isn't a race, and there's no standard timeline that applies to everyone. Some of your son's peers may be ready for certain experiences earlier, others later. The right experiences at the wrong time are still wrong experiences. Australian longitudinal research shows that early sexual initiation can have mixed outcomes, with some individuals experiencing negative consequences while others show resilience.[3] Around 53% of Australian secondary school students in Years 10 to 12 have not engaged in sexual intercourse, meaning many teenagers are choosing to wait for their first sexual experience (or are not having sexual opportunity).[4]

Using the Three Es framework, *explore* how your son feels about sex. What are his friends saying? How much does sexual content come up in conversation? What is the tone of conversation around sexual topics? How respectful is it? How much are boys pushing for details or for conquest? Boys pressure each other constantly – 'Did you score?' 'Tell me more!' This conquest mentality undermines genuine intimacy.

You might also explore what he thinks about intimacy, the values you've encouraged, the timing of sexual behaviour, and how to be respectful. *Explain* your ideas (with his consent) after you've explored and listened closely. And then *empower* him by developing a path forward together that explicitly outlines what he feels he can identify with and integrate into his developing values system.

The values conversation

For families with strong cultural or religious traditions around sexuality, these conversations require particular sensitivity. Many faith traditions offer wisdom about the sacred nature of sexual intimacy that can provide powerful guidance for young men. Similarly, cultural traditions often emphasise the importance of family honour, respect for women, and the responsibilities that come with intimate relationships. Sometimes these religious and cultural traditions are generous and wise. Other times, such traditions can be the source of pain, shame, and trauma. The key to helping your son make safe, healthy, wise sexual decisions revolves around the central concept of so much of this book: he must understand – and endorse – the 'why'. If he understands and buys into how these traditions serve as a benefit rather than a restriction (assuming they are positive and healthy traditions), he'll be more motivated to align with these norms and identify with – and integrate – these values.

Different families hold different values based on cultural backgrounds, religious beliefs, and personal convictions. Your family's framework might emphasise abstinence until marriage, focus on committed relationships and building friendship with an intimate partner, encourage an ability to communicate and navigate the fallout from a breakup after intimate involvement, and/or prioritise safety and consent. Engage your son in conversations about your family's specific values regarding intimacy and help him understand the 'why' behind those values.

Questions to explore:

- 'Who represents an appropriate partner given our family values?'
- 'When is the right time for sex according to our beliefs?'
- 'What are the right reasons for sex that align with our principles?'

These are sensitive conversations that require a delicate touch and plenty of time. And some children might have different views to their parents. This is where discussions of consent, safety, and respect become even more important.

The connection conversation

Sexual expectations are high for our teenagers. Pornography writes the sexual script and sets sexual expectations early – and peer groups discuss and police those scripts. Once your son is in a relationship, momentum can carry him in a sexual direction before he or his partner are ready for physical intimacy. Pressure is amplified by friends asking, 'Have you done it yet?'

Research shows engaging in physical intimacy before an emotional connection is established leaves both partners – particularly girls – regretful, with negative emotional outcomes.[5] Yale journalist Kyung Mi Lee noted, 'I've heard a joke on campus that goes something like this: "First base is hooking up, second base is talking, third base is going on a date, and fourth base is dating."'[6] This inverted relationship progression has left many without the tools they need to enjoy healthy, positive relationships. Emotional intimacy decoupled from physical intimacy often leaves at least one person with buyer's remorse the next day.

Help your son examine his motivations honestly: is potential sexual activity about connection or conquest? Is he seeking this for himself and his sexual partner, solely for his own pleasure, or to gain status with peers? If no one else would ever know, would he still want it?

Boys who focus on connection over conquest and selfishness help their partners feel safer and stronger. Boys who seek status through sex leave their partners feeling used: weaker, not stronger.

The protection conversation

If sexual activity is going to happen, protection is non-negotiable. Even if your religious or cultural (or personal) values are focused on abstinence, teaching your son about birth control, disease, and using condoms is important. Whether you think he's sexually active or not, you still need to teach about protection. Work on the assumption that one day your children will be sexually active. When that day arrives, they need to know how to protect against unwanted/unplanned pregnancy and reduce the likelihood of contracting or passing on sexually transmitted infections. Moreover, we must emphasise that not getting pregnant shouldn't just be the girl's responsibility. Teaching our boys to take responsibility for always having a condom is part of how he makes those around him feel and be safer. He also needs to know that penetrative sex is not required for pregnancy to occur. Pre-ejaculate can contain sperm, and pregnancy is possible from ejaculation (or semen leakage) near the vaginal opening. Many young people don't know this, and that ignorance has consequences.

Teach your son that asking about contraception isn't unromantic – it's responsible. Anyone who says, 'Don't worry, I'm clean,' probably doesn't know if they are. And if you know your son is sexually active, encourage him to get an STI check every three to six months, even if he says he uses condoms. STIs can be spread through oral sex too. Just as we go to the doctor to check our blood pressure, sexually active young people should get routine STI checks.

The take-home message

Understanding sex, consent, and staying safe doesn't happen automatically. It requires conversations and experience (and sometimes both). If your son and his eventual intimate partner/s follow these principles when they are behind closed doors – at the right time with the right person in the right place for the right reasons – they'll both be as excited about it the next day as they were in the moment. And that's adding value, being a bonus, being a healthy man.

17 Getting through school

Helping your son find meaning and motivation at school

In Chapter 1, we briefly examined the code red situation for boys in school.

If your son loves school, fabulous. But many are struggling to get through it. School feels like a years-long, never-ending experience of pain.

Imagine your day as follows. You wake up and race out the door for work. By 8.40, you're in your first meeting. You don't really know much about anything that is being discussed, but you're told it's critical that you understand it because you'll be tested on it and your future success hinges on understanding it. The meeting ends at 9.35, but you don't complete everything on the agenda. Your supervisor demands you do it at home because there will be more to cover tomorrow that builds on what you've just done (and not understood). You're confused and stressed, but you're late – as is your supervisor – so you rush to your second meeting. It's just like the first, including the 'do the rest at home' part, plus a big project due in a month. You're to complete that project with two workmates who refuse to talk and indicate they won't be contributing. At 10.30 you grab a 20-minute break to wolf down a snack, some water, and rush to the loo – only to find it locked. There's a sign on the door saying it's locked due to vaping. Plus the soap dispensers have been ripped off the walls and someone smashed the cistern – again. Then it's two more back-to-back meetings – more of the same, but about topics you aren't interested in – and a 40-minute lunch break. It's now 1 pm. You're frazzled. Then one more hour-long meeting where you sit, bored, getting lectured. You finally commute home, dreading the backlog of work you have to complete before tomorrow's meetings.

It doesn't sound like the kind of job any of us would want – but it's just another school day. And the data shows boys are switching off. It feels, for many, like the equivalent of psychological and educational waterboarding.

This chapter is your education blueprint, helping your son discover meaning, purpose, and satisfaction in education.

School matters

Education matters. Enormously. My advice to every young man I mentor or speak with: get all the education you can. This doesn't have to be formal education, but school really changes the game. Finishing Year 12 adds at least $300,000 in lifetime earnings versus not completing high school.[1] A university education improves outcomes even more. And post-graduate studies amplify earnings and life outcomes further again.

But for many, the idea of even finishing high school is awful. Doing another four to ten years post-school sounds stupefying.

And that's because of basic psychological needs. For so many of our sons, the school environment is need-frustrating rather than need-supportive.

Provocative? Yes. True for all? No. But it is the reality for far too many.

Here's a quick recap of the situation. Boys trail girls in every NAPLAN literacy indicator, with the writing gap widening from 21 points in Year 3 to 36 points by Year 9. Boys are also more likely to be suspended due to behavioural issues. At least three-quarters of suspensions across Australia are male students. In terms of school completion, 77.6% of boys complete high school compared to 85.3% of girls. The boys are dropping out of school. And fewer young men are starting university: 158,103 men commenced in 2024 compared to 252,590 women – with men's participation dropping 6% since 2015 despite population growth. This corresponds to higher numbers of female university graduates. In March 2026, Education Minister Jason Clare called a national enquiry into the gender gap in education, with Opposition Education Minister Julian Leeser offering bipartisan support, saying, 'The evidence on boys' education is compelling and speaks for itself. We are seeing gaps at almost every level.'

At the core, need-support is the fix. But because this is so individualised, this may not feel helpful. Let's break it down and see how it applies to your son.

Relatedness: finding his tribe

If your son doesn't like the people around him, his motivation for school disappears faster than pizza at a party. Friends are oxygen.

For your son to thrive at school, he needs two things: a friend who sees him walk through the school gate and says, 'Hey, come sit with us,' and an adult who knows him by name and shows genuine interest in his life or learning.

Does your son have people he's excited to see at school? Can he be his true self there? Does at least one adult know him by name?

If connection is an issue, there's often low-hanging fruit. Using the conversation principles from Chapter 11 (explore, explain, empower), you can discuss participation in extra-curricular experiences where your son can connect with like-minded peers. Host get-togethers. Have a party because it's Friday. Or the end of term. Find any reason to help him be social, even if it's wildly inconvenient.

Speak to teachers about class placement where he's more likely to connect with peers who share similar interests while still getting the work done. This can be tricky, so tread gently and work with your school collaboratively. And connect with school counsellors who can identify social opportunities if your son is struggling.

When your son feels like he has good connections, he'll choose to be at school.

One of the most consistent questions I receive on this topic relates to single-sex schools. 'Should I send my son to a boys' school or a co-ed school?' I have two answers here. One is black-and-white … and possibly wrong for your son. The other is nuanced, annoying … and probably right.

Here's the black-and-white response. Single-sex schools show the most consistent benefits for girls. Removing boys from the classroom is said to reduce stereotype threat (particularly in maths and science), and it frees girls from the social and attentional costs of mixed-gender dynamics. When I interviewed girls for my book *Miss-Connection*, they consistently told me that boys felt threatening and stifled their participation in school life. Being at an all-girls school, according to the data, allows girls to participate more freely in class and extra-curricular activities (they're more willing to attend a swimming carnival and wear their swimmers, for example) and builds a stronger sense of having academic competence. For boys attending a single-sex school, the research paints a weaker and less consistent picture – and there is a real argument that boys actually benefit from the 'civilising influence' of female peers. Research shows that higher proportions of girls in a classroom improve boys' behaviour and test scores. The important caveat to all of this comes from a landmark 2014 meta-analysis of 184 studies involving 1.6 million students across 21 nations, which found that once selection bias is properly controlled for – accounting for the fact that families who choose single-sex schools tend to be more motivated and resourced – the apparent academic advantages largely dissolve for both sexes.[2]

The second answer has less research behind it, but more individual focus. The school that supports your son's positive relationships and provides access to caring teachers, that he wants to go to (autonomy), and that fits with your lifestyle (and finances) will be the best choice. You could pick the best school in the country on paper, but if your son doesn't click with peers or if he struggles with his teachers, it's not the best school in the country *for him*. The variables we often look to – resources, reputation, and results – overlook the variables that matter more: friends, fit, fun, and philosophy.

Competence: the progress principle

Harvard education professor Teresa Amabile explains that 'the progress principle' is the great driver of interest and motivation.[3] Neurologically, your son's brain is like a slot machine with a design flaw that casino operators would kill for – it gets genuinely high off its own small wins. If your son feels like he's getting better at something, his brain comes alive. Each incremental step forward lights up the dopamine circuit like the local RSL pokies room. The progress principle is neurochemical rocket fuel.

But too many boys are not experiencing progress. They walk into the classroom, sit at their desk, and slump; head goes down onto the table. The teacher starts talking about history, calculus, or the circulatory system, and if the boy's brain doesn't catch the content quickly, the teacher blasts them for staring out the window and disengaging.

For a space shuttle to enter orbit, it must reach 28,000 kilometres an hour. A bullet fired from a handgun travels at about 1200 kilometres an hour. This means the shuttle in orbit travels about 23 times faster than a speeding bullet! In the first ten seconds after lift-off, the shuttle reaches 160 kilometres an hour. After one minute, it's travelling at 1600 kilometres an hour but still isn't free from gravitational pull. It takes 8.5 minutes of sustained burn to achieve orbit velocity.

Too often, your son looks at the lift-off process and says 'Nope'. The idea of putting in 8.5 minutes of sustained effort to reach orbit is awful. If it's work he's not familiar with or doesn't know how to do, he'll baulk. Avoidance is the standard strategy when competence is in question, and a *lot* of what happens at school fits that category.

Let's be clear. Your son *can* do the work. He is capable. But he's got to want to. (This is where competence overlaps with autonomy – and your relationship with him is integral to progress.) When things are tough, encourage him to 'be the space shuttle'. The first moments – getting started – are the hardest. He has to escape the gravitational pull of TikTok, Discord, Instagram, or Fortnite – even the fascinating interior of the fridge! But if your son can push through that first ten seconds, the first minute, and then 8.5 minutes without crashing back to earth, he reaches orbit. The external tanks drop off. He doesn't need massive quantities of fuel anymore. He's found momentum. And that's where real progress happens. It's a need-satisfying experience.

Progress is one of two sources of motivation that will really push him along. The other is structure, which we discussed in Chapter 7. If he comprehends the structure (or system, framework, process, etc) and can just make a start, he'll make progress, feel competent, and begin to value the activity. Motivation deepens. Success and completion are more likely. Engagement increases. And the chances of him finding school worthwhile will lift.

Here's how you can get him into orbit velocity.

- Help him break large tasks into steps.
- Connect learning to his interests.
- Create an environment that makes progress easy. (No screens or other distractions.)

- Teach him that the most powerful word in the English language is 'help'.
- The next most powerful word is 'yet'. (It turns 'I can't do this' into a work in progress, shifting the focus from victimhood to a willingness to get back up and have another crack.)

These practices intersect with relatedness. Your son is going to be more resilient in facing challenges when he has you beside him. Resilience is relational. You can do more push-ups when the personal trainer is encouraging you. You can get more work done when someone is working beside you. And you can push harder into a learning zone where frustration and distress are building up when you have a loving, supportive parent beside you, offering presence and help or guidance.

Autonomy: finding the 'why'

Perhaps the most useful explanation for the challenge boys are having in school sits in the autonomy space. Recall those key words that describe what happens when motivation is at a deep-enough level to support action: endorsement, identifying the value, buying in. This might be the very heart of our education gender gap.

My Year 9 daughter asked me if I knew what a 'surd' was. I laughed and made a comment about it sounding like a toilet joke. She told me it was a mathematical term. I confirmed I didn't know what a surd was. She then explained she had asked two teachers at school the same question and they didn't know. The only adult who knew was her maths teacher. Then she asked the critical question: 'If three well-educated adults can't tell me what a surd is even though they're functioning well in life, why am I learning it? I don't like this. I don't want to do it. And … it seems pointless.'

Some argue that it doesn't matter what you're learning. It's that you're learning how to learn. Rubbish. If you're going to learn, which is the default for our human brains anyway, let's make sure what you're learning has value.

Your son doesn't need easier work – he needs work that matters. When a boy can connect his learning to solving actual problems, building something tangible, or making a genuine contribution, his motivation shifts from external compliance to internal drive.

Autonomy doesn't mean your son has unlimited choice. Sometimes he just needs to know why something matters and agree that it does.

Assess your son's sense of choice.

- Does your son feel he has some choice and control over his learning experience?
- Does he understand and 'buy' the reasons behind school rules and expectations?
- Does he have opportunities to pursue topics that genuinely interest him?
- Does your son understand why he's learning what he's learning?

Encourage him to talk with his teachers about allowing some choice in topics, formats, or approaches. Sometimes this is effective. Other times teachers have limited power to say yes. Help him understand the 'why' behind requirements. And model respect for his perspective. If you listen to his concerns seriously, it's easier to work collaboratively on solutions.

When school isn't working

I hated school. And I failed. My relationships at school were poor. I don't think I'm overstating it to suggest I felt I was one of the most unpopular kids in my grade – for six years. I was placed into the 'dumb class' (back when we still had streaming) and so I thought I was stupid. But mostly, I wanted to be a radio announcer. I'd spent time in radio stations talking with on-air presenters. Few, if any, had completed high school. But they had the coolest job ever (in my mind). They were making good livings. So I saw no purpose in school. I didn't buy the need for an education. If I could have a radio career, school was irrelevant.

Your son's struggles with school may be different to mine, but regardless, the traditional school model is not working for many boys. If you've spent time discussing relationships, seeking academic support, and most importantly discovering whether he can identify value in his educational experience, I predict you'll find where the challenge lies fairly quickly. Hopefully there are simple remedies.

If there are no simple paths forward, the good news is there are alternatives that can lead to strong educational outcomes and career success. The central thing for your son is that he is productively engaged in something that matters to him. This is the whole box and dice – the entire game. If he is being asked to do something that doesn't matter to him, he'll avoid it. He'll be unproductive. He'll mope, sook, and avoid – usually with a screen in hand.

If your son is really struggling at school and you've exhausted your options, consider these alternatives.

- **Vocational schools (Year 10+):** Five weeks of school, five weeks of industry placement every term. Hands-on learning, real-world experience, access to apprenticeships. We placed one of our children into a school like this and, while still not without its challenges, it changed everything for the better. The schooling was less demanding but more relevant. And the work placement felt purposeful and offered direction.

- **School-based apprenticeships**: Begin trade qualifications while completing Year 12. Do three days of school, one day of TAFE, and one day of paid work, and transition to the workforce and a trade qualification. Once again, there's a reduction in academic emphasis, but daily work feels fulfilling and purposeful.

- **Distance education:** Full curriculum at your own pace. It's good for athletes, performers, and children who need reduced social pressure. Be aware work will be online and can feel isolating.

- **TAFE programs:** Practical, hands-on learning environments with smaller class sizes.

All of these tend to be low- or no-cost for families (although prices will vary depending on what you're enrolling your son in). And most metro and central areas are well serviced. This may not feel like your ideal, but the goal is completion – not conformity.

A NEET boy – that is, a boy who is Not in Education, Employment, or Training – is a boy who is at risk of languishing or struggling. These are our non-thriving boys – and they need something to live for. Education, employment, and training generally provide these things because they help boys feel manly. If they're in education, employment, and training (and it's purposeful/meaningful to them), they'll feel like they're on the path to being a better provider, a useful partner, and a contributor to society.

The take-home message

Getting your son through school can feel like your very own Everest. But there are flexible options, and people and organisations who can support you. Central to his success, however, will be connections, competence, and a sense of purpose. Purpose *is* the pathway. If his education or training means something to him, any education motivational issues will resolve.

If purpose and motivation for education is your biggest struggle, the next chapter – about work and career choices – will be just what you need to guide your son through this tricky stage.

18 Career plans

How to help your son find direction

'So, what do you want to be when you leave school?'

It's a standard and common question that people love to ask. Most people think it's fair game to ask it. Wharton psychologist Adam Grant doesn't agree.

In his book *Think Again*, Grant argues that asking young people what they want to be nudges them towards identity foreclosure: locking prematurely onto a career before they've had the life experience to know what they actually value. When who we are becomes tied to what we do, he argues, we stop exploring and start defending. We commit to paths we chose too young, and we stay on them long after we should have changed course.[1]

And the numbers bear this out. Surveys consistently find that only around one in ten adults are actually working in the career they dreamed of as teenagers – which matches almost exactly what I see when I ask parents in my audiences to put up their hands if they're doing what they thought they'd be doing when they left school. About one in ten hands goes up. The rest? Life took them somewhere they never planned, and for most of them that turned out just fine.

Boys are particularly vulnerable to the pressure of this question. Underneath the words 'What do you want to do after school, for the rest of your life?' they hear pressure: 'How will you provide?' They feel overwhelmed: there are so many choices. For some, it invites them to plant a flag – and boys often feel compelled to look certain even when they're not.

In my conversations with young men, I consistently hear confusion about career decisions. I tell them they're exactly where they should be right now. They're not supposed to know all the answers yet. (Most adults are still trying to figure it out.) They need to give it time.

Take the pressure off your son in terms of career choice. He's not supposed to know what he'll do for the rest of his life while he's still at school – or even as he starts life after school. Even if he does know what his plans are, he'll probably change his mind.

However, there are six principles he can start employing now to find more satisfaction at school and to prepare for career success, and one big thing not to do.

Get all the education you can

I am pro university. Heavily. I loved my university experience and value it as one of the most important things I did – and note, I didn't go to university until I was 27 (after a year at TAFE … more on that shortly). University graduation is associated with positive financial, health, emotional, and relational outcomes. It's genuinely valuable despite recent arguments about the cost and usefulness. If your son doesn't do well at school, university will still be an option (should he identify the value in it and possess the depth of motivation uni requires). Alternative pathways, bridging courses, and a range of other options are available at almost any stage for him to make the shift to tertiary education. And once *he* is making the decision for reasons that make sense to him, he'll be able to achieve.

But education isn't just university degrees. It's any learning that builds capability. Trade certifications, apprenticeships, international experience that teaches languages, working on farms in regional areas. They're all education. They all count. Getting certified in something is a powerful strategy that makes your son more viable economically and socially.

I've met parents who feel that if their child doesn't go to university, they've failed. Let's dispel that now. Only around 30% of Aussie adults have a university degree.[2] Plenty of people are doing great and making valuable contributions without one. Further, Australia faces decades-long trade shortages. We have massive opportunities for young men willing to learn practical skills in a trade. Add in the generational transfer of mum-and-dad businesses in the coming decades. There are countless successful small-business owners who face the prospect of closing up their shops. They'd much rather sell them on to young business-minded people who can jump-start their lives by taking on a pre-existing, valuable enterprise.

I have two sons-in-law with trades (an electrician and a builder – how handy!) and they're thriving because they pursued education through trades. They didn't enjoy school and were checking out. They wanted to be active, use their hands (and their brains), and start earning. And, in the eyes of my daughters, these young men made themselves viable by getting certified, earning money, developing competence, and demonstrating they could do work that was purposeful and made a contribution.

Build range over depth

Many parents push their children to make a career or study decision, lock in, and go hard. But that's rarely what *we've* done, and it's not what works for most people, particularly over the long term.

The average worker changes careers between three and seven times, and they switch jobs every 2.7 years.[3] That sounds a lot until you consider the maths. We're talking a new career for your son every ten years (believable, and not that scary), and 15 or more jobs across the five decades he'll be working. Demanding your son choose his life's work at 17 (or 15) makes no sense.

David Epstein, author of *Range*, found that generalists often outperform specialists over time.[4] Encourage your son to try anything that comes his way if it piques his interest until somewhere between 25 and 30. If he doesn't like it, he can find something new. If he likes it, more opportunities will develop and he should say yes. After the age of 30, he'll start to become very clear on his areas of strength and interest and can start saying no to anything that doesn't progress him.

If that sounds too broad, there's another way to look at it. Imagine your son is interested in engineering. He should pursue that, whether through TAFE or university (depending on his school scores). Perhaps partway through his studies he'll receive an email offering an overseas experience, or a chance to study elsewhere. Maybe he'll be asked to write a piece for a trade publication and discover he loves the creativity of writing an essay on a topic he cares about, or he'll have a business idea that combines his newfound engineering skills with a hobby he had as a boy. Building range over depth means that practical experience across as many areas as possible opens up new opportunities no one has exploited yet. This leads to my next idea that, over time, can allow your son options.

Develop your 'and'

Scott Adams created the cartoon *Dilbert* not because he was the world's best artist or funniest writer, but because he combined two things he was reasonably good at: drawing and humour. He argues if you can be in the top 25% of one thing (in his case, drawing) and the top 25% in another thing (humour), you'll find a niche … and success.[5]

Most successful people excel at this intersection strategy – being very good at two things beats being exceptional at one. The combination creates unique value specialists can't replicate. There doesn't need to be any pressure around this. It's probably going to take years. Perhaps decades. We don't need to rush this stuff. Your son's 'and' may evolve as he pursues interests while building a foundation in an area where it's easy to gain employment. For example, the electrician specialising in heritage buildings, the accountant serving creative businesses, the nurse developing healthcare software: magic happens at intersections. I met a guy from the Netherlands at an Indonesian surf resort who hated the corporate life but knew about software in hospitality and had discovered a passion for surfing. He quit his corporate job and began developing software for surf resorts to handle bookings and customer experience. I had a radio career for a decade after school. I learned how to present, entertain, and communicate complex ideas concisely. When I quit radio I felt that I had wasted a decade. But I took my media learnings and applied them to communicating psychology.

Master character over skills

Employers consistently rank character traits as more important than technical skills.[6] Your son needs five non-negotiables:

- reliability (show up on time, every time);
- initiative (see what needs doing and do it without being asked);
- communication (look people in the eye, hold conversations);
- adaptability ('It's not my job' kills careers); and
- integrity (do the right thing even when no one is watching).

These traits are perpetually scarce. James Clear, author of *Atomic Habits*, notes: 'You can carve out a very good career simply by being the most reliable person on the team.'[7]

Work with excellence

Silicon Valley didn't emerge randomly – critical mass of talent drives innovation. As a radio announcer, my performance developed massively in a capital-city market compared with regional markets. Your son will develop greater competence and passion for his work when he seeks environments where he's surrounded by people better than him. Higher standards, better resources, expanded networks. Whether university, apprenticeships, or entry-level jobs, proximity to excellence accelerates development faster than talent. This typically (though not always) means moving to major cities, working in larger organisations, and seeking out mentors to accelerate development.

Provide value

All the money your son will ever need already exists. The trouble for him is it's in other people's bank accounts. Your son's job is to develop an appropriate, ethical strategy to get it from their bank account to his. And the answer is: solve problems people will pay for.

A lawn-mowing or car-detailing business solves a problem. It adds value. People will pay for it. A software solution for booking guests at a surf retreat in Indonesia solves a problem, adds value, and people will pay for it (and it will fund a tropical surf lifestyle!).

A clothing brand that is practical and edgy; an ability to develop business strategy; an understanding of personal finance; the list is endless. Career success and financial stability are based on your son's ability to add value – to be a bonus – in the lives of others.

All of the ideas here require more than just the skill to program or work or design. They also require sales and marketing skills, creative skills, a willingness to take risks, hiring and firing skills, and more. This is partly why entrepreneurs are often older, with broad skill sets and experience. They've gained education. They've had experience and developed range. They've found an 'and'. They've matured and developed the characteristics and discipline that make them stand out. They've often worked with excellent people who have elevated their vision.

But not everyone wants to (or should be) an entrepreneur. Adding value to a business increases your employability, income, and security. Employers are desperate for employees who are a bonus.

Be careful pursuing passions

There's an irony in what I'm going to say here. I'm about to give you advice I've ignored twice in my career. First, I chased and was successful in a media career when everyone said it was 'a lottery'. Second, I chose an entrepreneurial path when I had the potential of a stable academic career. Both times, following passion over practicality worked brilliantly.

But I don't advise your son to 'follow his passion'. I get to write this chapter because I succeeded. The hundreds of wannabe radio hosts who didn't make it? They're not writing career-advice books. The countless people who wanted to create a successful business? Stats on business failure are shocking. Writing books and speaking for a living? Only the top 1% of books sell more than 50,000 copies.[8] Those are low odds. It's the same (or worse) for the arts, sports, podcasting, online influencing, and more – the 'vanity' careers.

We hear about the success stories. But this creates survivorship bias – we celebrate the exceptions and forget the rule. The advice that works for 1% of people becomes the standard advice given to 100% of people. Most who follow passions fail quietly, often changing professions or living in financially challenging circumstances while they keep chasing the dream. That's why my 'boring' advice is more credible, not less. I've lived both sides.

The 'follow your passion' mantra has three fatal flaws. First, many boys have no clear passion. They feel like there's something wrong with them when adults keep asking about their 'calling' and they have no idea what that means. Ask a boy how he's going to do something purposeful and make a contribution to the world, and he will go blank. It feels way too big. Second, when they do identify passion, it's usually vanity careers – gaming, influencing, content creation. Only 2% of professional actors make a living from their craft. The 97th percentile of YouTube creators earn $15,000 yearly.[9] These are lottery odds, rather than career strategies. Third, passion is unreliable. It changes. The kid passionate about marine biology at 16 might discover by age 30 that he hates being wet, sandy, and salty. The kid who wants to be a personal trainer at 19 might decide early mornings and late evenings don't work at 33 with two young kids. Building your future on teenage enthusiasm is shortsighted.

If your son knows what he wants and is passionate, he should go for it. Music, a restaurant, a sport career ... go for it. But rather than pursuing a passion, I'd contend many boys – particularly those who are unsure – should be consistent, try a bunch of things (range), and find an area where they can be economically viable and do something that is generally satisfying. If your son chooses fields where most people who want to find employment have been able to, he's likely to be successful simply because he has a productive job. Then I'd encourage him to be better than 95% of people in his industry. Do a business degree and be better than 95% of the cohort. Get a trade and be better than 95% of other tradies. In so doing, he'll become an industry leader. He'll be sought out for his expertise. People will laud him for his knowledge and experience. He'll acquire the recognition and reward of excellence, and will probably find that passion follows his competence and consistency.

I know this may sound harsh. We usually celebrate passion and purpose, so telling your son to choose the boring route feels almost un-Australian. But boring doesn't mean meaningless or dull. It means sustainable. Vanity careers promise everything and deliver for only the very few. Boring careers provide sustainable success for those who show up and excel. And it's surprising just how passionate people can become about almost anything, from stonemasonry to HVAC, from landscape design to shipping logistics.

Finding passion

If your son follows these fundamentals, he's going to learn a lot, be around great people, develop competence and mastery, have a range of experience … and in so doing, he will likely become passionate about what he's doing.

Now for the counter-example – because this stuff is complex, and there are no guarantees.

My friend Rich worked as a forklift driver on the docks after high school. He was incredibly good at it – top 5% good. He was so good that he was approached by a criminal consortium (the mafia, literally), to do some extra work on the side for them so he could make his earnings a little more … lucrative. Rich told me he stopped driving forklifts, not because of the mafia, but because ultimately the work didn't feel fulfilling and purposeful. For many people, it's not enough to just be good at something. It must matter. Purpose and meaning are vital ingredients to having a great career. Just because you're competent doesn't mean you should pursue it. Autonomy matters too. Rich went on to find a way into university study and a stunningly successful 50-year academic career. It worked out well, but it started unseriously, culminating in a life of influence and purpose.

The advice in this chapter is oriented towards safety. Viability. Risk-reduction. The sure thing. But there is a question that has driven me and the most inspiring people I've known throughout my life that is worth considering: 'Do you love it?'

After school I chose radio and enjoyed a successful decade-long career. By my late-20s, I was a father of two. My marriage was not strong. My parenting was a disaster. And I was in crisis. Moreover, I had fallen out of love with radio, and it was clashing with my sense of identity – my values. (No surprise: motivation was shallow when this happened.)

Because I felt so incompetent at home, I wanted to progress. I became passionate about parenting, quit my radio career, and pursued qualifications in psychology. This meant a year at TAFE, completing four years of undergraduate psychology, and then earning a doctorate (a further 3.5 years). The process was incredibly need-supportive – and hence motivating. My relationships were improving as I learned my subject. I felt an ongoing sense of progress. And I saw the value of the learning. I was buying the purpose for what I did.

My short-lived stint as a university tutor and lecturer ended because I didn't see the value, and because I felt more competent speaking and writing to help others. And the next 15 to 20 years was built on creating a more need-supportive environment in which to work.

The take-home message

If your son follows these fundamentals, he's going to learn a lot, be around great people, develop a high level of competence, have a load of experience … and in so doing, he will likely become passionate about what he's doing. Passion doesn't drive success. Success drives passion. When your son has successful experiences, he'll discover he is passionate about the place his success comes from.

Passion is a luxury that follows competence, not a prerequisite for it. Choose boring, get good, build from there.

19 The gap-year advantage

Why stepping back before university might be your son's smartest move

In one of my favourite blog posts ever, Brett McKay, founder of website and podcast The Art of Manliness, describes famous men of previous generations. He describes that before Steve McQueen's 18th birthday, the future movie star had worked on a farm, joined a circus, sold pens at a travelling carnival, hitchhiked across the US, worked as a lumberjack, laboured on a chain gang, served in the Merchant Marine (underage) and joined the Marine Corps. One more time for emphasis: he did it all *before* he turned 18. Sean Connery served in the Royal Navy as a teenager, worked as a milkman, lifeguard, truck driver, and once took on six gang members single-handedly, fighting them and earning their respect. Jack London tramped around the US by rail, sailed the Pacific aboard a seal-hunting schooner, and ventured into Western Canada's Klondike region seeking gold – all before turning 22.[1]

Sure, there's some selection bias. But the stories are compelling, and a stark contrast to the experiences of many of today's young men. Moreover, these weren't cherry-picked celebrities with exceptional backgrounds. Many young men of previous generations accumulated rich, varied experiences – often physically demanding, occasionally dangerous – that built their capacity and character. They discovered their capabilities by testing their boundaries in real-world contexts. They mastered challenges, built relationships and steered their lives volitionally. Their histories document purpose, satisfaction, and happiness.

Today's boys encounter a different landscape. Regulatory constraints, safety concerns, parental anxiety, supervised schedules, and the need to win the rat-race have crowded out the space for autonomous and healthy exploration and risk-taking. As McKay notes, contemporary youth follow predictable, sanitised paths with few opportunities for consequential choices and real-world testing. Perhaps, as he suggests, our youth today are 'the least interesting generation'.

Is that what we're going for, though? Do we want our boys to have interesting lives, or successful ones? My contention is they're not mutually exclusive, but we behave like they are. Like a river diverted into a concrete channel, we've contained boys' natural energy into narrower, 'safer' paths. We have sacrificed exploration and experience for consistency, and strategic planning for 'fulfilled potential'. Consequently, something valuable has been lost.

In our last chapter, we discussed career decisions. In this chapter I'm going to make the argument for a gap year – or two or three, or even five – after school. It's provocative. But it deserves consideration.

Mention 'gap year' and some parents recoil in shock. Kids need to get out in front, they respond. It's a race and everyone's sprinting for the finish line. We must help our children achieve their potential!

A couple of points: first, there is no finish line when it comes to adult life. Year 12 represents the end of compulsory schooling, but beyond that, who is racing and what for? Second, this idea of fulfilling potential makes no sense. Have you fulfilled yours? Have you capped out, done all you can, developed yourself to your fullest? Are you now maxed out in terms of growth, learning, and possibility? And even if you really do believe that you have fulfilled your potential, did you achieve it by 18? Stop putting that pressure on your son. Third, university is the focus of this chapter, but it's not essential. Education and career success take many forms, and university is just one pathway – albeit an effective and positive one.

We *should* have high expectations for our boys. They need to work out where they're going and what they're doing. But sending them straight into university may be the least useful way to help them hit the heights we hope they'll find.

My provocation: at least 80% to 90% of kids should *not* go straight to university. They're not ready for a university education – and I say this as a former university lecturer. Most students I taught weren't ready. University is for adults, not kids, and 18-year-olds are still developing the neurological maturity and architecture needed for independent learning and decision-making.

I'm in good company. Professor Laurence Steinberg, the world's leading adolescence researcher, confirmed this when he told me a gap year is a wise choice 'if it's spent in the right way. It's got to be productive. A gap year is not for sitting on the couch watching YouTube. It might be working instead of going to school, volunteering, starting your own business – there are lots of productive, interesting things you can do.'[2] Goals and direction matter.

Researchers Jonathan Haidt and Greg Lukianoff encourage gap years too: 'We don't think 18-year-olds should be on campus … a year or two of some sort of activity away from the home' is beneficial.[3] In their book *The Coddling of the American Mind*, they identified that the maturity and growth that comes from a year of learning, development, and experience before university almost always yields benefits for students when they resume study. These men are two of the most relevant and iconic researchers globally and they are pointing to gap years as productive and attractive.

Gap years are the norm in Nordic countries like Denmark and Norway, and Germans are increasingly encouraging a year or two away from full-time education. South Korea, Israel, Singapore, Finland, Switzerland, Austria, Sweden, and Greece all require military or civil service between school and study for several months to nearly two years. It's common. (I think this would be incredibly good for Australian youth too and wish our leaders would get behind it.) A gap year has clear advantages over the approach we take in Australia.

Despite these facts, many parents are shocked when I suggest gap years. 'What if he never goes back to university?' 'What about scholarships and academic momentum?' 'What if he falls behind?'

The research is overwhelming

Research shows 90% of gap-year students enrol in university within a year of taking their gap year.[4] And as for scholarships, most universities allow deferred enrolment for gap years. Sure, your son might be a year or two older than his cohort, but it's not a race. And that extra year or two of maturity will almost certainly play to his advantage.

The data is compelling. Research involving over 900 first-year students at Sydney University revealed taking a year off between high school and university had a positive effect on students' motivation and performance in those first semesters at university.[5] My hypothesis: a year off gives a young person the chance to think about what they value. If they value and endorse more education, returning to study feels inspiring and motivating. It gives them purpose. It is need-satisfying.

Australian data shows that high school students who deferred university entry and took a gap year were equally likely to complete their degree as those who entered straight from high school. Gap-year students showed significantly improved academic performance when they went to university, with the strongest improvement for students who had applied with lower grades when they left high school.[6]

Gap-year students consistently outperform their peers academically, even when that time off exceeds a year, and most gap-year students feel like it increases their likelihood of completing their degree.[7] Maturation, insight, and motivation develop during gap years so that when they return to study some years later, they are far more likely to do well.

Ninety-eight percent of US and Canadian gap-year participants say their gap year increased their maturity, 97% say it improved their self-confidence, and 82% felt it gave them a competitive advantage when applying to college and for jobs.[8]

Slowing down speeds up success.

What a productive gap year looks like

A well-planned gap year isn't a binge-drinking 12-month holiday or an extended gaming marathon. I'm not advocating for that (although much of the gap-year research I've reviewed is agnostic on what kids do during their 'time off'). A gap year, ideally, is a strategic pause in formalised education that builds maturity, discipline, and purpose.

If you're open to your son taking a gap year, the following blueprint is my recommendation.

Work full-time or close to it

Real paid employment teaches responsibility, time management, and the value of money. Whether it's construction, retail, landscaping, changing tyres, furniture removals, working in a call centre, providing tech support, or selling clothes in a retail outlet, the experience of showing up every day builds character. And minimum wage is fine – the financial lessons are powerful and the motivation for further education will likely increase. Your job is not to support your son to 'find himself', but if he's willing to put in the work, you can be his number one cheerleader. If he's not, deeper conversations about his motivation, his environment, his basic psychological needs, and his output and productivity will be helpful. Now that he's an adult, it's reasonable to expect he will be mature enough to engage with you meaningfully. Remember, deep down he wants to do well. Sometimes he might just feel stuck.

Save for something meaningful

Whether it's a car, house deposit, or international travel, having a concrete financial goal teaches delayed gratification and planning. Have this conversation early so he doesn't blow it all on gaming, gambling, or beers.

Pay board or rent

For a son who still lives at home, paying board teaches responsibility and contribution and important lessons in budgeting. It might be a small sum – always lower than market rate if parents can afford it – or a percentage of his pay.

Pro tip: if you don't need the money, put it into a savings account for him and return it to put towards a big trip or a house deposit (or as a marriage gift). Don't tell him. It makes a wonderful surprise.

Gain certification in something valuable

Whether it's first aid, forklift operation, hospitality certifications, or trade-related qualifications, additional credentials stack up over time and demonstrate initiative to future employers or universities. Plus, they'll often give him a pay bump. If he can pay for it himself, encourage him to. If he's baulking, tell him to pay for it and you'll pay him back once he completes the course (or offer a 50% refund, depending on your budget position).

Volunteer in the community

SES, parkrun, aged care, fire brigade, surf club, churches, charities, supporting refugees, manning the phones for a charity, feeding the homeless – there are countless ways to contribute. Volunteering builds empathy, develops networks, and shifts perspective; plus it provides massive wellbeing benefits.

Cool stat: students who perform voluntary community service are 19% more likely to graduate from tertiary education, and it also improves long-term health-related behaviours.[9]

Take an Australian Defence Force gap year

This might be one of my favourite gap-year options. The Australian Defence Force (ADF) offers a compelling opportunity for school-leavers: a 12-month paid gap-year program for school-leavers aged 18 to 24 who've completed high school.[10] After that introductory year of initial military training, participants can continue with ADF work if they choose. Leo, a graduate of the ADF gap-year program, told me that 'the structure, discipline, and responsibility change your life'. The program pays extremely well for a role that requires no qualifications: an amount close to the median Australian full-time wage, plus 16% superannuation and other benefits. This is a terrific start for a kid who's unsure where he's going at 18.

The maturity dividend

Gap-year students develop what psychologists call 'career maturity' – the ability to make informed and confident decisions about pursuing careers and education.[11] Many students report that their gap year instilled a deeper appreciation and desire for learning when it came time to attend university. A small study of medical students found nearly all who had taken a gap year (77 out of 79) would advise current school-leavers to take one.[12] They consistently credited work–life experiences from their gap years for enhanced adaptability, patient-interface skills, greater maturity, empathy, humility, and patience.

A gap year potentially supports all three basic psychological needs: relatedness (real-world relationships through networking, travel experience), competence (developing work skills or volunteering), and autonomy (choosing how to spend the year). After a gap year, a young man who has worked for eight months and volunteered at a homeless shelter on weekends approaches his business and economics degree or his psychology or social work degree with very different motivation (and wisdom) than his peers who enrolled straight from school.

Consider these statements that I heard when I lectured at university: one was said by recent school-leavers, the other by mature-aged students. See if you can pick who was more likely to say which statement:

- 'I've just got to get through uni so I can get on with my life.'
- 'I've got to get uni through me so I can make more of my life – and give more of my life.'

If you picked the mature-aged students for the second statement, you'd be correct.

When school-leavers asked a question during my psychology lectures, it was often, 'Will this be on the test?' When mature-aged students raised their hand it was because they wanted to go deeper on what we were discussing: their goal wasn't to pass, it was to learn. (And school-leavers rolled their eyes at the 'old' students who asked questions ...)

The take-home message

A productive gap year is a wellbeing amplifier. The competence, confidence, and capacity your son develops will set him up with an advantage over his peers. The gap year provides an extra year (or three) of neurological maturation and pushes big decisions down the road to when he'll have greater clarity because of life experience that stretches beyond the school fence. It gives him range. He might learn 'that one more thing'. A gap year offers an opportunity to do the inner work that can't happen if you're drifting aimlessly on a path someone else chose for you or that you felt compelled to take.

If he's lost, it gives him time. If he comes back unsure about direction, reassure him that's normal. So long as he continues to do *something* he'll develop range, breadth, and experience. Before he discovers what he will do for a career, encourage him to do more experimentation and exploration. Too often, boys are told to 'make a decision and get on with it'. This is poor advice. Range and breadth are more likely to lead to long-term commitment once he has discovered what he wants to do. Then he can shift from experimentation and exploration to locking in.

As I've said, I've found that it's not as useful to listen to what people say as it is to look at what they do. In my family, we do gap years. My gap-decade set me up for a better life and I'm grateful for the years of experience before I returned to formal education. At the time of publication, my fourth child was on her gap year. Each of her three older siblings also took gap years. At the ages of 25, 22, and 21, each returned to study and was completing a university degree (locking down commitments after some experimentation and changing of minds), and were passing with the highest honours. The gap years, in every case, served them well and set them up for maturity and success. (Be aware, you may find you're supporting your child financially until they are well into their 20s, although a gap year *could* short-circuit that.)

If your son is currently in Year 12, he has been at school for 13 years. Consider what it would look like to give him a year or two (or more) to discover what school was preparing him for. It might be university. It could be a trade. He might become a business owner and entrepreneur. You don't need the answers now and neither does he. Slowing it down with a gap year can offer clarity and support for everyone in the family, particularly your son. Have a conversation with him aligned with the principles we outlined in Chapter 11. Explore. Explain. Empower.

The boy who emerges from a productive gap year isn't just older; he's wiser, more motivated, and more capable of living a life of purpose and making the most of whatever path he chooses next.

20 The finish line

What it really means to raise a good boy into a good man

I have learned that it is the weak who are cruel, and that gentleness is to be expected only from the strong.

Leo Rosten[1]

When the fictitious English soccer coach Ted Lasso delightedly sprang onto our screens in 2020 with his big moustache, folksy humour, and kind character, we saw and fell in love with something rarely seen on television: a surprisingly human, fully fleshed-out man. He didn't swear. He wasn't neurotic. He didn't have anger issues. Wounded and prone to anxiety from losing his father to suicide as a teen, he was nevertheless thoughtful, articulate, and approachable. Lasso was, in a word, 'kind'.

If you've watched the show, you know that, despite being a soccer coach, Lasso didn't coach soccer. He left that to his coaching staff. Instead, Ted Lasso coached *character*. Lasso demonstrated what it looks like when a man's primary goal is to leave people better than he found them. He sought – not always successfully; ask his ex-wife – to be a bonus in every life he touched *despite* his anxiety issues and his agonising divorce and public humiliation.

Further, this likeable American grid-iron-turned-football coach wasn't obsessed with what most coaches focus on most: winning. When asked to define success, Lasso humbly stated: 'Success isn't about the wins and losses. It's about helping these young fellas become the best versions of themselves on and off the field.'[2]

In those two sentences, Lasso captured what we've been exploring for this entire book: the essence of healthy masculine development. Not domination. Not competition at all costs. Not toxic self-reliance. But growth, connection, and positive impact. Helping those around him feel safer and stronger. Being a bonus.

This represents a revolutionary shift. Instead of measuring manhood by conquest, consumption, or control, we can measure it by contribution. Instead of asking, 'What can I get from others?' we ask, 'What can I give to others?' It's not just *a* model. It's *the* model. Our goal is to teach our sons to become the best versions of themselves. When our sons embrace this mindset they create a better world. They break cycles of disconnection and entitlement that damage so many men. This is what it means to provide surplus value. This is what it means to help others feel safer and stronger. This is what it means to be, in the clearest sense, a good man.

Throughout this book, I've emphasised that individual boys are not the problem. They are, in many ways, casualties of a society still working out how to nurture them correctly. But society can change. And we're the ones to change it – in our families and by our examples. As Richard Reeves noted, masculinity must be taught, learned, and, above all, shown: 'boys believe their eyes more than their ears. When the job is done well, men know they are needed, and for what.'[3] That's our job: to show them what healthy masculinity looks like. Our boys need fewer critics and judges, and more good role models.

One caring adult

In 1955, on the Hawaiian island of Kauai, psychologist Emmy Werner embarked on what would become one of the most illuminating studies of human resilience ever conducted.[4] Kauai's population was facing significant challenges. Nearly one-third of the families in this community lived in poverty. Many parents had minimal education. There were intergenerational challenges around alcohol and other drugs. Unemployment was a problem too.

Fascinated by why some children thrived despite adversity while others collapsed under its weight, Werner tracked every single baby born in that Kauai community that year: 698 infants in total. Werner and her team would follow these children's lives for over 40 years, creating a never-before-seen window into human development from birth until middle age.

Emmy Werner's landmark study identified several protective factors that promoted resilience in children. They're applicable as we raise our sons. The most crucial factor: having at least one stable, caring adult in their lives focused on helping them feel connection – to know they matter, *no matter what*. Often it wasn't a parent. Sometimes it was a teacher, a church leader, a sports coach, or a relative. But that one person – that one caring adult who was there no matter what – was the critical element.

Boys thrive when they have great relationships with safe, healthy adults in their lives – particularly you. And to have that great relationship with your son requires time together – and conversations. Most of the time you'll drop the agenda and find yourself listening, soaking him up and delighting in the man he's becoming. It's all about connection. T-I-M-E.

There are other times you'll have an agenda. You'll be proactive. You'll address something you know is coming up in his life. Or you'll be responding to the latest drama, crisis, or emergency. The chapters in this book should be helpful guides when these conversations are required. And while we haven't covered everything, you will find yourself drawing on the ideas as you address other problems that arise.

Making time for connection

There's one final idea to highlight.

As each of our children has approached the age of 16, Kylie and I have offered them a treat. 'Around your 16th birthday, we'd like to take you away somewhere for a few nights. Just you and us.' Our birthday child can choose any location within a three- or four-hour flight away. Before our trip, we brief our child on the purpose of the time away: to have important conversations. Fun is important and we lock in experiences. Celebration is important. This *is* their birthday gift, after all. But 16 is a key moment in their development from child to adult. At 16 they're thinking about life after high school. Romantic interests may be developing. They're working, gaining independence, and thinking about the world and their future in ways they never have before.

Arriving at our celebration location, we map out a clear agenda and arrange time for important conversations. Conversation one: careers, schooling, and finance. Conversation two: romance, relationships, consent, and intimacy. In our third discussion: physical health, including making healthy choices with diet and exercise, and discussing alcohol and other drugs. Finally, our fourth big discussion: beliefs, values, and things of a deeper, more spiritual and religious nature. We talk about purpose in life, service, contribution, and ensuring the most important factors and priorities are never at the mercy of the least.

Each of these discussions is a dance, back and forth. Our child feeling seen, heard, and valued is at the heart of it. We explore their experience and perspective, explain what we would prioritise for them, and listen some more. Eventually we empower them to set goals in each of these domains that will support a good life, and we ask them how they want us to support them. They are *their* goals, after all. Not every family will have the means to go on a holiday for such an occasion, but you can do a different version of this that suits your family. The important thing is that you talk – and listen. We cannot leave our children's development to chance. Meaningful conversations are at the heart of their growth.

The message every boy needs to hear

In a world that too often either demonises boys or dismisses their struggles, we are the ones who must be their greatest supporters. Fewer fault-finders. More advocates.

Our boys are not the problem. They're the solution. And with the right guidance and example – with *your* guidance and example – they will grow into men who make the world better and help those around them feel safer and stronger. They'll be the bonus in the lives of everyone they touch. Can we help them be the best versions of themselves? The data and the principles in this book give you every shot.

Inspired in part by Ted Lasso's definition of success, and Emmy Werner's research into the need for one caring adult in boys' lives, I close now with the key message I want your son to hear – from you.

> You matter. You matter so much.
>
> Nothing – no mistake you make and nothing you ever do – will be bigger than our love for you.
>
> You can come to us at any time for anything. We're here for you.
>
> There is no one like you in all the world. The world needs you, and the best you can offer it.
>
> Your job is simple: work out how to give more than you take. Be a bonus.
>
> Our job is simple too. We have to support you to get there and be an example of that very thing we ask of you – to leave others feeling safer and stronger; to be a bonus.
>
> Try stuff. Get at it. Smile. Have a crack. But always make sure you're helping the people around you feel safer and stronger.
>
> You've got this. I believe in you. I love you. No. Matter. What.

In the end, raising healthy, happy boys who become strong, caring, healthy, contributing men comes down to one thing: love.

Not the soft, permissive love that avoids difficult conversations and boundaries and allows kids to abrogate ownership, accountability, and responsibility. But the fierce, protective love that says, 'I see you. I accept you. And I believe in you enough to help you become the best person you can be.'

This is serious work, helping these fellas become the best version of themselves. It's not easy. But it is possible. And it begins with you.

Acknowledgements

I began this book with a dedication to my nephew, Logan Steinwede. We lost him to suicide when he was 20 years old. It tore our hearts out.

The message of this book is the message I wish Loges could have lived – for many decades to come. The tragedy is that he can't.

To Karina, Jaxson, Phoenix, Paris, Jet, and Teanu – I love you. I hope this book honours Logan and offers something lasting in remembrance of someone we all loved and miss every day.

There was a second dedication – to my dad.

My dad gave me life, and then spent his life showing me how to live it well. The goodness, generosity, and love he modelled is woven into every page of this book. This one's for you, Dad. I love you.

*

To write a book about boys and masculinity is the most daunting project I've ever taken on. But it's needed. And the time is now. Writing a book like this is a lonely pursuit, but it's been made so much better because of the generosity and skin-in-the-game approach so many collaborators and supporters have offered me.

I extend great globs of gratitude to experts who were generous in their conversations (or emails) with me and who shared their wisdom freely. Melissa Abu-Gazaleh from Top Blokes gave in-depth, boots-on-the-ground insights that enriched much of what is in these pages. Marshall Ballantine-Jones and Maree Crabbe provided insights into the world of pornography that we'd all rather not know but really need to. Michael Flood shared concepts of masculinity that broadened my perspective. Man Box researchers Matt Tyler and Drew Hanger were enthusiastic supporters from the start, and I loved our conversations; it's a delight and pleasure to know you. Brad Marshall consistently delivers in our discussions about screens, tech, and its impact on our young people. Luke Mead was inspiring, and his work on problem gambling deserves its own book. Peggy Orenstein was generous in outlining her insights from *Boys & Sex* and sharpened my thinking in so many areas. And Laurence Steinberg, one of the world's most recognised adolescence researchers, has contributed so much to my knowledge.

The readers who took on the colossal task of working through a messy manuscript well before it was truly done deserve special appreciation. Thank you Melissa Abu-Gazaleh (again!), Christine Gregory, Mim Hammonds, Evelynne Hatchard, Caroline Martel, Mel McLean, Daniel Principe, and Victoria Vanstone.

To Beck Delahoy, enormous gratitude for proofreading, fact-checking, referencing, and generally being over the top in ensuring what I wrote was appropriately supported by credible evidence.

To the team at ABC Books, the extra edits and additional reading made life harder for all of us and the book better for every parent. It was worth it. I am grateful to you for being such taskmasters on this one. And thanks so much to the entire ABC Books and HarperCollins team for getting the book out there, with specific recognition to Mary Rennie.

I'm a dad to six kids, and husband to a wife I adore beyond description. And so …

To my kids: I hope my daughters are loved well by good men – and that the strength, wisdom, and warmth each of them carries is matched by the men they choose. Seeing my first two, Chanel and Abbie, select such outstanding husbands gives me tremendous hope. Jared and Elijah – you're doing it right. Thank you. I can't wait to see who Ella, Annie, Lilli, and Emilie choose for themselves. May those 'chair stackers' bless your life by helping you feel – and be – safer and stronger.

Finally, my longsuffering wife, Kylie – who endured my late nights, early mornings, frustrations, flip-outs, insecurities, and statements of 'I've just got to get this book done and then we'll slow down and spend more time together' for close to four years. Thank you. This work will change lives. It will make a difference. And I promise that's it … for a while at least.

Endnotes

Author's note

1 A.H. Eagly & J.A. Hall, 'The kernel of truth in gender stereotypes: Consider the avocado, not the apple', *Journal of Experimental Social Psychology*, 118, 2025, 104713.

2 L. Jussim, T. Cain, J. Crawford et al., 'The unbearable accuracy of stereotypes' in T. Nelson (ed.), *Handbook of prejudice, stereotyping, and discrimination*, 2009, pp.199–227; S.B. Kaufman, 'Taking sex differences in personality seriously', *Scientific American*, 12 December 2019.

Introduction

1 David Cunliffe, 2014.

2 R. Neely, 'Well it's really ramping up', Facebook [Residents for Noosa], 10 June 2025.

3 F. Hunter, '"Spit on homeless man": Shore School year 12s plan crime-filled muck-up day', *Sydney Morning Herald*, 22 September 2020.

4 A. Mowle, S. Ewing & T. Perry, 'Sexual Harassment of Teachers in Schools', Collective Shout, 2024.

5 ABC News In-depth, 'How the "manosphere" is fuelling teen misogyny inside Australian schools', *Compass*, video, YouTube, 13 July 2025.

6 B. Mathews, R.E. Pacella, J.G. Scott et al., 'The prevalence of child maltreatment in Australia: findings from a national survey', *Medical Journal of Australia*, 2023, S13-S18.

7 C. Flanagan, 'In praise of heroic masculinity', *The Atlantic*, 30 August 2023.

8 R.V. Reeves, *Of Boys and Men: Why the modern male is struggling, why it matters, and what to do about it*, Brookings Institution Press, 2022.

9 A. Rubinstein, *The Making of Men: Raising boys to be happy, healthy and successful*, Brio Books, 2013.

Chapter 1: Code red

1 A. Todd, 'The world is choosing daughters, but here is my case for the "boy mum"', Mamamia, 27 January 2026.

2 'FREE FOR ALL: Dr. Vivek Murthy on why American men are in crisis', The Ink, 24 April 2024.

3 M. Brooks, M. Bell & C. Badley, '"A Boy Today": The world into which a boy today in the UK is growing up', All-Party Parliamentary Group on Issues Affecting Men and Boys, September 2021.

4 Ibid.

5 Ibid.

6 'Completion rates of higher education students – cohort analysis, 2005–2022', Department of Education, 18 December 2023.

7 'People with disability in Australia', Australian Institute of Health and Welfare, 2024.

8 'Alcohol, tobacco & other drugs in Australia', Australian Institute of Health and Welfare, 2025.

9 Ibid.

10 'Education and work, Australia', Australian Bureau of Statistics, May 2024.

11 'People with disability in Australia', Australian Institute of Health and Welfare, 2024.

12 'Key work health and safety statistics Australia 2022', Safe Work Australia, 2022.

13 'Alcohol, tobacco & other drugs in Australia', Australian Institute of Health and Welfare, 2025.

14 Ibid.

15 Ibid.

16 'Recorded crime – victims', Australian Bureau of Statistics, 2023.

17 '2023 suspensions and expulsions', NSW Department of Education, 2023.

18 'Deaths, Australia', Australian Bureau of Statistics, 2023.

19 'Autism in Australia, 2022', Australian Bureau of Statistics, 11 October 2024.

20 'Alcohol, tobacco & other drugs in Australia', Australian Institute of Health and Welfare, 2025.

21 'Causes of Death, Australia', Australian Bureau of Statistics, 2023.
22 'Australia's children', Australian Institute of Health and Welfare, 2022.
23 D. Lawrence, S. Johnson, J. Hafekost et al., 'The mental health of children and adolescents. Report on the second Australian Child and Adolescent Survey of Mental Health and Wellbeing', Department of Health, Canberra, 2015.
24 '2023 suspensions and expulsions', NSW Department of Education, 2023.
25 'Recorded crime – victims', Australian Bureau of Statistics, 2023.
26 'Prisoners in Australia', Australian Bureau of Statistics, 2024.
27 'Key work health and safety statistics Australia 2022', Safe Work Australia, 2022.
28 R. Reeves, *Of Boys and Men: Why the modern male is struggling, why it matters, and what to do about it*, Brookings Institution Press, 2022.
29 See T. Tao, L. Wang, C. Fan & W. Gao, 'Development of self-control in children aged 3 to 9 years: perspective from a dual-systems model', *Scientific Reports*, 2014; A. Sullivan, N. Tippett, B. Johnson & J. Manolev, 'Understanding disproportionality and school exclusions', School Exclusions Study Key Issues Paper No. 4. University of South Australia, 2020; S.A. Hemphill, D.J. Broderick & J.A. Heerde, 'Positive associations between school suspension and student problem behaviour: Recent Australian findings', Australian Institute of Criminology, June 2017; '2023 suspensions and expulsions', NSW Department of Education, 2024; J. Lacoe M.P. & Steinberg, 'So suspensions affect student outcomes?', *Educational Evaluation and Policy Analysis*, 41(1), 2019; S.J. Prins, R.T. Shefner, S. Kajeepeta et al., 'Longitudinal relationships among exclusionary school discipline, adolescent substance use, and adult arrest: Public health implications of the school-to-prison pipeline', *Drug and Alcohol Dependence*, 251, 2023, 110949; and A.L. Noltemeyer & R.M. Ward, 'Relationship between school suspension and student outcomes: a meta-analysis', *School Psychology Review*, 44(2), 2015, pp.224–40.
30 S. Mullola, N. Ravaja, J. Lipsanen et al., 'Gender differences in teachers' perceptions of students' temperament, educational competence, and teachability', *British Journal of Educational Psychology*, 2012;

B. Hartley & R. Sutton, 'A stereotype threat account of boys' academic underachievement', *Child Development*, 84(5), 2013, pp.1716–33.

31 C. Cornwell, D.B. Mustard & J. Van Parys, 'Noncognitive skills and the gender disparities in test scores and teacher assessments: Evidence from primary school', IZA Discussion Papers, No. 5973, 2011.

32 'PISA 2018 Results (Volume II): Where All Students Can Succeed', PISA, OECD, 2019.

33 F. Larkins, 'Examining gendered differences in participation in higher education', Melbourne Centre for the Study of Higher Education, 2024.

34 D. Maywald, 'In Australia, men and boys are lagging on a broad range of indicators', Save, 24 January 2025.

35 D.M. Buss, 'Sex differences in human mate preferences: evolutionary hypotheses tested in 37 cultures', *Behavioral and Brain Sciences*, 12(1), 1989, pp.1–14.

36 B. Neyt, S. Vandenbulcke & S. Baert, 'Are men intimidated by highly educated women? Undercover on Tinder', *Economics of Education Review*, 73, 2019.

37 L. Bursztyn, T. Fujiwara & A. Pallais, '"Acting wife": Marriage market incentives and labor market investments', *American Economic Review*, 107(11), 2017, pp.3288–3319.

38 J. Quill & E. Ludlow, 'Reports reveal youth homelessness crisis in Australia', World Socalist Web Site, 1 April 2025.

39 'Obesity trends in Australian children', Obesity Evidence Hub, 2025.

40 'Australia's youth: Mental illness', Australian Institute of Health and Welfare, 2021.

41 E.M. Robson, H.M. Husin, S.G. Dashti et al., 'Tracking the course of depressive and anxiety symptoms across adolescence (the CATS study): a population-based cohort study in Australia', *Lancet Psychiatry*, 12(1), 2025.

42 D. Lawrence, S. Johnson, J. Hafekost et al., 2015, 'The mental health of children and adolescents. Report on the second Australian Child and Adolescent Survey of Mental Health and Wellbeing', Department of Health, Canberra, 2025; 'Autism in Australia, 2022', Australian Bureau of Statistics, 11 October 2024; A.S. Rommel, F. Rijsdijk, C.U. Greven et al., 'A longitudinal twin study of the direction of effects between

ADHD symptoms and IQ', *PLoS ONE*, 10(4), 2015, e0124357; I. Park, J. Gong, G.L. Lyons et al., 'Prevalence of and factors associated with school bullying in students with autism spectrum disorder: a cross-cultural meta-analysis', *Yonsei Medical Journal*, 61(11), 2020, pp.909–22; A.L. Accardo, N.M.H. Pontes & M.C.F. Pontes, 'Heightened anxiety and depression among autistic adolescents with ADHD: findings from the National Survey of Children's Health 2016–2019', *Journal of Autism and Developmental Disorders*, 54(2), 2022, pp.563-76; 'Autism in Australia, 2022', Australian Bureau of Statistics, 11 October 2024; E. Atkinson, S. Wright & H. Wood-Downie, '"Do my friends only like the school me or the true me?": school belonging, camouflaging, and anxiety in autistic students', *Journal of Autism and Developmental Disorders*, 2024.

43 R. McHale, N. Brennan, B. Boon et al., 'Youth Survey Report 2024', Mission Australia, 2024; 'Men's mental health', Beyond Blue, 18 June 2025.

44 I. Chowdhury, '5 charts that show how young Australians are getting screwed', The Conversation, 27 October 2025.

45 'Deaths in Australia', Australian Institute of Health and Welfare, 2025.

46 G. Poole, '10 new facts about male suicide in Australia. Australian Men's Health Forum', 2025.

47 S. Bricknell, 'Statistical report 42: homicide in Australia 2020–21', Australian Institute of Criminology, 2023; 'Recorded crime – victims', Australian Bureau of Statistics, 2023; 'Crime victimisation', Australian Bureau of Statistics, 2023–24; 'Personal safety, Australia, 2021–22', Australian Bureau of Statistics, 2023.

48 'Testimonies', Teach Us Consent.

49 'Recorded crime – victims, 2023', Australian Bureau of Statistics, 2024.

50 'Youth justice in Australia 2022–23', Australian Institute of Health and Welfare, 2024.

51 S. Johnson, 'Warrnambool school sorry for making boys stand in apology for "behaviours of their gender"', ABC News, 25 March 2021.

52 S. Marin, 'What exactly is toxic masculinity? And could the term's overuse have unintended consequences?', ABC News, 26 October 2024.

53 Quoted in Richard Reeves, 'We must pay more attention to young men', Of Boys and Men, substack, 28 January 2024.

Chapter 2: Hardwired

1 C. Hooven, T: *The story of testosterone, the hormone that dominates and divides us*, Henry Holt & Company Inc, 2021.

2 K. Steinbeck, 'Health Check: do boys really have a testosterone spurt at age four?', *The Conversation*, 23 October 2017; Interestingly, girls exposed to testosterone in-utero due to genetic conditions show increased male-typical behaviour due to the effects of androgens (man-makers) on the developing brain, even when they have been socialised as girls their entire lives; M. Hines, V. Pasterski, D. Spencer et al., 'Prenatal androgen exposure alters girls' responses to information indicating gender-appropriate behaviour', *Philosophical Transactions of the Royal Society B*, 371(1688), 2016; H.A. Feldman, C. Longcope, C.A. Derby et al., 'Age trends in the level of serum testosterone and other hormones in middle-aged men: longitudinal results from the Massachusetts Male Aging Study', *The Journal of Clinical Endocrinology & Metabolism*, 87(2), 2002, pp.589–98; Research on AFAB (assigned female at birth) people who transitioned to men (transgender men) using gender-affirming hormone treatment has found that testosterone can change brain structure at any point, not just during childhood and puberty, and that the continued presence of androgens in the brain is essential for maintaining sex-specific brain-differences; H.E. Hulshoff Pol, P.T. Cohen-Kettenis, N.E.M. Van Haren & J.S. Peper, 'Changing your sex changes your brain: Influence of testosterone and estrogen on adult human brain structure', *European Journal of Endocrinology*, 155(1), 2006; L. Zubiaurre-Elorza, S. Cerdán, C. Uribe et al., 'The effects of testosterone on the brain of transgender men', *Androgens: Clinical Research and Therapeutics*, 2.1, 2021.

3 C. Bohannon, *Eve: How the Female Body Drove 200 Million Years of Human Evolution*, Hutchinson Heinemann, 2023; N.E. Holton, T.R. Yokley, A.W. Froehle & T.E. Southard, 'Ontogenetic scaling of the human nose in a longitudinal sample: Implications for genus: Homofacial evolution', *American Journal of Physical Anthropology*, 2013.

4 D. Crozier, Z. Zhang, S. Park & D. Sternad, 'Gender differences in throwing revisited: sensorimotor coordination in a virtual ball aiming task', Frontiers in Human Neuroscience, 13(231), 18 July 2019; S.K. Hunter, S.S. Angadi, A. Bhargava et al., 'The biological basis of sex

differences in athletic performance: consensus statement for the American College of Sports Medicine', *Medicine and Science in Sports and Exercise*, 55(12), pp.2328–60.

5 'Australia women's team loses 7–0 to Under-15 men's side', *GOAL*, 26 May 2016.

6 W.R. Charlesworth & C. Dzur, 'Gender comparisons of preschoolers' behavior and resource utilization in group problem solving', *Child Development*, 58(1), 1987, pp.191–200.

7 J.F. Benenson & H. Markovits (collaborator), *Warriors and Worriers: The survival of the sexes*, Oxford University Press, 2014; D.C. Geary, 'Male, female: The evolution of human sex differences, 2nd ed., *American Psychological Association*, 2010; J.A. DiPietro, 'Rough and tumble play: A function of gender', *Developmental Psychology*, 17(1), 1981, pp.50–58.

8 R. Henderson, 'The Male Monkey Dance', Rob Henderson's Substack, 11 September 2022.

9 E.P. Shulman, K.P. Harden, J.M. Chein & L. Steinberg, 'Sex differences in the developmental trajectories of impulse control and sensation-seeking from early adolescence to early adulthood', *Journal of Youth and Adolescence*, 44(1), 2015, pp.1–17.

10 J. Archer, 'The reality and evolutionary significance of human psychological sex differences', *Biological Reviews*, 94(4), 2019, pp.1381–1415; J.F. Benenson, C.E. Webb & R.W. Wrangham, 'Self-protection as an adaptive female strategy', *Behavioral and Brain Sciences*, 45, e128, 2021.

11 J. Frankenbach, M. Weber, D.D. Loschelder et al., 'Sex drive: Theoretical conceptualization and meta-analytic review of gender differences', *Psychological Bulletin*, 148(9–10), September–October 2022, pp.621–61.

12 D.P. Schmitt, L. Alcalay, J. Allik et al., 'Universal sex differences in the desire for sexual variety: tests from 52 nations, 6 continents, and 13 islands', *Journal of Personality and Social Psychology*, 85(1), 2003, pp.85–104.

13 S. Galloway, 'Slow dopa', Medium, 3 January 2026.

14 S. Stewart-Williams & L. Halsey, 'Men, women, and STEM: why the differences and what should be done?', *European Journal of Personality*, 35(1), January 2021.

15 Ibid.

16 D. Voyer, S. Voyer & M.P. Bryden, 'Magnitude of sex differences in spatial abilities: a meta-analysis and consideration of critical variables', *Psychological Bulletin*, 117(2), March 1995, pp.250–70.
17 A. Falk & J. Hermle, 'Relationship of gender differences in preferences to economic development and gender equality', *Science*, 362, 19 October 2018, p.6412.
18 C. Hooven, *T: The story of testosterone, the hormone that dominates and divides us*, Henry Holt & Company Inc, 2021.

Chapter 3: Boxed in

1 The Men's Project & M. Flood, 'Unpacking the Man Box: What is the impact of the Man Box attitudes on young Australian men's behaviours and wellbeing?', Jesuit Social Services, 2020.
2 R.F. Baumeister, 'Stalking the true self through the jungles of authenticity: problems, contradictions, inconsistencies, disturbing findings – and a possible way forward', *Review of General Psychology*, 23(1), 2019, pp.143–54.
3 J.A. Vandello, J.K. Bosson, D. Cohen et al., 'Precarious manhood', *Journal of Personality and Social Psychology*, 95(6), 2008, pp.1325–39.
4 J.K. Bosson, M. Wilkerson, N. Kosakowska-Berezecka et al., 'Harder won and easier lost? Testing the double standard in gender rules in 62 countries', *Sex Roles*, 87, 2022, pp.1–19.
5 A. Delaney, 'The "Run It Straight" challenge went viral for teen boys. It's already killed one of them', Mamamia, 5 June 2025.
6 J.R. Mahalik & M.P. Harris, 'Precarious manhood, precarious nations: The contribution of cultural beliefs comprising masculinity to national happiness', *Social Science and Medicine*, 388, 2026.
7 M. Greene, 'The history of the "Man Box", Medium, 16 January 2019.
8 The Men's Project & M. Flood, 'Unpacking the Man Box: What is the impact of the Man Box attitudes on young Australian men's behaviours and wellbeing?', Jesuit Social Services, 2020.
9 William Pollack, *Real Boys*, Random House, 1998.
10 The Men's Project, & M. Flood, 'Unpacking the Man Box: What is the impact of the Man Box attitudes on young Australian men's behaviours and wellbeing?', Jesuit Social Services, 2020.
11 Ibid.

Chapter 4: Screen lords

1 E.O. Wilson, 'Looking back looking forward: a conversation with James D Watson and Edward O Wilson', Harvard Museum of Natural History, video, YouTube, 9 September 2009.

2 S. Galloway, 'Attentive', *No Mercy/No Malice*, 16 September 2022.

3 A. Huxley, *Brave New World*, Chatto & Windus, 1932.

4 J. Haidt, *The Anxious Generation: How the great rewiring of childhood is causing an epidemic of mental illness*, Penguin Press, 2025.

5 J.E. Brand, T.W. Wilson, J. Jervis & P.M. Huggins, 'Australia Plays 2023', *Interactive Games and Entertainment Association*, 2023.

6 A. Kandola, N. Owen, D.W. Dunstan & M. Hallgreen, 'Prospective relationships of adolescents' screen-based sedentary behaviour with depressive symptoms: the Millennium Cohort Study', *Psychological Medicine*, 52(15), 2021, pp.3531–39; B.W. Hygen, V. Skalická, F. Stenseng et al., 'The co-occurrence between symptoms of internet gaming disorder and psychiatric disorders in childhood and adolescence: prospective relations or common causes?', *Journal of Child Psychology and Psychiatry*, 61(8), 2020, pp.890–98; M. Vuorre, N. Johannes, K. Magnusson & A.K. Przybylski, 'Time spent playing video games is unlikely to impact well-being', *Royal Society Open Science*, 9(7), 2022, 220411.

7 S. Marinos, 'Younger Australians are more likely than their parents or grandparents to feel alone in the world, finds the annual HILDA survey', Pursuit, 12 February 2024.

8 B. Marshall, W.A. Warburton, M. Kangas & N. Sweller, 'Internet gaming disorder (IGD) and smartphone overuse in Australian primary school and secondary school children: prevalence and developmental impacts', *Current Psychology*, 2025.

9 'How's life for children in the Digital Age?', Organisation for Economic Co-operation and Development, 15 May 2025.

10 B. Marshall, W.A. Warburton, M. Kangas & N. Sweller, 'Internet gaming disorder (IGD) and smartphone overuse in Australian primary school and secondary school children: prevalence and developmental impacts', *Current Psychology*, 2025.

11 S. Galloway, 'The crisis of men and boys – with Jonathan Haidt and Richard Reeves | Prof G Conversations', video, YouTube, 15 August 2025.

12 H. Kang, C. Suh & H.K. Kim, 'Match experiences affect interest: Impacts of matchmaking and performance on churn in a competitive game', *Heliyon*, 10(3), 2024, e24891.

13 S. Chaiklin, 'The zone of proximal development in Vygotsky's analysis of learning and instruction', in A. Kozulin, B. Gindis, V.S. Ageyev & S.M. Miller (eds.), *Vygotsky's Educational Theory in Cultural Context*, Cambridge University Press, 2003, pp. 39–64.

14 W. Siu, 'I make video games. I won't let my daughters play them', *New York Times*, 2 October 2022.

15 S. Galloway, 'The crisis of men and boys – with Jonathan Haidt and Richard Reeves | Prof G Conversations', video, YouTube, 15 August 2025.

16 R. Riordan, *Percy Jackson and the Olympians: The Lightning Thief*, Puffin, 2023.

17 T. Puolitaival, M. Sieppi, R. Pyky et al., 'Health behaviours associated with video gaming in adolescent men: a cross-sectional population-based MOPO study', *BMC Public Health*, 20, 2020, pp.1–8; S. Peracchia & G. Curcio, 'Exposure to video games: effects on sleep and on post-sleep cognitive abilities. A sistematic review of experimental evidences', *Sleep*, 11(4), 2018, pp.302–14; R. Kowert, E. Domahidi, R. Festl & T. Quandt, 'Social gaming, lonely life? The impact of digital game play on adolescents' social circles', *Computers in Human Behavior*, 36, 2014, pp.385–90; O.R.W. Pergams & P.A. Zaradic, 'Is love of nature in the US becoming love of electronic media? 16-year downtrend in National Park visits explained by watching movies, playing video games, internet use, and oil prices', *Journal of Environmental Management*, 80(4), 2006, pp.387–93.

18 M.E. Raichle, 'The brain's default mode network', *Annual Review of Neuroscience*, 38, 2015, pp.433–47.

19 L. Wang, Z. Zhang, S. Wang et al., 'Deficient dynamics of prefrontal-striatal and striatal-default mode network (DMN) neural circuits in internet gaming disorder', *Journal of Affective Disorders*, 323, 2023, pp.336–44.

20 'Gallup Familial and Adolescent Health Survey', Gallup Panel, 2023.
21 'Teens, social media and technology 2022', Pew Research Center, 2022.
22 J. Taylor, 'We unleashed Facebook and Instagram's algorithms on blank accounts. They served up sexism and misogyny', *The Guardian*, 21 July 2024.
23 C. Baker, D. Ging & M.B. Andreason, 'Recommending toxicity: The role of algorithmic recommender functions on YouTube Shorts and TikTok in promoting male supremacist influencers', DCU Anti-Bullying Centre Dublin City University, 2024.
24 J. Davey, 'Gamers who hate: an introduction to ISD's Gaming and Extremism Series', Institute for Strategic Dialogue, 11 September 2021.
25 Ibid.
26 A. Tate, 'Fact. Women are sex workers', @Cobratate, X, 30 December 2024.
27 M. Gaines, *Why Women Deserve Less*, 2023.
28 *Louis Theroux: Inside the Manosphere*, Netflix, 2026.
29 J.M. Richardson, 'Hypermasculine influencers can be good role models for boys too', *The Conversation*, 10 April 2025.
30 M. Faverio & O. Sidoti, 'Teens, social media and AI chatbots 2025', Pew Research Center, 9 December 2025.
31 'Talk, trust, and trade-offs: How and why teens use AI companions', Common Sense Media, July, 2025.
32 E. Musk, @ElonMusk, X, 21 August 2025.
33 K. Miller, 'Gen Bet: has gambling gatecrashed our teens?', Victorian Responsible Gambling Foundation, 2017.
34 'Gambling advertising in Australia: placement and spending', Australian Commmunications and Media Authority, 2023.
35 M. Saunders & M. Harrington et al., 'Teenage gambling in Australia', Australia Institute, 7 April 2025.

Chapter 5: The porndemic

1 S. Gilbert, *Girl on Girl: How pop culture turned a generation of women against themselves*, Penguin Press, 2025.
2 M.A.H. Horvath, L. Alys, K. Massey et al., 'A rapid evidence assessment on the effects that access and exposure to pornography has on children and young people', Children's Commissioner, 30 June 2013.

3 S. Galloway, 'Porn', Medium, 22 March 2025.

4 'Bringing Up Boys Summit', video, Happy Families, 2022.

5 P.J. Wright, D. Herbenick, B. Paul & R.S. Tokunaga, 'U.S. parents underestimate their child's pornography use and learning', *Archives of Sexual Behavior*, 52, 2023. pp.373–83; S. Liu, F.C. Chang, C.H. Chiu et al., 'Parent–child discrepancies in reports of exposure to violence/pornography on mobile devices and the impact on children's psychosocial adjustment', *Cyberpsychology, Behavior, and Social Networking*, 24(6), 2021.

6 M. Ballantine-Jones, 'Inquiry into impacts of harmful pornography on mental, emotional, and physical health (Submission No. 34)', Standing Committee on Social Issues, NSW Parliament House, 2024.

7 M.S.C. Lim, P.A. Agius, E.R. Carrotte et al., 'Young Australians' use of pornography and associations with sexual risk behaviours', *Australian and New Zealand Journal of Public Health*, 41(4), 2017, pp.438–43.

8 M. Crabbe, M. Flood & K. Adams, 'Pornography exposure and access among young Australians: a cross-sectional study', *Australian and New Zealand Journal of Public Health*, 48(3), 2024, pp.100–35.

9 C. Sun, A. Bridges, J.A. Johnson & M.B. Ezzell, 'Pornography and the male sexual script: an analysis of consumption and sexual relations', *Archives of Sexual Behaviour*, 45(4), 2016, pp.983–94.

10 D. Kolitz, 'The Goon Squad', *Harper's Magazine*, November 2025.

11 A. Srinivasan, *The Right To Sex*, Farrar, Straus & Giroux, 2021.

12 R.S. Tokunaga, P.J. Wright & L. Vangeel, 'Is pornography consumption a risk factor for condomless sex?', *Human Communication Research*, 46(2–3), 2020, pp.273–99; M.S.C. Lim, P.A. Agius, E.R. Carrotte et al., 'Young Australians' use of pornography and associations with sexual risk behaviours', *Australian and New Zealand Journal of Public Health*, 41(4), 2017, pp.438–43; J.M. Farré, A.L. Montejo, M. Agulló et al., 'Pornography use in adolescents and its clinical implications', *Journal of Clinical Medicine*, 9(11), 2020, 3625; E.A. Marshall & H.A. Miller, 'The role of sexual scripts in the relationship between pornography use and sexual coercion', *Journal of Interpersonal Violence*, 38(7–8), 2022; J.B. Grubbs. P.J. Wright, A.L. Braden et al., 'Internet pornography use and sexual motivation: a systematic review and integration',

Annals of the International Communication Association, 43(2), 2019, pp.117–55; R. Mikorski & D.M. Szymanski, 'Masculine norms, peer group, pornography, Facebook, and men's sexual objectification of women', *Psychology of Men & Masculinity*, 18(4), 2017, pp.257–67; K.R. Rasmussen & A. Bierman, 'Risk or release?: porn use trajectories and the accumulation of sexual partners', *Social Currents*, 5(6), 2018; P.J. Wright, R.S. Tokunaga, A. Kraus & E. Klann, 'Pornography consumption and satisfaction: a meta-analysis', *Human Communication Research*, 43, 2017, pp.315–43; M.H. Butler, S.A. Pereyra, T.W. Draper et al., 'Pornography use and loneliness: a bi-directional recursive model and pilot investigation', *Journal of Sex & Marital Therapy*, 2017.

13 P.J. Wright & R.S. Tokunaga, 'Women's perceptions of their male partners' pornography consumption and relational, sexual, self, and body satisfaction: toward a theoretical model', *Annals of the International Communication Association*, 42(1), 2018, pp.55–73.

14 T. Gana & L.M. Hunt, 'Young women and anal sex', *British Medical Journal*, 2022; D. Herbenick, C. Patterson, P.J. Wright et al., 'Sexual choking/strangulation during sex: a review of the literature', *Current Sexual Health Reports*, 15, 2023, pp.253–60; M.A. Dunkin & Z. Sheikh, 'Anal sex safety: what to know', WebMD, 11 April 2024; H. Douglas & L. Sharman, 'Choking during sex: many young people mistakenly believe it can be done safely, our study shows', *The Conversation*, 2 February 2025; A. Hedrick, 'A Meta-analysis of media consumption and rape myth acceptance', *Journal of Health Communication*, 26(9), 2021, pp.645–56.

15 M.L. Ybarra, K.J. Mitchell, M. Hamburger et al., 'X-rated material and perpetration of sexually aggressive behavior among children and adolescents: is there a link?' *Aggressive Behavior*, 37(1), 2011, pp.1–18.

16 B. Mathews, R.E. Pacella, J.G. Scott et al., 'The prevalence of child maltreatment in Australia: findings from a national survey', *Medical Journal of Australia*, 2023, S13–S18.

17 A. McKee, K. Litsou, P. Byron & R. Ingham, *What Do We Know About the Effects of Pornography After Fifty Years of Academic Research?*, Routledge, 2022.

18 'Bringing Up Boys Summit', video, Happy Families, 2022.

19 J. Coulson (host), '#935 A Real World Honey Trap', Happy Families, audio podcast, 26 February 2024.

20 J. Coulson (host), '#936 The Sordid World of Honey Traps With Julie Inman Grant', Happy Families, audio podcast, 27 February 2024.

21 Ibid.

22 'Bringing Up Boys Summit', video, Happy Families, 2022.

Chapter 6: Character

1 OpenAI, ChatGPT (September version), Large Language Model, 2025.

2 D. Brooks, *The Road to Character*, Random House, 2015.

3 S. Milgram, 'Behavioral study of obedience', *The Journal of Abnormal and Social Psychology*, 1963, 67(4), pp.371–78.

4 J. Coulson, 'Raising rebels', video, TEDx, September 2017.

5 S. Galloway (host), 'Choosing between career and family: Scott's best relationship advice, and being a dad', Prof G podcast, audio podcast, 5 September 2025.

6 Aristotle, *The Nichomachean Ethics of Aristotle*, R. Browne, trans., George Bell & Sons.

7 D. Brooks, *The Road to Character*, Random House, 2015.

Chapter 7: Your son's psychological engine

1 J. Clear, 'Do more of what already works', jamesclear.com/checklist-solutions.

2 E.L. Deci & R.M. Ryan, 'The "what" and "why" of goal pursuits: human needs and the self-determination of behavior', *Psychological Inquiry*, 11(4), 200, pp.227–68. See also C.E. Ackerman, 'Self determination theory and how it explains motivation', PositivePsychology.com, 21 June 2018.

3 E.E. Werner, 'Vulnerable but invincible: high-risk children from birth to adulthood', *Acta Paediatrica – Supplement*, 422, 1997, pp.103–05.

4 R.J. Waldinger & M.S. Schulz, *The Good Life: Lessons from the world's longest scientific study of happiness*, Simon & Schuster, 2023.

5 M. Pooravari, S. Ghanbari, A.Z. Mohammadi et al., 'The comparison of tendence to risky behaviour, in secure/insecure attachment in parents', *International Journal of Applied Behavioural Sciences*, 2(2), 2015, pp.7–14; S. Perren & R. Hornung, 'Bullying and delinquency in adolescence:

victims' and perpetrators' family and peer relations', Swiss Journal of Psychology, 64(1), 2006; A. Miller, 'Family influences on adolescent sexual and contraceptive behavior,' *The Journal of Sex Research*, 39(1), 2002, pp.22–26.

6 M. Stafford, D.L. Kuh, C.R. Gale et al., 'Parent–child relationships and offspring's positive mental wellbeing from adolescence to early older age,' *Journal of Positive Psychology*, 11(3), 2016, pp.326–37; A.K. Fishel, 'Home for dinner: mixing food, fun, and conversation for a happier family and healthier kids', American Management Association, 2015.

7 D. Sivers, 'How to live: 27 conflicting answers and one weird conclusion', Hit Media, 2021.

8 T. Amabile & S. Kramer, *The Progress Principle: Using small wins to ignite joy, engagement, and creativity at work*, Harvard Business Review Press, 2011.

9 A. Hormozi, 'You don't become confident by shouting affirmations in the mirror', @AlexHormosi, X, 30 October 2022.

Chapter 8: Motivation

1 A. Kohn, 'Why lots of love (or motivation) isn't enough', 23 April 2016.

2 R.M. Ryan & E.L. Deci, 'Self-determination theory and the facilitation of intrinsic motivation, social development, and well-being', *American Psychologist*, 55(1), pp.68–78.

3 C. Kamii, 'Obedience is not enough', *Young Children*, 39(4), 1984, pp.11–14.

4 A. Kohn, *Punished by rewards: the trouble with gold stars, incentive plans, A's, praise, and other bribes*, Houghton Mifflin, 1993.

5 M. Csikszentmihalyi, *Flow: The psychology of optimal experience*, Harper, 1990.

6 M. Wizla & K. Lewczuk, 'Compulsive sexual behavior disorder and problematic pornography use in the context of social Ties', *Current Addiction Reports*, 11, 2024, pp.275–86; A. Štulhofer, A. Rousseau & R. Shekarchi, 'A two-wave assessment of the structure and stability of self-reported problematic pornography use among male Croatian adolescents', *International Journal of Sexual Health*, 32(2), 2020, pp.151–64; S. Kármen, K.K. Janosi & I. Kotta, 'The highs and lows of pornography

use: does motivation affect users' life satisfaction?', *Studia Universitatis Babeş-Bolyai Psychologia-Paedagogia*, 69(1), 2024, pp.183–200.

Chapter 9: Emotions

1 Oprah Daily, 'Oprah talks with Brené Brown about the power of being able to name your emotions', 6 January 2022.

2 T.M. Chaplin & A. Aldao, 'Gender differences in emotion expression in children: a meta-analytic review', *Psychological Bulletin*, 139(4). 2013, pp.735–65; G. Domes, L. Schulze, M. Böttger et al., 'The neural correlates of sex differences in emotional reactivity and emotion regulation', *Human Brain Mapping*, 31, 2010, pp.758–69.

3 M. Oransky & J. Marecek, '"I'm not going to be a girl": masculinity and emotions in boys' friendships and peer groups', *Journal of Adolescent Research*, 24, 2009, p.218.

4 M. Baker & K. Milligan, 'Boy-girl differences in parental time investments: evidence from three countries', NBER Working Paper No. 18893, March 2013; M.W. Clearfield & N.M. Nelson, 'Sex differences in mothers' speech and play behavior with 6-, 9-, and 14-month-old infants', *Sex Roles*, 54(1/2), 2006; T.M. Booth, 'the effect of child gender on parental nonverbal communication', master's thesis, University of Maryland, 2019; E.W. Lindsey & P.R. Cremeens, 'Gender differences in mother-toddler and father-toddler verbal initiations and responses during a caregiving and play context', *Sex Roles*, 2010; T.M. Chaplin, P.M. Cole & C. Zahn-Waxler, 'Parental socialization of emotion expression: gender differences and relations to child adjustment', Emotion, 5(1), 2005, pp.80–88; M. Cassano & C. Perry-Parrish, 'Influence of gender on parental socialization of children's sadness regulation', *Social Development*, 16(2), 2007, pp.210–31; E. Randell, L. Jerdén, A. Öhman et al., 'Tough, sensitive and sincere: how adolescent boys manage masculinities and emotions', *International Journal of Adolescence and Youth*, 21(4), 2016, pp.486–98.

5 T.M. Chaplin, P.M. Cole & C. Zahn-Waxler, 'Parental socialization of emotion expression: gender differences and relations to child adjustment', *Emotion*, 5(1), 2005, pp.80–88; R. Fivush, M.A. Brotman, J.P. Buckner & S.H. Goodman, 'Gender differences in parent-child emotion

narratives,' *Sex Roles*, 42(3), 2000, pp.233–53; R.B. Garside & B. Klimes-Dougan, 'Socialization of discrete negative emotions: gender differences and links with psychological distress', *Sex Roles*, 47, 2002, pp.115–28.

6 L. Damour, *The Emotional Lives of Teenagers: Raising Connected, Capable and Compassionate Adolescents*, Ballantine Books, 2023.

7 J.A. Crowell, 'Development of Emotion Regulation in Typically Developing Children', *Child and Adolescent Psychiatric Clinics of North America*, 30(3), 2021, pp.467–74.

8 J.T. Gross & J. Cassidy, 'Expressive suppression of negative emotions in children and adolescents: theory, data, and a guide for future research', *Developmental Psychology*, 55(9), 2019, pp.1938–50.

9 L. Damour, *The Emotional Lives of Teenagers: Raising Connected, Capable and Compassionate Adolescents*.

10 A. Kumari & S. Gupta, 'A study of emotional intelligence and frustration tolerance among adolescent', *Advance Research Journal of Social Science*, 6(2), 2015, pp.173–80.

11 A. Bracken, *The Darkest Minds*, Disney Hyperion, 2012.

12 L. Kogler, V.I. Müller, E. Wermminghausen et al., 'Do I feel or do I know? Neuroimaging meta-analyses on the multiple facets of empathy', *Cortex*, 129, 2020, pp.341–55.

13 L. Nummenmaa, J. Hirvonen, R. Parkkola & J.K. Hietanen, ,Is emotional contagion special? An fMRI study on neural systems for affective and cognitive empathy', *NeuroImage*, 43, 2008, pp.571–80.

14 J. Van der Graff, S. Branje, M. De Wied et al., 2014 ,Perspective taking and empathic concern in adolescence: Gender differences in developmental changes', *Developmental Psychology*, 50(3), 2014, pp.881–88.

15 Ibid.

16 H. Yoo, X. Feng & R.D. Day, 'Adolescents' empathy and prosocial behavior in the family context: a longitudinal study', *Journal of Youth and Adolescence*, 2012.

Chapter 10: The father factor

1 T. Real, *I Don't Want To Talk About It: Overcoming the secret legacy of male depression*, Scribner, 1997.

2 The Men's Project, 'Adolescent Man Box: preliminary findings for advisory group', manuscript in preparation, Jesuit Social Services, 2025.
3 K.D. Pruett, 'The role of the father', *Pediatrics*, 102(5), 1998, pp.1253–61.
4 N. Pancsofar & L. Vernon-Feagans, 'Mother and father language input to young children: Contributions to later language development', *Journal of Applied Developmental Psychology*, 27(6), 2006, pp.571–87; L. Rollè, G. Gullotta, T. Trombetta et al., 'Father involvement and cognitive development in early and middle childhood: a systematic review', *Frontiers in Psychology*, 10, 2019, pp.2405; C.S. Tamis-LeMonda, J.D. Shannon, N.J. Cabrera & M.E. Lamb, 'Fathers and mothers at play with their 2- and 3-year-olds: contributions to language and cognitive development', *Child Development*, 75(6), 2004, pp.1802–20; E. Pougnet, L.A. Serbin, D.M. Stack & A.E. Schwartzman, 'Fathers' influence on children's cognitive and behavioural functioning: A longitudinal study of Canadian families', *Canadian Journal of Behavioural Science / Revue canadienne des sciences du comportement*, 43(3), 2011, pp.173–82.
5 D.J. Eggebeen, 'Do Fathers Uniquely Matter for Adolescent Well-Being?' in W.B. Wilcox & K.K. Kline (eds.), *Gender and Parenthood: Biological and social scientific perspectives*, Columbia University Press, 2013, pp.249–70.
6 T. Real, *I Don't Want to Talk About It: Overcoming the secret legacy of male depression*, Scribner, 1997
7 J.R. Moehringer, *The Tender Bar: A memoir*, Hyperion, 2006.

Chapter 11: Communication

1 J. Green, *Turtles All the Way Down*. Dutton Books for Young Readers, 2017.
2 'How to fight smarter: soften your start-up', Gottman, 15 March 2013.
3 L.M. Padilla-Walker, A.M. Fraser & J.M. Harper, 'Walking the walk: the moderating role of proactive parenting on adolescents' value-congruent behaviors', *Journal of Adolescence*, 35(5), 2012, pp.1141–52.

Chapter 12: Learning self-control

1 Dunedin Multidisciplinary Health & Development Research Unit, 'Home'.

2 T. Moffit, R. Poulton & A. Caspi, 'Lifelong impact of early self-control', *American Scientist*, 101(5), 2013, p.352.

3 'The Assessments', Dunedin Multidisciplinary Health & Development Research Unit.

4 L.S. Richmond-Rakerd, A. Caspi, A. Ambler et al., 'Childhood self-control forecasts the pace of midlife aging and preparedness for old age', *Proceedings of the National Academy of Sciences of the United States of America*, 118(3), 2021, e2010211118.

5 K.L. Bates, 'Self-controlled children tend to be healthier middle-aged adults', *Duke Today*, 5 January 2021.

6 T. Moffit, R. Poulton & A. Caspi, 'Lifelong impact of early self-control, *American Scientist*, 101(5), 2013, p.352.

7 J. Burn-Murdoch, 'The troubling decline in conscientiousness', *Financial Times*, 8 August 2025.

8 J. Haidt, *The Anxious Generation: How the great rewiring of childhood is causing an epidemic of mental illness*, Penguin Press, 2024.

9 N. Webster, *A Collection of Essays and Fugitive Writings on Moral, Historical, Political and Literary Subjects*, Scholars' Facsimiles & Reprints, 1977.

10 A. Pandey, D. Hale, S. Das et al., 'Effectiveness of universal self-regulation-based interventions in children and adolescents', *JAMA Pediatrics*, 172(6), 2018, pp.566–75.

11 G.W. Fincham, C. Strauss, J. Montero-Marin & K. Cavanagh, 'Effect of breathwork on stress and mental health: A meta-analysis of randomised-controlled trials', *Scientific Reports*, 13, 2023, p.432.

12 M.Y. Balban, E. Neri, M.M. Kogon et al., ‚Brief structured respiration practices enhance mood and reduce physiological arousal', *Cell Reports Medicine*, 4(1), 2023, 100895.

13 J. Li, Z. Huang, W. Si & T. Shao, 'the effects of physical activity on positive emotions in children and adolescents: a systematic review and meta-analysis', *International Journal of Environmental Research and Public Health*, 19(21), 2022, 14185.

14 F. Hedigan, H. Sheridan & A. Sasse, 'Benefit of inhalation aromatherapy as a complementary treatment for stress and anxiety in a clinical setting – A systematic review', *Complementary Therapies in Clinical*

Practice, 52, 2023, 101750; M. Lee, S. Lim, J.A. Song et al., 'The effects of aromatherapy essential oil inhalation on stress, sleep quality and immunity in healthy adults: Randomized controlled trial', *European Journal of Integrative Medicine*, 12, 2017, pp.79–86; D.I. Sánchez-Vidaña, S.P. Ngai, W. He et al., 2017, 'The effectiveness of aromatherapy for depressive symptoms: a systematic review', *Evidence-Based Complementary and Alternative Medicine*, 2017, 5869315.

15 M.M. Hansen, R. Jones & K. Tocchini, 'Shinrin-yoku (forest bathing) and nature therapy: a state-of-the-art review', *International Journal of Environmental Research and Public Health*, 14(8), 2017, 851; R. Ivers & T. Astell-Burt, 'Nature Rx: nature prescribing in general practice', *Australian Journal of General Practice*, 52(4), 2023.

16 T. Field, 'Touch for socioemotional and physical well-being: A review', *Developmental Review*, 30, 2010, pp.367–83.

17 M.V. Thoma, R. La Marca, R. Brönnimann et al., 'The effect of music on the human stress response', *PLOS One*, 2013.

18 G. Lee, K. Han & H. Kim, 'Risk of mental health problems in adolescents skipping meals: The Korean National Health and Nutrition Examination Survey 2010 to 2012', *Nursing Outlook*, 65(4), 2017, pp.411–19.

Chapter 13: Friends

1 M. Giletta, S. Choukas-Bradley, M. Maes et al., 'A meta-analysis of longitudinal peer influence effects in childhood and adolescence', *Psychological Bulletin*, 147(7), 2021, pp.719–47.

2 J. Chein, D. Albert, L. O'Brien et al., 'Peers Increase adolescent risk taking by enhancing activity In the brain's reward circuitry', *Developmental Science*, 14(2), 2011, F1–F10.

3 J.A. Hall, 'How many hours does it take to make a friend?', *Journal of Social and Personal Relationships*, 36(4), 2018, pp.1278–96.

4 J. Twenge, *The Real Differences Between Gen Z, Millennials, Gen X, Boomers, and Silents – and What They Mean for America's Future*, Atria Books, 2023.

5 L.M. Jaremka, R.R. Andridge, C.P. Fagundes et al., 'Pain, depression, and fatigue: loneliness as a longitudinal risk factor', *Health Psychology*, 33(9), 2014, pp.948–57.

6 I. Pollak, M. Mitic, J. Birchwood et al., 'A systematic review of intervention programs promoting peer relationships among children and adolescents: methods and targets used in effective programs', *Adolescent Research Review*, 8, 2023. pp.297–321.

7 L. Keijsers, S. Branje, S. Hawk et al., 'Forbidden friends as forbidden fruit: parental supervision of friendships, contact with deviant peers, and adolescent delinquency', *Child Development*, 83(2), 2011, pp.651–66.

8 Ibid.

9 S. Pallini, R. Baiocco, B.H. Schneider et al., 'Early child-parent attachment and peer relations: a meta-analysis of recent research', *Journal of Family Psychology*, 28(1), 2014, pp.118–23.

Chapter 14: Screen wars

1 M. Allen, 'Sean Parker unloads on Facebook: "God only knows what it's doing to our children's brains."', Axios, 9 November 2017.

2 M. Zuckerberg, 'Testimony before the U.S. Senate Judiciary Committee: Big Tech and the online child sexual exploitation crisis', hearing testimony, United States Senate Judiciary Committee, 31 January 2024.

3 'Trapped online: Watch teens speak about their smartphone addiction', *The Australian*, video, YouTube, 16 August 2025.

4 A.J. Skiera, 'What Gen Z thinks about its social media and smartphone usage', The Harris Poll, 10 September 2024.

5 T.C. Thiagarajan, J.J. Newson & S. Swaminathan, 'Protecting the developing mind in a digital age: a global policy imperative', *Journal of Human Development and Capabilities*, 26(3), 20 July 2025, pp.493–504; 'Age of first smartphone/tablet and mental wellbeing outcomes', Global Mind Project, Sapien Labs, 15 May 2023; S.Y. Sohn, P. Rees, B. Wildridge et al., 'Prevalence of problematic smartphone usage and associated mental health outcomes amongst children and young people: a systematic review, meta-analysis and GRADE of the evidence', *BMC Psychiatry*, 19, 2019, 356; 'Teens, screens and mental health', World Health Organization, 25 September 2024.

6 B. Marshall, W.A. Warburton, M. Kangas & N. Sweller, 'Internet gaming disorder (IGD) and smartphone addiction: parent intervention trial', *Australian Journal of Psychology*, 76(1), 2024 2396961.

7 W. Siu, 'I make video games. I won't let my daughters play them', *New York Times*, 2 October 2022.

8 E. Grosemans & R. De Cock, 'From gambling-like elements in and around video games to monetary gambling: Testing a pathway model among adolescents', International Gambling Studies, 25(3), 2025, pp.472–94.

Chapter 15: Tackling the porndemic

1 G. Grace, 'What happens when porn replaces sex education', *GQ*, 26 February 2021.

2 Top Blokes Foundation, 'Submission to the Standing Committee on Social Issues: inquiry into impacts of harmful pornography on mental, emotional and physical health', 2024.

3 K. Dawson, S.N. Gabhainn, R. Friday & P. MacNeela, 'Barriers and recommendations for parent-child conversations about pornography', *Frontiers in Sociology*, 25(9), 2024, 1349549.

4 C. McKenna, 'All homes need five layers of digital protection', Institute for Family Studies, 22 September 2025.

5 K. Dawson, S.N. Gabhainn, R. Friday & P. MacNeela, 'Barriers and recommendations for parent-child conversations about pornography', *Frontiers in Sociology*, 25(9), 2024, 1349549; E.E. Rasmussen, R.R. Ortiz & S.R. White, 'Emerging adults' responses to active mediation of pornography during adolescence', *Journal of Children and Media*, 9(2), 2015, pp.160–76.

6 M. Ballantine-Jones, 'Inquiry into impacts of harmful pornography on mental, emotional, and physical health (Submission No. 34)', Standing Committee on Social Issues, NSW Parliament House, 2024.

7 J. Power, T. Norman, A. James et al., 'Beyond "The Talk" – Supporting parents and carers to speak with children about sex, relationships and consent,' Australian Research Centre in Sex, Health and Society, La Trobe University, 2025; I. Higgins & S. Wallen, 'Dads leaving sex education to mums, report finds, with concerns young boys are missing out', ABC News, 15 September 2025.

8 Top Blokes Foundation, 'Submission to the Standing Committee on Social Issues: inquiry into impacts of harmful pornography on mental, emotional and physical health', 2024.
9 C. McKenna, 'All homes need five layers of digital protection', Institute for Family Studies, 22 September 2025.
10 J.W. Patchin & S. Hinduja, 'It is time to teach safe sexting', *Journal of Adolescent Health*, 66(2), 2019.
11 Australian Institute of Health and Welfare, 'Bullying and negative online experiences', 2021.
12 S. Rose, 'New eSafety report raises child safety concerns for image-based abuse', Moores, 18 October 2019.
13 eSafety Commissioner, 'Deepfake damage in schools: How AI-generated abuse is disrupting students, families and school communities', 27 July 2025.
14 Headspace National, 'Inquiry into Impacts of Harmful Pornography on Mental, Emotional, and Physical Health. Submission No. 47', 31 January 2025.

Chapter 16: Encouraging healthy sex

1 Centers for Disease Control and Prevention, 'Youth risk behavior survey data summary & trends report: 2013–2023', U.S. Department of Health and Human Services, 2024.
2 L. Widman, S. Choukas-Bradley, S. M. Noar et al., 'Parent-adolescent sexual communication and adolescent safer sex behavior: a meta-analysis', *JAMA Pediatrics*, 170(1), 2016, pp.52–61.
3 L.E. Prendergast, J.W. Toumbourou, B.J. McMorris & R.F. Catalano, 'Outcomes of early adolescent sexual behavior in Australia: longitudinal findings in young adulthood', *Journal of Adolescent Health*, 64(4), 2020, pp.516–22.
4 Australian Institute of Health and Welfare. 'Intimate relationships', 2021.
5 R. Wesche, S.E. Claxton & E.A. Waterman, 'Emotional outcomes of casual sexual relationships: A systematic review', *The Journal of Sex Research*, 58(8), 2020.
6 K.M. Lee, 'Settling down: romance in the era of Gen Z', *Yale News*, 14 February 2020.

Chapter 17: Getting through school

1 R. Browne, 'More educations equals more pay: report', *Sydney Morning Herald*, 24 October 2012.
2 E. Pahlke, J.S. Hyde & C.M. Allison, 'The effects of single-sex compared with coeducational schooling on students' performance and attitudes: A meta-analysis', *Psychological Bulletin*, 140(4), 2014, pp.1042–72.
3 T. Amabile & S. Kramer, *The Progress Principle: Using Small Wins to Ignite Joy, Engagement, and Creativity at Work*, Harvard Business Review Press, 2011.

Chapter 18: Career plans

1 A. Grant, *Think Again: The power of knowing what you don't know*, Penguin, 2023.
2 Australian Bureau of Statistics, 'Education and Work, Australia', May 2024.
3 University of Queensland Australia, 'How many career changes in a lifetime?', 19 June 2023.
4 D. Epstein, *Range: Why generalists triumph in a specialized world*, Riverhead Books, 2019.
5 S. Adams, 'Career advice', Dilbert, blog, 20 July 2007.
6 M. Salas Velasco, 'More than just good grades: candidates' perceptions about the skills and attributes employers seek in new graduates', *Journal of Business Economics and Management, 13*(3), 2012, pp.499–517.
7 J. Clear, '3-2-1: On self-worth, how to have style, and how to build a great career', The 3-2-1 Newsletter, 5 September 2024.
8 D.K. Wall, 'Musing: fewer than a dozen books sold?', 4 September 2022.
9 S. Galloway, *The Algebra of Wealth: a simple formula for financial security.* Portfolio, 2024.

Chapter 19: The gap-year advantage

1 B. McKay & M. McKay, 'The least interesting generation', The Art of Manliness, 6 July 2021.
2 Happy Families, 'Bringing Up Boys Summit, video, 2022.
3 YWAM Seven Peaks, 'Why Take a Gap Year – Greg Lukianoff and Jonathan Haidt, The Coddling of the American Mind', video, YouTube, 25 January 2023.

4 Gap Year Association, 'Gap Year to College'.
5 A.J. Martin, 'Should students have a gap year? Motivation and performance factors relevant to time out after completing school', *Journal of Educational Psychology, 102*(3), 2010, pp.561–76.
6 Department of Education, Skills and Employment. 'Completing Higher Education – The impact of taking a gap-year', Australian Government, 2019; P.W. Miller & E.R. Birch, 'The characteristics of "gap-year" students and their tertiary academic outcomes', *Economic Record*, 83(262), 2007, pp.329–44.
7 Ibid; M. Marchant, '*The Impact of Gap Years on Academic Outcomes for Women: A Case Study from the Missionary Age Change*', honours thesis, Brigham Young University, 2018; N.H. Gallagher & K. Blythe, 'Gap year alumni survey 2020 supplemented with 2015 Americorps national civilian community corps survey data', Gap Year Association, 2020.
8 N.H. Gallagher & K. Blythe, 'Gap year alumni survey 2020 supplemented with 2015 americorps national civilian community corps survey data', Gap Year Association, 2020.
9 C.W. Moore & J.P. Allen, ,The effects of volunteering on the young volunteer', *Journal of Prevention*, 17, 1996, pp.231–58; J.S. Nakamura, R. Wilkinson, M.A. Nelson et al., 'Volunteering in Young Adulthood: Complex Associations With Later Health and Well-Being Outcomes', *American Journal of Health Promotion*, 39(1), 2025, pp.39–51.
10 ADF Careers, ADF Gap Year.
11 S. Rabie & T. Naidoo, 'The value of the gap year in the facilitation of career adaptability', *South African Journal of Higher Education*, 30(3), 2016.
12 L. Paterson-Brown, F. Paterson-Brown, E. Simon et al., 'The Influence of a "Gap Year" on Medical Students', *Journal of Education and Training Studies*, 3(4), 2015.

Chapter 20: The finish line

1 L. Rosten, *Captain Newman, M. D.*, 1962, p.328.
2 B. Lawrence, J. Sudeikis, B. Hunt et al. (executive producers), *Ted Lasso*, television series.

3 R.V. Reeves, 'Why Lone Ranger masculinity is a dead end', Of Boys and Men, 2 September 2023.

4 E.E. Werner, 'Vulnerable but invincible: high-risk children from birth to adulthood', *Acta Paediatrica – Supplement, 422*, 1997, pp.103–05.

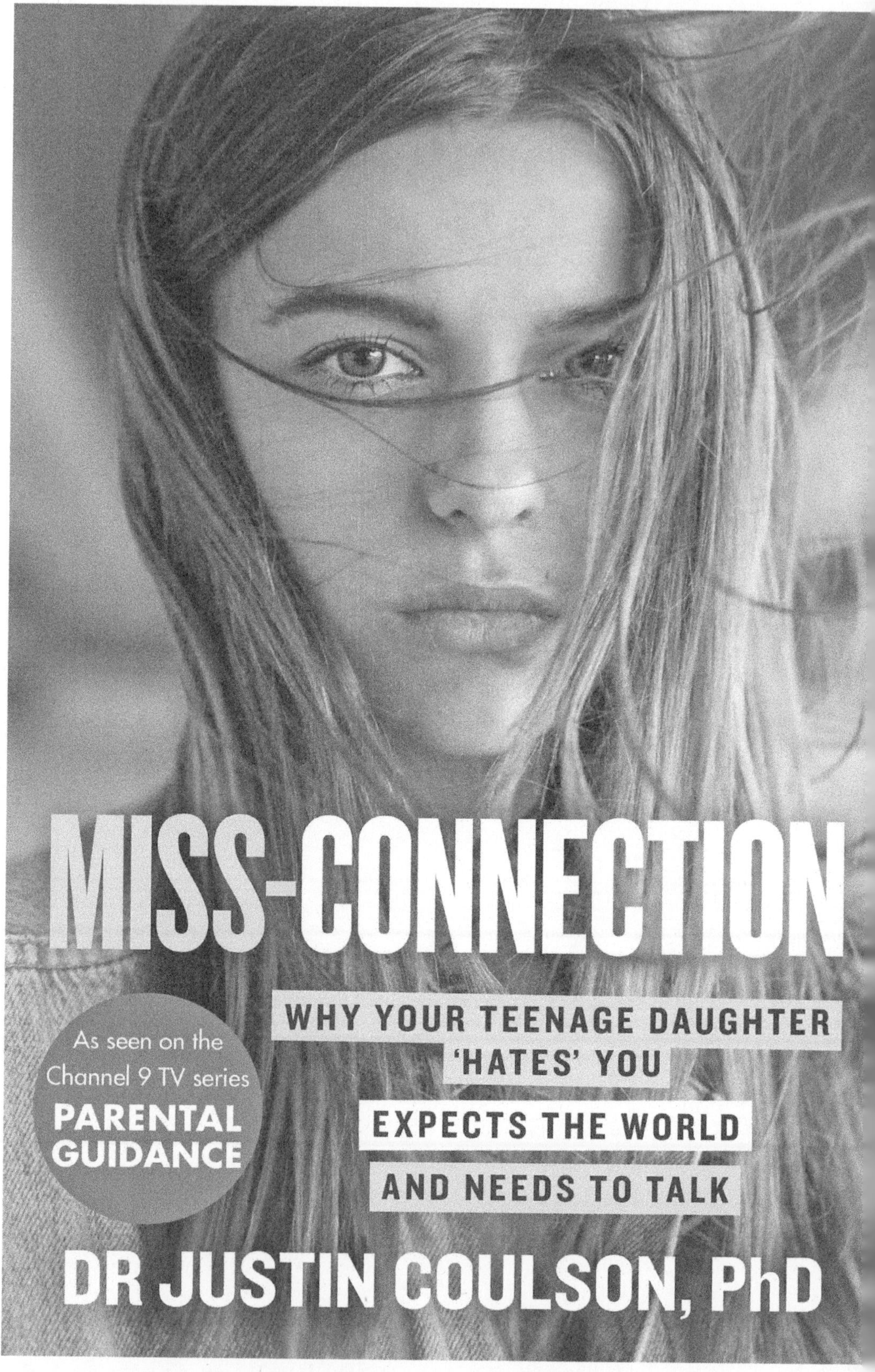
MISS-CONNECTION
WHY YOUR TEENAGE DAUGHTER 'HATES' YOU
EXPECTS THE WORLD
AND NEEDS TO TALK
As seen on the Channel 9 TV series PARENTAL GUIDANCE
DR JUSTIN COULSON, PhD

What is the best thing about being a teenage girl right now? *'My friends!' 'Independence!' 'Discovering who I am.'*

What is the worst thing about being a teenage girl? *'My friends.' 'Not knowing what the future holds.' 'Pressure to be perfect and look a certain way.'*

What do teenage girls wish they could talk to us about? *'I'm sick of pretending to be happy all the time.' 'My face; if anyone is ever going to love me despite how grotesque my face is.' 'I sometimes don't want to be here.'*

There has never been a better time to be a teenage girl. But perhaps there has never been a harder time. We know that connection is at the heart of our teenage daughters' happiness. And we do our best to have strong connections with our girls. But despite this, we often feel a disconnect. Or perhaps, more precisely, a *mis-connect*.

If you're looking to understand your teen daughter better and deepen your connection with her, this book is your guide. Drawing on cutting-edge psychology research along with interviews and surveys from close to 400 teenage girls, *Miss-connection* will take you into the world your teen girl experiences and help you connect with her the way she needs you to.

As the girls themselves set out the challenges they face – with social media, friends, boys, identity – you will find connection and solutions.

THE
PARENTING
REVOLUTION
A guide to raising resilient kids
Co-host of
the popular
TV program
Parental
Guidance
Dr Justin Coulson

What does it mean to be a good parent? Are you a good parent when your child is compliant, but a bad parent when they're not? What if they're perfect at age three and challenging at thirteen? And what if your child has additional needs?

This is a book about parenting styles and what it takes to be a great parent. We know about tiger parents, helicopter parents, free-range parents, but have you heard of Tesla parents, leaf-blower parents or iPhone 6 parents?

So many styles, but is there one that actually works?

Justin Coulson believes so. Drawing on up-to-the-minute research in parenting science as well as studies of childhood development, he shows:

- how our children thrive when we understand and meet their basic psychological needs;
- how our job is not to fix our kids, but to create an environment that supports their growth and development; and
- how children flourish when we minimise control, but maximise our warmth and involvement, and establish healthy boundaries.

Not all children are the same, and Justin considers a range of circumstances that you or your child might be in – including children with non-typical development.

His revolutionary approach and practical strategies will encourage you to change the way you parent forever.